Illustrated Chronology and Index

Other Publications:
AMERICAN COUNTRY
VOYAGE THROUGH THE UNIVERSE
THE THIRD REICH
THE TIME-LIFE GARDENER'S GUIDE
MYSTERIES OF THE UNKNOWN
TIME FRAME
FIX IT YOURSELF
FITNESS, HEALTH & NUTRITION
SUCCESSFUL PARENTING
HEALTHY HOME COOKING
LIBRARY OF NATIONS
THE ENCHANTED WORLD
THE KODAK LIBRARY OF CREATIVE PHOTOGRAPHY
GREAT MEALS IN MINUTES
THE CIVIL WAR
PLANET EARTH
COLLECTOR'S LIBRARY OF THE CIVIL WAR
THE EPIC OF FLIGHT
THE GOOD COOK
WORLD WAR II
HOME REPAIR AND IMPROVEMENT
THE OLD WEST

This volume is one of a series that examines
various aspects of computer technology and the
role computers play in modern life.

UNDERSTANDING COMPUTERS

Illustrated Chronology and Index

BY THE EDITORS OF TIME-LIFE BOOKS

TIME-LIFE BOOKS, ALEXANDRIA, VIRGINIA

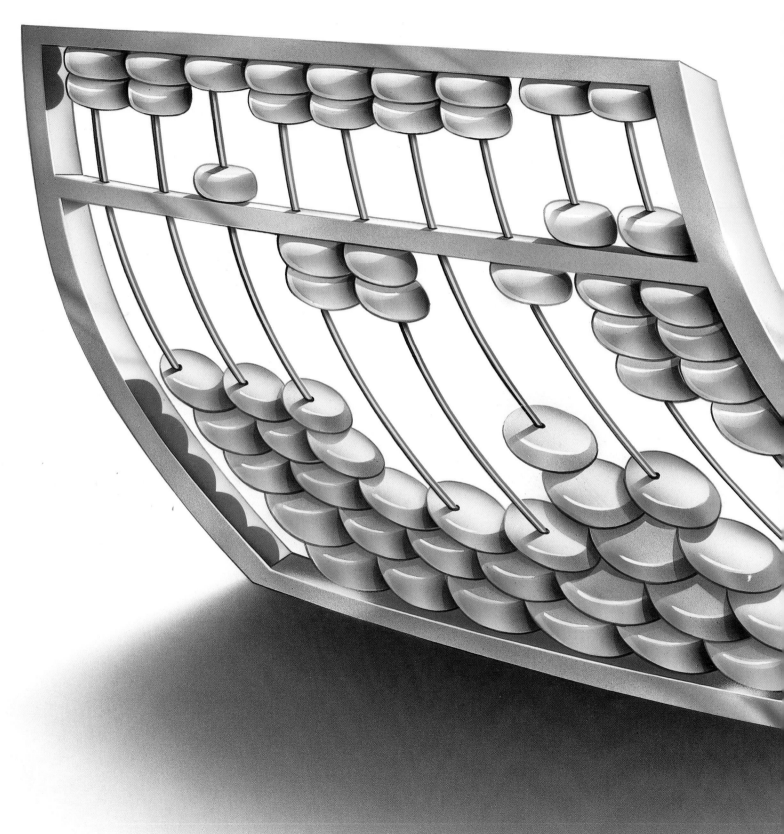

Fifty Centuries of Computing

From the invention of the abacus by the Babylonians around the year 3000 BC to the creation of today's electronic marvels, the history of computing spans nearly five millenniums. In this book, an illustrated time line traces that fascinating journey through 300 milestone events.

The abacus, shown at left in a stylized version of the form it had assumed by about the third century AD, was the first calculating machine—an efficient device whose beads could be manipulated to add, subtract, multiply, and divide. Progress from this humble but promising beginning was at first fitful. The eighteenth century, for example, saw not a single noteworthy contribution to computing. After the middle of this century, however, the pace accelerated dramatically—even dizzyingly—and shows no signs of slowing. If anything, future advances are likely to make today's supercomputers seem as quaint as yesteryear's abacus.

Accompanying the time line that runs through this book is a master index to the preceding twenty-three volumes of the Understanding Computers series. The index includes a glossary of important terms. A key along the tops of the pages translates the two-letter codes that signify titles in the series. Italicized page numbers indicate illustrations in the books.

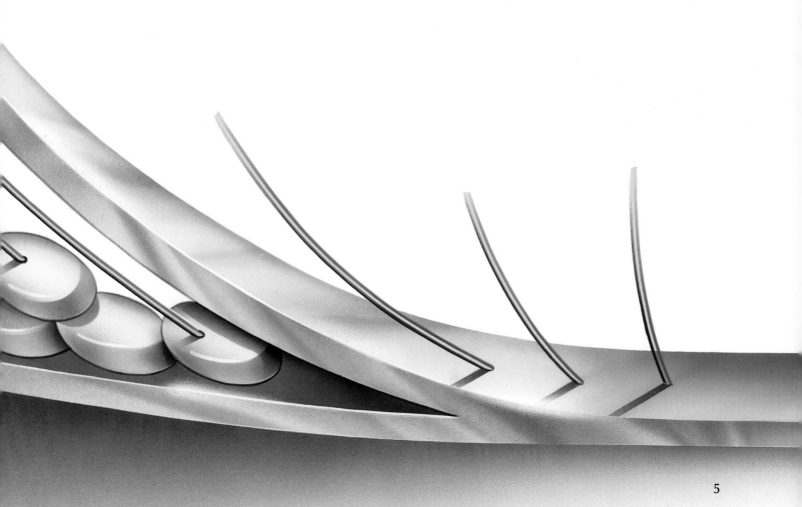

Abacus: CB 7-8, 10, *11*

Abdomen: HB *51*

Abelson, Robert: AI 69

Abrahams, Paul: LA 71

Abrahamson, James: MF 109

A-C bacterium: HB 67

Accelerometers: TR 52, *58*

Access control: *the use of either physical safeguards such as locks, or software guards such as passwords to prevent unauthorized access to a computer.* CS 41-42, *43*, 45, *46-57*, 69, 73, *74-85*

Access-Control List (ACL): CS *76-77*; circumvention, CS *78-81*

Accuracy: limitations in computation, RV *16-17*

ACE (Acceptance Checkout Equipment): IC *50*, SP 41

ACE (Automatic Computing Engine): CB 64, IC *24*

ACH (automated clearinghouse): SO *80-81*

ACM (Association for Computing Machinery): LA 73

Acoustic coupler: *a type of telecommunications equipment that permits the transmission of computer data over the telephone network through the handset of a telephone.* CO 20, IC 60

Acoustic delay line: *an early form of computer memory consisting of a mercury-filled glass tube with quartz crystals at either end. The crystals convert electrical pulses representing data into vibrations that travel as sound waves through the mercury.* IC *15*, MS 9-10, *11*

ACP (Airline Control Program): SO 39, 41, 44, 47, 48, 49, 51

Actuators: RO 47, 48, *50*, 51

Ada: IC 96, LA 82-84, MF 102-103, SC 20; origins, LA 79-82

ADALINE: AC 50, 52

Adaptive filters: AC 50

Adaptive routing: CO 73, *74-75*

Adaptive Suspension Vehicle (ASV): IC *117*, RO 68, 70, 77

Adder: *a circuit that performs addition.* See Adder circuit.

Adder circuit, design of: CM 35, *36-49*

Adding: LA *26-27*

Address: *the location of a specific cell in a computer's memory.* See Memory: addresses.

Address bus: *the wires in a computer that carry signals used to locate a given memory address.* See Computers: structure and operations.

Addressing memory: MS *26-27*

Adleman, Leonard: CS 100-101, 112

Adobe Systems: PostScript, PC 51

ADP: SC 21

Advanced Automation System (AAS): for air traffic control, TR 105

Advanced Inertial Reference Sphere (AIRS): MF 74, 78

Advanced Micro Devices (AMD): CM 54-55, 73, 74

Advanced Research Projects Agency: *See* ARPA

LOGARITHMS eased the chore of multiplying and dividing large numbers. Invented by Scottish mathematician John Napier, logarithmic notation represents a number as a power of a base number (usually 10). For example, 100 can be written as 10^2; the exponent 2 is the logarithm. The logarithm of 200 is 2.3, and that of 1,000 is 3. Numbers are multiplied by adding their logarithms and divided by subtracting them. The invention led to several calculating devices, including the slide rule.

JOHN NAPIER'S "BONES," numbered rods crafted of wood or ivory, reduced multiplication problems to simple addition. After the bones were arranged side by side to represent a pair of numbers, the product was found by adding single-digit values in adjacent segments. Although they were invented by the father of logarithms, these numbered rods made no use of them and were soon rendered obsolete by the slide rule.

THE PASCALINE digital adding machine, built by French philosopher and mathematician Blaise Pascal in more than fifty versions, summed numbers by means of an ingenious mechanism that would be used in calculators for the next 300 years. Numbered dials on the device, turned according to the numbers to be added, advanced a complex arrangement of cogs inside the Pascaline's fourteen-inch-long polished brass box. This internal mechanism displayed a running total in windows across the top of the calculator.

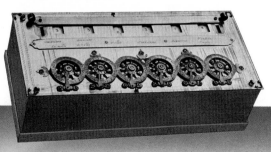

1614

1617

1642

and Index; IO Input/Output; LA Computer Languages; MF The Military Frontier; MS Memory and Storage; PC The Personal Computer; PM The Puzzle Master; PO Speed and Power; RO Robotics; RV Revolution in Science; SC The Software Challenge; SO The Computerized Society; SP Space; SW Software; TR Transportation

*Adventures of Andrae &
Wally B., The:* CI 89, 90
AED (ALGOL Extended for
Design): LA 68
Aegis ship defense system: MF
94-96; cruiser, MF *96-97*
Aerodynamics: RV 35, 39
Aerospace industry: CIM, CI
106; graphics, CI 106
Aetna Life and Casualty: CO
96
Ahl, David: PC 10
AI: *See* Artificial intelligence
AIDS: HB 67, 71

Aiken, Howard: CB 52, *55*, 58,
65, LA 72, MS 17, RV 14, 15,
18, SC 24, SW 11
AIMACO (Air Matériel Com-
mand language): LA 41, 42
Airborne Integrated Data
System: TR 17
Airbus Industrie A320: IC *121*,
TR *20-21*
Aircraft applications: autopilot,
TR 18; autothrottle, TR 18;
computerized cockpit, TR
20-21; conservatism, TR 16;
EICAS, TR 18, 19; flight-data

acquisition units, TR *12-13*;
Flight Management Com-
puter System, TR 18-19;
fly-by-wire controls, TR
20-21, 22-23; graphic
reconstructions of flight
data, TR *14-15*; inertial
navigation systems, TR 17;
instrument panels, TR 17;
Traffic Alert and Collision
Avoidance System (TCAS),
TR *116-117*, 118; weather
radar, TR *118-119*. *See also*
Air traffic control system;
Supercockpit
Aircraft design: PO 19, *22-23*,
44
Airline reservation systems:
SO 40-41, 50-52, SW 86-87
Air pollution, automotive: TR
8-9, computer solutions, TR
10, 27; noncomputer
solutions, TR 9-10
Air traffic: changes in, TR 99,
100, 104
Air traffic control system: IC
84, SW 89-90, TR 8, *110-115*;
Advanced Automation
System (AAS), TR 105;

backup system (DARC), TR
103-104; computer for, TR
100-101; computer reliability,
TR 102; cost, TR 101; early
system, TR 98-99; National
Air Space System, TR 109,
110-121; and radar, TR 99,
112-113; software for, TR 101,
104, 105; Traffic Alert and
Collision Avoidance System
(TCAS), TR *116-117*; U.S.
federal control over, TR 98
Air warfare, and AWACS: MF
96-98
Akers, John F.: CO 8
Albers-Schönberg, Ernst: MS
19
Albrecht, Allan J.: SC 53
Albrecht, Robert L.: LA 99-100,
101, 102
Albus, James S.: RO 33, 62, 112
Alcyone: TR 25
Aldrin, Buzz: SP 47, 117
Aldus Corporation: IC 118, PC
67
Al Faiha: TR 91
ALGOL (Algorithmic
Language): IC 40, LA 44-45,
47, SC 87, 91, SW 29; ALGOL

A HAND-CRANKED CALCULATOR devised by German mathematician Gottfried Wilhelm Leibniz lightened the burden of lengthy calculations. Leibniz, a mathematical prodigy who spurned academe for diplomacy, later surpassed this achievement by perfecting binary arithmetic—the lingua franca of twentieth-century digital computing.

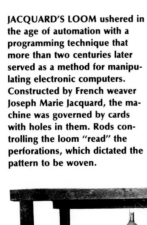

JACQUARD'S LOOM ushered in the age of automation with a programming technique that more than two centuries later served as a method for manipulating electronic computers. Constructed by French weaver Joseph Marie Jacquard, the machine was governed by cards with holes in them. Rods controlling the loom "read" the perforations, which dictated the pattern to be woven.

CHARLES BABBAGE, an eccentric English mathematician, drew up plans for a device he called a Difference Engine. The machine was intended for computing and printing mathematical engineering tables, whose accuracy Babbage pursued with fanatical zeal. Discouraged by waning government support, Babbage never built the machine. Instead, he conceived a far more ambitious mechanism *(right)*.

1673   1804   1822

ALGOL (continued)
60, LA 48-49, 67, 76; ALGOL 68, LA 77, 81; ALGOL W, LA 76; design committee for ALGOL 60, LA *49;* design committee for ALGOL 68, LA 76

Algorithm: *a set of clearly defined rules and instructions for the solution of a problem. A computer program consists of the step-by-step procedures for executing an algorithm.* LA *17-19,* SW 30, 33, 42

Algorithms to Silicon: CM 102-103

Aliasing: CI *55, 58*

Alignment: *in chip manufacturing, the arranging of the mask and the wafer, one with respect to the other, usually followed by exposure to light. See Aligners.*

Aligners: CM 63

Allen, Paul: CB *99,* 100, IC *82,* LA 102, SW 62-63, *70*

Allen, Ron: CC 42

Allen-Bradley, Inc.: RO 43, 46

Alliant FX/8: PO 98

Allison, Dennis: LA 101

Alohanet: CO 57, 62

Alpert, Martin: PC 18

Alphanumeric: *pertaining to the characters (letters, numerals, punctuation marks, and signs) used by a computer. See ASCII.*

Altair: CB *92,* 94-100, 102, 103; 8800, IC *81,* LA 100, 101, 102, SO 101-102, SW 57, *63;* add-ons, CB *100;* bus, CB 100; limitations, CB 99-100; programming, SW 57, 62-63

Alternative computers: AC entire volume

Altimetry: radar, RV 99, *100-101*

Alto: CI 60, IC *78,* PC 59-60, SC 104. *See also* Xerox PARC

ALU (arithmetic logic unit): CB *82-83,* 109, CM 102, SW 21

Aluminum conductors: CM *14-15;* on gigachip, CM 89-90; resistance, CM 27

Aluminum gallium arsenide (AlGaAs): *a synthetic semiconductor, often paired with gallium arsenide in the formation of high-speed transistors. See Semiconductors.*

Alvin: RO 102

Amateur Computer Society: CB 94

AM (Automated Mathematician): AI 80, IC 83

American Airlines: SO 40-41, 52

American Medical Association: HB 74; AMA/NET, HB 74

American Research & Development (ARD): PO 69

American Science & Engineering, Inc. (AS&E): CC 66, 67, 68

American Standard Code for Information Interchange: *See* ASCII

American Standards Association (ASA), X3: CO 49

American Telephone and Telegraph Company: *See* AT&T

Amino acid: *the basic chemical constituent of proteins. The sequence of a protein's amino acids determines its structure and function.* RV *82-83,* 91

PLANNING THE ANALYTICAL ENGINE, the earliest expression of the idea for an all-purpose, programmable computer, monopolized Babbage's attention. Intended to be "a machine of the most general nature," it would have carried out all manner of mathematical chores. But blueprints called for an unwieldy device the size of a locomotive, and except for a few isolated components *(below)*, the computer was never built.

THE COUNTESS OF LOVELACE, the mathematically gifted daughter of the poet Lord Byron and assistant to Charles Babbage in his efforts toward the Analytical Engine, wrote the first examples of programs to control a computing machine.

GEORGE BOOLE, a self-taught genius, devised a system of symbolic logic now called Boolean algebra. Published as *The Mathematical Analysis of Logic* and later wed to the binary number system, his ideas became the foundation for electronic digital computing.

1834

1843

1847

Amorphous semiconductors: MS 105

Ampex Corporation: MS 36

Amplitude-shift keying: *a technique for representing the binary digits zero and one by varying the amplitude of a wave-shaped signal between two designated levels. See* Modems: amplitude-shift keying.

AMR: Confirm system, PC 104

AMRAAM (Advanced Medium-Range Air-to-Air Missile): MF 72-73

Amyotrophic lateral sclerosis (ALS): HB 89-90

Analog: *the representation of a continuously changing physical variable (temperature, for example) by another variable (such as the height of a column of mercury). See* Computers, analog.

Analog and digital signals: CO 29, *30-31;* advantages of digital, CO 95

Analog computer: *a computer in which continuous physical variables such as the* movement of gears or the magnitude of voltage represent data. *See* Computers, analog.

Analog-digital conversion: CI 8, *9*

Analog-to-digital converter: *a device that changes an analog signal into digital information. See* Analog-digital conversion. IO 19, *20-23,* 113

Analytical Engine: IO 8-9, SW 9-*10*

Anderson, Harlan: PO 68, 69

Anderson, James A.: AC 45, 53, 54, 67, AI 108

Anderson, Philip: CM 91

Anderson, Richard W.: CM 67, 70, 73

AND gate: *a logic circuit whose output is TRUE (or one) only when all inputs are TRUE. See* Logic gates.

Anelco: CM 53

Angel, Roger: CC 23, 24, 28

Angiography, Digital Subtraction (DSA): HB *62-65*

Animation, computer-assisted: CI *78-79, 88, 89;* film, PO 44; human, CI *86-87. See also* Motion picture graphics

Animation languages: LA 68

Antarctica: ozone hole, PM *8-9,* 106-108

Anthropology: RV 93, 95-98

Antiaircraft gun directors: RO 10-11, 14, 15-17

Antialiasing: CI *55,* 585

Antibodies: RV 91

Antisubmarine rocket torpedo (ASROC): MF 95

Aperture synthesis: with radio telescopes, CC 57-58, *78-82*

APL (A Programming Language): IC *61,* LA 72-73

Apollo, Project: SP 33, 39-48, 87; abort guidance system, SP 47; acceptance check-out equipment system, SP 40-41; *Apollo 1,* SP 46, 117; *Apollo 7,* SP 46, 117; *Apollo 9,* SP 46-47, 117; Apollo 10, SP 47, 117; *Apollo 11,* SP 47-48, 117; *Columbia,* SP 47; command module (CM), SP 39-40, 44, 47; DSKY, SP 47; *Eagle,* SP 47-48; guidance

A WORKING DIFFERENCE ENGINE was constructed by Swedish printer and inventor Georg Scheutz. Based on Charles Babbage's design, the machine won a gold medal in the 1855 Paris Exhibition, vindicating the Englishman's incomplete efforts. Ironically, the British government, which had abandoned Babbage, bought one of Scheutz's machines to calculate insurance actuarial tables in its registrar-general's department.

A PUNCH-CARD TABULATOR *(below, left)* tripled the speed of processing data for the U.S. census and helped inventor Herman Hollerith launch the company that would evolve into the computer giant IBM. Metal pins in the reader passed through holes punched in cards the size of dollar bills, momentarily closing electric circuits. The resulting pulses advanced counters assigned to details such as income and family size. A sorter *(below, right)* could be programmed to pigeonhole cards according to patterns of holes, an important aid to analyzing census statistics.

THE VACUUM-TUBE TRIODE was patented by Lee De Forest. Used for decades as the voltage-multiplying component of amplifiers, the vacuum tube could also act as a switch to turn a current on or off. This binary function made the tube invaluable to builders of early electronic digital computers.

1853

1890

1906

Apollo, Project (continued)
system, IC *63*, SP 43-47, 48;
lunar-landing module (LM),
SP 40, 44, 47; lunar-orbit
rendezvous (LOR), SP 34, 39;
memory, MS 22; service
module, SP 40; software, SP
45-46

Apollo Computer: IC *104*, PC
89

Apple Computer Company: CB
93, 103, 104-108, IO 74, MS
52, PC 45-46; Apple I, CB
104, *105*; Apple II Plus, IO
95, 96; and enthusiasts, PC
47-48; logos, PC *9*; reshaping
after Macintosh, PC 65-68;
strategy, PC 47, 67-68;
working environment, PC
48-49, 62. *See also individual
computers*

Apple LaserWriter: PC 68

Apple Lisa: IC *107*, IO 74, PC
49, 58, 59, 60-61, 63;
canceled, PC 66; graphical
interface, PC 59-60;
software, PC 61, 63

Apple Macintosh: IC *110*, IO
75, PC *12*, 65; developers,

PC *48-49*; development, PC
58-60, 61-65; Mac Plus, PC
68; Mac II, IC *122*, PC 68, 89;
marketing, PC 64-65;
memory, PC 64; software,
PC 65; user interface, PC
59-60, 64, 68

Apple II: CB *99*, 105, *106*, 108,
IC *90*, PC 7, *11*, 18, SW 68;
early success, PC 8, 47; engineering, PC 45; software, PC
47; and VisiCalc, PC 10

Apple III (Sara): PC 49, 58

Apple Writer: SW 74

Application programs: SW 19;
in everyday life, SW 91, *92-99*

Application-specific integrated
circuits (ASICs): CM 101-102,
IC 115

Applied Dynamics Inter-
national (ADI): AC 30

APT (Automatically Pro-
grammed Tools) language:
IC 42, LA 68, *70*

APT (Automatically Pro-
grammed Tools) System: CI
32, IC 42

APT (Automatic Photoelectric
Telescope): CI *20-21*

AQ11: AI 76, IC 87

Aquila: MF *69*

Aquinas, Thomas: PM 53, 58

Arbib, Michael: AI 12

ARC (Augmentation Research
Center): IO 64, 66, 67

ARC (Average Response
Computer): RV 61

Archaeology: PM 29-32, *33*

Arches: AI 75-76

Archimedes: PM 35

Architectural graphics: CI 91,
92-99; engineering
simulation, CI *95*, 96, *98*;
floor plans, CI 94, *95*

Architecture: *the design of a
computer system, including
both its hardware configuration and its software strategies for handling data and
running programs.*

Architecture, computer: PO
33; massively parallel, PO
96, 98, 102-104, 105-106;
modified von Neumann, PO
52-65; non-von Neumann,
PO 49, 89-106; parallel, PO
33-34, 49, *54-65*, 96-98,
102-104, 105-106; von

Neumann, PO 33, 49, *50-53*,
96, 98, 105, 106

Architecture, flexible: and
WWMCCS, MF 102

ARCO: PO 44

Argo (underwater vehicle): LA
7, RO 104

Arithmetic logic unit (ALU): *a
part of the central processor
that performs arithmetic operations, such as subtraction,
and logical operations, such
as TRUE-FALSE comparisons.
See ALU*

Armor, reactive: MF 67, 70

Armstrong, John: CM 92, 93

Armstrong, Neil: SP 39, 47-48,
117; quoted, CB *28-29*

Arnold, John: LA 101

Aronson, Marc: CC 106

ARPA (Advanced Research
Projects Agency): CO 40, IO
64, 66, 67, RO 63, RV 45;
Arpanet, CO 43, 44-47, 48;
and time sharing, CO 40, 43

ARPANET: AC 86, IC 66

Array: *a data structure containing elements that have some
feature in common; the*

CHESS WAS THE FORTE of this Boolean network of electromagnetic relays. The work of Spanish inventor Leonardo Torres y Quevedo, the device was one of the earliest attempts to imitate complex human thought processes. The machine always prevailed in the only game it was able to play—a lopsided denouement pitting its king and rook against a human opponent's king. The device automatically assessed the legality of its adversary's moves and formulated winning responses based on distances between the pieces.

FREQUENCY-DIVISION MULTIPLEXING, which permits a single communications link to carry multiple conversations or streams of data simultaneously, passed a field test staged with a pair of telephone wires between Maumee, Ohio, and South Bend, Indiana. A year later, AT&T established the first commercial service—a five-channel phone line between Baltimore and Pittsburgh. Today, the technique is indispensable for transferring data between computers.

THE TERM ROBOTS was first used in Karel Čapek's play *R.U.R. (Rossum's Universal Robots)*. Čapek extracted the now-common name for automaton from *robota*, the Czech word for work. The humanoid mechanical servants in his drama rebelled and destroyed their human masters.

1912

1917

1920

computer equivalent of a table of information. See Data structures: arrays.

Array processing: *a processing technique in which a single control unit directs the activities of a group of processors, commanding them to perform the same operation simultaneously on different sets of data. See Array processors.*

Array processors (AP): PO 73-76; uses, PO *75, 76*

Art, computer: *See* Computer art

Artifacts, computerized study of: PM 37; atomic analysis, PM *46-49;* dating, PM *44-45;* infrared art probes, PM *40-41;* monitoring condition, PM *38-39;* restoration, PM *42-43*

Artificial intelligence (AI): *the ability of a machine to perform functions that are normally associated with human intelligence, such as comprehending spoken lan-guage, making judgments, and learning.*

AI entire volume, IC 37, RO 17-18, SC 89, 91, SW 112; beginnings, AI 8-9, IC 35; expert systems, RO 18; founders, AI 56-57; machine learning, AI 73-84; naming, AI 56-57; neural-modeling approach, AI 11-14, 103, 108-110; and neural networks, AC 48, 51, 52, 54; perception, AI 100-109; potential consequences, AI 7; in space, AI 111; and space station: SP 71-72; and supercomputers, PO 89, 97, 104, 106; thinking, AI 109-110. *See also* Expert system

Artificial intelligence (AI) languages: LA 69, *118-121;* IPL, LA 69; LISP, LA 69, 71; Prolog, LA 71, 119

ART 2 (Adaptive Resonance Theory 2): AC 53

ARU (audio response unit): SO 82, 83

ASCII: *the acronym for American Standard Code for Infor-mation Interchange, a widely used system for encoding letters, numerals, punctuation marks, and signs as binary numbers.*

CB 32, CO 49, 54, IC 52, IO 45, 51, MS 76, SW 23; examples, CB *28-29, 32-35*

Ashton-Tate: SC 21

Asimov, Isaac: RO 9

Assembler: *a program that converts the mnemonic instructions of assembly-language programs into the zeros and ones of binary machine code.*

LA 15, 23, *32-33,* SW 36

Assembly language: *a low-level programming language, specific to a computer, just above the zeros and ones of machine code, that employs short mnemonic codes to tell the computer to carry out operations.*

IO 38, LA 7, 9, 15-16, 21, 23, *24-35,* 87, RV 40, 41, SW 25, 26, 36

Association for Computing Machinery (ACM): SC 85

A

THE DIFFERENTIAL ANALYZER, the most accurate calculating device of its day, was completed by M.I.T.'s Vannevar Bush. An analog device, the analyzer was designed to speed the solution of complicated differential equations, which sometimes took months to work out with pencil and paper. Bush's purely mechanical machine was programmed with a wrench and a screwdriver, a task that often required two to three days of oily labor.

A MATHEMATICAL SIEVE demonstrated the ability to sift whole numbers at the rate of 30,000 per minute in search of primes—integers that are divisible only by one and themselves. Invented by mathematician Derrick Lehmer of the University of California at Berkeley, this concatenation of motors, wheels, pulleys, and belts was a digital device that signaled the discovery of a prime number with an automobile headlamp.

IBM ADOPTED THE EIGHTY-COLUMN PUNCH CARD, setting a de facto industry standard that endured for decades. Data or programs, recorded as patterns of holes at the intersections of eighty columns and twelve rows, were retrieved in one of two ways: shining light through the openings or penetrating them with fine bristles of a wire brush, in much the same way as Hollerith's census-tabulating equipment had functioned nearly forty years earlier.

1928

1930

1932

Association of American Railroads (AAR): TR 76, 80; tracking of rail cars, TR *80-89*

Associative memory: *a machine's ability to recall an entire set of data when given only a part; a capability of one type of neural network.* AC *40-43*, 53

Asteroids: SP 102

Astrolabe: *the earliest analog computer; a device for making astronomical calculations.* AC 9

Astronomical Image Processing System (AIPS): CC 60-61

Astronomy: *See* Celestial mechanics

Astrophysical research: PO 19, *28-29*, 74-75

ASV: *See* Adaptive Suspension Vehicle

Atalla, John: CM 30

Atanasoff, John: CB 37, 59, 65, IC 15

Atanasoff-Berry Computer: IC *15*, IO *12*

AT&T: CM 67; Bell Laboratories, CO 14, 15, 18, 19, 46, 79, 82, 87-89, 100, LA

73; and CASE, SC 68-69; connecting foreign equipment to system, CO 21; Dataphone, CO 18, 19, IC *44*; and IBM, CO 97; and microwaves, CO 82, 83-84; and multiplexing, CO 14; network, CO *16-17*; satellites, CO 79-80, 87-89, 94, 96; and telecommunications network, CO 47, 49; *Telstar*, CO 79-80, 88-89. *See also* Bell Laboratories

Atari Corporation: CB 106, IC

72, IO 74, SW 70

Athena 2000 (sewing machine): SO 99

Atkinson, William: IC *123*, PC *49, 59*, 60, 61, 64

Atlantis (space shuttle): SP 71, 121; electrical problem, CS 28-29

Atlas I: MS 82, 83

Atlas rocket: SP 18

ATM (automatic teller machine): IC *67*, SO 79, *84-85*, SW 88, 89; early off-line models, SO 85; multibank

networks, SO 74-75, *84, 85*; and OLTP, SO 75-77

Atmosphere, general-circulation models of: PM 107; and chaos theory, PM 108

Atmospheric interference: CC 28, 29, *83*

ATOLL (acceptance, test or launch language): SP 42-43

Atomic-scale computers: AC 107-108

Attractors: PM *116-119*; bifurcation diagram, PM *120-121*; Lorenz, PM 110, 111, 116, *117, 118-119*; strange, PM *111*

Aurora 7: SP 7-8

Authorship, analysis of: PM 61-62

AutoCad: PC 96

AUTOCODE: IC 30, LA 20, 21

Automated clearinghouse (ACH): *a computerized facility that sorts electronic payment transactions originating at many banks into groups of payments, each of which is routed to a single bank.* SO *80-81*

ALAN TURING published the seminal paper "On Computable Numbers." The Cambridge mathematician's monograph set forth a hypothetical "universal machine" that would perform any calculation or logical operation a human could devise.

THE FIRST ELECTRICAL BINARY ADDER consisted of cast-off telephone relays, old batteries, flashlight bulbs, and strips cut from a tin can. This elementary but essential computer component was assembled by Bell Laboratories mathematician George Stibitz working evenings in his kitchen. Gangs of adders formed the basis of his 1940 Complex Number Calculator.

CLAUDE SHANNON, an M.I.T. graduate student, wedded binary numbers, Boolean algebra, and electric circuitry into a theoretical foundation for electronic computing in his master's thesis, "A Symbolic Analysis of Relay and Switching Circuits." From M.I.T., Shannon went to Bell Labs, where he earned a reputation as a leading communications theorist.

1936

1937

1938

A

Automated Commercial System (ACS): TR 70-72

Automated guided vehicles (AGVs): RO *107-109*

Automated Manifest System: TR 71

Automated Quota System: TR 72

Automated teller machine (ATM): *a computer terminal used by bank customers for conducting routine transactions, such as making deposits, withdrawing money, or transferring funds from* one account to another. *See* ATM.

Automated traffic management: for aircraft, TR 92; for automobiles, TR 105-108; for vessels, TR 91-92

Automatic Language Processing Advisory Committee (ALPAC): PM 76

Automatic Photoelectric Telescope (APT): CC *20-21*

Automatic Sequence Controlled Calculator (Mark I): RV 15

Automatic target recognition: MF 66-67

Automatic teller machine: *See* ATM

Automation in manufacturing: IO 77-79

Automobile design: PO 19, 25

Automobile industry: CAD, CI 103, 104; CAE, CI 103-105; CAM, CI 105-106

Automobiles: shipment of, TR 77-78

Automobile traffic, automated management of: TR 105-108; limited access highways, TR 106-108; traffic lights, TR 106

Automotive applications: TR 7, 10-11, 16, 27, *28-41;* air pollution control, TR 10, 27; brakes, TR 7, *36-37;* climate control, TR *39;* cost of electronics, TR 11; engine control, TR *30-31;* four-wheel steering, TR *32-33;* instruments, TR *40-41;* navigation system, TR 41, 54; seats, TR *38-39;* sensors, TR *28-29;* shock absorbers, TR *34-35;* simplifying wiring, TR 11, 16, 27

Autonomous land vehicle (ALV): IC *114,* RO *30-31,* 76, *77*

Autonomous underwater vehicle (AUV): RO 104-105

AutoSketch: PC 94

Aviation navigation: inertial systems, TR 17

Aviram, Ari: AC 97, 104

AWACS (Airborne Warning and Control System): MF 96-98, 100

Ayres, Robert: RO 46

Axon: *the impulse-transmitting fiber of a nerve cell; the part of a neural network that emulates its function. See* Neural networks: synapses.

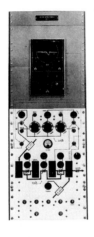

POLYPHEMUS, THE COMPUTING CYCLOPS, became the first fully electronic analog computer and another ally against the engineering drudgery of differential equations. For the shaft rotations that Vannevar Bush's differential analyzer used to signify values, inventor George Philbrick substituted voltages. Results were displayed on the circular screen of an oscilloscope, prompting Philbrick to name his creation for a one-eyed character of Greek mythology.

1938

THE COMPLEX NUMBER CALCULATOR closeted at Bell Laboratories' headquarters in New York City was the first computer to communicate a long distance with a remote terminal. Members of the American Mathematical Society meeting at Dartmouth College in Hanover, New Hampshire, were invited to transmit problems over a teletype circuit to the calculator, which responded from New York a minute or so later.

1940

B-1B bomber: MF 49
Babb, Del: SP 36, 37
Babbage, Charles: AI 8, CB 10-13, IC *7, 8*, IO 8-9, SW 9-*10*
Babbitt, Milton: IO 100
Babcock, Horace: CC 30
Bachman Information Systems: Bachman Re-Engineering Product Set, SC 64, 69
Back-propagation algorithm: *the formula by which a neural-network computer calculates how close it has come to a correct response and adjusts the strengths of relationships between its neurons to improve its performance.*
Backus, John: AI 102, IC *31*, 36, 93, LA 38-39, *40*, 45, 48, *49, 50*, RV 40, SC 20, 85-86, 99, 100, 106, SO 15, 18, SW 29, 57
Backward error propagation: *a process in neural-network*

computing whereby the computer learns from its mistakes.
Backward-error-propagation algorithm: AC 32, 55, 60
BACON: AI 77, 80, IC 91, SW 111
Bacon, Roger: AC 110
Bacteriorhodopsin: *a purple light-sensitive protein that is used to create an ultrafast, high-capacity optical digital storage disk.* AC *102-103*, 105
Bailey, David: PM 36
Baird, John Logie: MS 97-98
Bakalinsky, Eric: LA 101
Bales, Steve: SP 61
Ballard, Robert D.: RO 103
Ballistic computations: RV 12, 15
Ballistics uses: CB 52, 53, 59
Banana printers: PC 24
Banchoff, Thomas: CI 111

Bandwidth: *the range of frequencies occupied by an information-bearing signal or that can be accommodated by a transmission medium such as copper wires, microwaves, or optical fibers. The greater the bandwidth, the more data can be transmitted.* See Electromagnetic spectrum.
BankAmericard: SO 49
Banking: credit checks, SO *68-69;* direct deposits, SO *80-81;* electronic, SO 79, *80-87;* and fault-tolerant computers, SO 74-77; funds transfers, SO *86-87;* multibank ATM networks, SO *84, 85;* software, SW 88-89; by telephone, SO *82-83*
Barak missile: MF 72
Baran, Paul: CO 44-45
Bar code: *a series of dark bars and light spaces used to rep-*

THE FIRST FLIGHT SIMULATOR was perfected by Helmut Hoelzer, circumventing much costly flight testing during the development of Germany's V-2 rocket. An analog computer in the device generated voltages that imitated those sent to the missile's guidance system as a result of external influences such as wind. The guidance system in turn produced flight-control voltages that could be analyzed to determine whether they were appropriate to bring the missile back on course.

GERMANY'S KONRAD ZUSE built the Z-3, the first operational program-controlled computer. Performing arithmetic by means of 2,600 second-hand telephone relays, the electromechanical Z-3 incorporated features of two earlier prototypes: the use of binary numbers to perform logical operations, and the storage of programs by means of holes punched in discarded movie film.

BANKS OF VACUUM TUBES added to Vannevar Bush's differential analyzer did away with the oily manual labor required to program the computer to solve differential equations, reducing setup time from days to minutes. The improved device was dubbed the Rockefeller Differential Analyzer (RDA2) in honor of its partial funding by the Rockefeller Foundation.

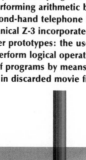

1941

1941

1942

B

resent a number keyed to a computer file containing information, usually about an item of inventory.
SW *94-95;* on automobiles, TR 77; and Federal Express, SO 110-111; optical scanners for, SO *104-107;* in retail merchandising, SO *116-119;* UPC, IC *77,* SO *92-97*
Bardeen, John: CB *57, 70, 71, 72,* CM 17, *20*
Barnaby, John: IC *97,* SW 69, *71*
Barnes, Henry: SW 85
Baroyan, Oganes Vagarshako-vitch: HB 70
Base: *region of a bipolar transistor that controls the flow of current between the emitter and the collector. See* Manufacturing of chips.
Base register: SC 27
Bash, James C.: MF 98
BASIC (Beginners All-Purpose

Symbolic Instruction Code): IC 54, LA *17, 46,* 71, 99-100, SC 36, SW 26, 27-28, 30, 31-32, 37, *38;* for Altair, CB 99, 100; and microcomputers, LA 99, 100-103; tiny, LA 101
Batch processing: *a method of executing programs in which instructions and data are submitted to the computer at one time and the results are released when the entire job is complete.*
SO *17, 22, 46, 47,* SW 26, 27
Baudot, Emile: CO 9, 12

Beard, Kenneth V.: RV 94-95
Beast, the (robot): RO 70
Becker, Douglas: MS 106-107
Becker, Eric: MS 107
Beck-Sagué, Consuelo: HB 67-70
Bednorz, Johannes Georg: CM 92
BEFORTRAN: LA 99
Bell, Alexander Graham: CO 13
Bell, Gordon: PO 70
Bell, Gwen: CO 40
Bell Laboratories: AC 54, 65, CB 70, 97, CC 32, 53, 95, CM 17, 20, 57, 102, IO 11, 101, 106, LA 73, RO 10, 11, SC 34; Model I, IO 11, *12;* optical technology, AC 86-87, 92, 94; and superconductivity, CM 91, 92, 93; and UNIX, RV 73. *See also* AT&T; Transistors
Belzer, Jack: RV 13
Bennington, Herbert: MF 110
Bentley: PC 95
Berndt, Bruce: PM 36
Bernstein, Jeremy: AC 48, 51
Berry, Clifford: CB 59
Bethe, Hans: RV 13
Beth Israel Hospital (Boston): HB 60
Bible: concordances, PM 53, *54-57,* 59-60
Big Bang: CC 16, 23; confirmation of theory, CC 95; origins of theory, CC 89, 94; simulations, CC 96-97, 105-108, 109
Bigelow, Julian: AI 10, RO 16
Billings, John Shaw: CB 14
Bill of lading: TR 84
BINAC (Binary Automatic Computer): IC *23,* IO 15, MS 37, SW 16

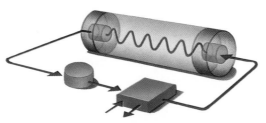

THE ACOUSTIC DELAY LINE was the first type of memory fast enough to keep up with a vacuum-tube electronic computer. Devised by William Shockley, later a coinventor of the transistor, the delay line briefly stored data by converting it from electrical pulses to much-slower sound waves passing through a tube of mercury. Improved versions of the delay line could hold as many as one thousand bits of data for increments of one-thousandth of a second, until the computer was ready for it.

THE FIRST ELECTRONIC DIGITAL COMPUTER, constructed by John Atanasoff and Clifford Berry at Iowa State College, utilized vacuum tubes and capacitors arranged on a drum. With logic built from the vacuum tubes and memory lodged in the capacitors, the single-purpose machine was fed information on punch cards. The Atanasoff-Berry Computer, which never advanced beyond the prototype stage, lay unappreciated until 1974, when a federal judge voided the patent granted to ENIAC (page 18) and declared Atanasoff and Berry the inventors of the modern computer.

COLOSSUS cracked German codes during World War II. Named for its 2,000 glowing vacuum tubes, Colossus was pitted against the Germans' Enigma machine, which could encode messages 100 billion different ways. Confronted with so many possibilities, Allied cryptanalysts relied heavily on trial-and-error code-breaking methods even though Enigma's internal secrets had been compromised. Colossus brought the necessary brute force to the task. Using photoelectric readers to examine encrypted communications punched into paper tape, the computer searched for telltale patterns in the messages at the rate of 25,000 characters per second.

1942

1943

1943

Binary: *having two components or possible states; usually represented by a code of zeros and ones.*

Binary adders: CB 39, *44, 45;* cascading, CB *46-47*

Binary arithmetic: IO 23, LA *12-13*

Binary code: *a system for representing things by combinations of two symbols, such as one and zero, TRUE and FALSE, or the presence or absence of light or voltage. See also Binary notation.*

Binary code, optical: AC *72-73*

Binary logic: CI *8*

Binary notation: *a number system that uses two as its base and expresses numbers as strings of zeros and ones.*

Binary number system: CB 9, 37-38, 39, *40-41,* SW 11; as computer code, CB 29-31, 36-38; and neurons, AI 11-12

Binary search: *a technique for rapidly isolating the object of a search through a sequentially arranged database by dividing it into successively smaller halves. See Database, relational: binary searches.*

Binary star interferometry: CC 31

Binary tree architecture: *a hardware design incorporating many layers of processors, beginning with a conventional serial processor that branches into two processing elements, each connected in turn to two more processors. See Binary tree network.*

Binary tree network: PO 103-104

Binary trees: PM *54-57*

Biochemistry: CI *109,* 112; crystallography, RV 81, *82-91*

Biochip: *a hypothetical device for molecular computing, which would be "grown" from organic substances, analogous to an electronic integrated circuit.* AC *98-103,* 105-107

Biomechanics: CI 101, 107-108, HB *14-15*

Biomedical research: computers in, RV 59-67

Biometric identification systems: CS 45, *46-47;* data recording, CS *46-47;* fingerprint, CS *56-57;* hand geometry, CS 11, *54-55;* retinal, CS 11, *52-53;* signature, CS *48-49;* voice, CS 11, *50-51*

BIONET: HB 43

BIOS: copiers of IBM PC, PC 22-24

Bipolar: *transistors in which current is carried by both positive and negative particles, holes, and electrons. See Transistors: bipolar.*

Birge, Robert: AC 105, 107

Bistability: *the property that allows a material to maintain either of two opposite states (a positive or negative charge, for example) without external aid; most substances are naturally stable in only one state.* AC 94

Bit: *the smallest unit of information in a digital computer, equivalent to a single zero or one. The word "bit" is a contraction of "binary digit."* CB 36, SW 22; origin of term, RV 42

Bit map: *a temporary memory for a graphic display in which each dot, or pixel, of the display is represented by one or more bits.* CI 54

Black boxes, aircraft: TR 12. *See also* Flight-data acquisition

Black Hole, The: CI 77

Black holes: CC *13,* 16, 74, PO 74, 75

Blair, Janet Braintree: CS 18
Blake, William: PM 82-89, *90*, 91
Blanchard, Malcolm: CI 89
Bletchley Park: CS 91
Blidberg, D. Richard: RO 105
Blind: computerized aids for the, HB 93-96, 107
Blinn, James: CI 49, 58-59
Blizzard, Edward: SP 101
Block, Richard: SW 16-17
Blocking: CS *104*
Block structure: LA 49
Blood flow: HB *55*; and DSA, HB *63-65*
Blue Cross/Blue Shield of Maryland: MS 107
Blue Gasmeter Job: TR 44
BMEWS (Ballistic Missile Early Warning System): malfunction, MF 23
BNF (Backus Naur Form; Backus Normal Form): IC 42, LA 48, 49
Boeing: SC 61, TR 17-18, 54
Boeing Artificial Intelligence Center: SP 72
Bogue, Allan: PM 19
Bolt Beranek and Newman Inc.: CO 46, 47

Boltzmann machine: AI 109
Bomb, guided: MF 62, *70, 71*
Bondi, Hermann: CC 94
Bonding: CM *110-111*
Bonn, Ted: MS 37, 38
Bonner, Dick: TR 69
Bonner, William: SW 104
Boole, George: AI 12, CB *31*, 36, 39, IC *8*
Boolean algebra: *a method for expressing the logical relationships between entities such as propositions or on-off computer circuits.* CB 31, 36, 38, *42-43;* early electronic devices, CB 36, 37-38, IC 8
Boone, Greg: SC 63
Booth, Andrew D.: MS 44, PM 67
Bootstrapping (booting): CB *112-121*
Bootstrap program: *built-in instructions that take effect when a computer is turned on and that prepare the computer for operation. See* Bootstrapping.
Borland International: LA 104-105

Borman, Frank: SP 38, 116, 117
Borwein, Jonathan and Peter: PM 36
Bottom-Up Design (BUD): CM 103
Bottom-up model: CC 96-97, 106, 107
Bottom-up school: AI 7, 12-14, 103, 108
Bottom-up theory: *an approach to artificial intelligence aimed at mechanically duplicating the human brain to create adaptive networks. See* Bottom-up school.

Bouldin, Barbara: SC 68-69
Bouldin, Eric: MS 105
Boulez, Pierre: IO 106
Boundary analysis: SC 8-9, 114-115
Boyd, Jim: PC 87
Boyle, Willard S.: CC 32
Braille: HB 93
Brain: computer simulation, HB *24-25*, 26, *27-29*, *32-33*; cross-field research, HB 33; mental illness, HB 30, 33, 75-78; and mind, HB 24-25, 30; research approaches, HB 30; three-dimensional structure, HB 31, *114-115*
Brain tissue: AC 46
Brakes: antilock, TR 7, *36-37*
Branch, conditional: SW 30
Branching: testing, SC 12-13
Branch instructions: LA *30-31*; conditional, LA *58-59*
Brattain, Walter: CB 57, *70, 71, 72*, CM 17, *20*, IC 20
BRAVE 3000: MF 68
Bricklin, Daniel: IC 97, PC 9, *11*, SW 69-70, *72*
Brigham Young University: BYU Concordance Program, PM 60

THE HARVARD MARK I, developed by IBM and Howard Aiken, was the first American calculating device to offer the convenience of loading instructions from punched paper tape. A mechanical dinosaur, the machine was fifty-one feet long and contained 3,304 electromechanical switches able to add or subtract twenty-three-digit numbers (decimal, not binary) in three-tenths of a second. Although made obsolete by electronic computers such as ENIAC and EDVAC, it did yeoman service for sixteen years calculating ballistics tables for the United States Navy.

A BASIC PLAN FOR COMPUTERS appeared in mathematician John von Neumann's famous "First Draft" memorandum. Incorporating ideas from computer giants Alan Turing, John Mauchly, and J. Presper Eckert, von Neumann's scheme called for a central arithmetic logic unit (ALU), a central control unit, provisions for input and output, and—most important—a memory for storing programs.

STANISLAW ULAM invented the Monte Carlo method, an early means of solving by computer inexact problems in fields ranging from aerodynamics to traffic control, to trace nuclear fusion reactions leading to the H-bomb. The idea came to the Polish-born mathematician while he was playing solitaire during a hospital stay. Ulam saw that the outcome of the game could be predicted approximately from the results of many, many games. The same method works, he realized, for any process in which each step (in card games, fusion, or weather), though random, depends partly on the step preceding it.

1944

1945

1945

Bright, Herb: LA 37
British Leyland: RO 42
British Telecom: MS 107
Bromberg, Howard: LA 44
Brookhaven National Laboratory: CM 107
Brookings Institution: econometric model, PM 96
Brooks, Frederick: SC 24, 26, 31-32, 33, 38
Brother Industries: RO 33
Brown, Ernest: CC 86, 87, RV 10
Brown, Gordon S.: CI 9, 12, RO 14
Brown, T. H.: RV 14
Brown University: AC 46, PM 83

Browser, hypermedia: PM *88-89*
Brunner, Theodore F.: PM 60
Buchanan, Bruce: AI 40, HB 72, SW 111, 112
Buffer: *a temporary memory used to hold data being transferred from one device to another, such as from a computer to a printer.* refresh, CI 38; screen, CI *16*
Buffer, frame: bit map, CI 60; core, CI 50; RAM, CI 51, 54; rotating drum, CI 50; shift-register, CI 51
Bug: SW *17*
BUGSYS (Bug System language): LA 68-69
Bunnell, David: CB 99
Bunting, Robert: SW 104-105
Burger, Robert: CM 73
Burke, William: PM 110
Burnham, David: MS 72
Burroughs Corporation: LA 42,

PO 33, SO 20, 23, 89, SP 17, 19; B5000, MS 83-84; B5500, PM 97; computers, CB *98*, SO 23, SP 17, 19; ILLIAC IV, PO 34, 96; and virtual memory, MS 83
Burton, Tony: HB 68
Bus: *a set of wires for carrying signals around a computer.* CB 100, *112-113*, 117, IO *26-27*; Altair-100, CB 100; S-100, CB 100; and speed, PO 51
Busa, Roberto: PM 53, *58*-59
Bush, Vannevar: AC 10, 11, *13*, CB 36, *54*, CC 87, IC *11*, 14, PM 78-79, 90-91, RO 15, SP 9
Bushnell, Nolan: CB 106, IC *72*, SW 70
Busicom: SO 89, 90, 91, 100
Business graphics: CI 7
BusinessLand: PC 25
Business languages: LA 41-44
Butterfly Effect: PM 110
Byron, Augusta Ada: CB 11, 12, IC *8*, IO 8-9, 111, SW 9-10, *11*
Byte: *a sequence of eight bits, treated as a unit for computation or storage.* SW 22; definition, CB *36*

ENIAC was the first electronic digital computer, solving H-bomb problems before turning to its steady job of calculating artillery-aiming tables for the U.S. Army. The machine was twice as large as the navy's Harvard Mark I, but because it operated with vacuum tubes rather than electromechanical switches, it was also a thousand times faster. Even so, designers Mauchly and Eckert realized that ENIAC was obsolete before its first run. Not only did it manipulate decimal numbers rather than binary ones, but it lacked internal storage of programs, which had to be wired into the circuitry. To change from one program to another, a technichian unplugged and replugged hundreds of wires, a task that could take two days.

1946

C: IC 74, LA 7, 8, 9, 73, 76, 105, SC 20, 36

C++: SC 20, 89, 105

C3 (C-cubed): MF 93-94; and battlefield communications, MF *103;* and EMP, MF 106-107; interservice, MF 98; and SDI, MF 108; strategic, MF 100-102, 106, 107; tactical, MF 93-100; and VHSICs, MF 100. *See also* Aegis; AWACS; Joint STARS; JTIDS

Cabell, Charles: MF 97

Cache: *a high-speed intermediate memory unit between main memory and the CPU that accelerates the fetching of data and instructions. See* Memory: cache.

Cache memory: *See* Memory: cache

CAD: *See* Computer-aided design

CAD/CAM: CI 107, IO 78, 79. *See also* Computer-aided design; Computer-aided manufacturing; Computer-integrated manufacturing

CADUCEUS: AI 40-41, HB 74, IC 99, SW 111

Cadwell, Carlton: HB 77, 78

Cadwell, John: HB 77

Cahill, Thaddeus: IO 98

Calculators: electronic, RV 71-73, SO 90; mechanical, SO 89-90

California Institute of Technology (Caltech): AC 46, PO 102, SP 86, 87; Jet Propulsion Laboratory, RO 7; Stanford/JPL hand, RO *76,* 79

Caltech: *See* California Institute of Technology

Caltech-Xerox project: CM 31-32

Calvert, Thomas: IO 110

CAM: *See* Computer-aided manufacturing

Cameras, computerized: CB *18-19*

Cameras, monitor: CI 16, *28-29*

Campbell, Robert: SW 16-17

Canary: SC 59

Cancer: and 3-D imaging, HB *112-113*

Canine, Ralph: MF 47

Canion, Rod: PC 22, *25*

Capacitance tactile sensors: RO 79-80

Capacitor: *a device that stores electrical energy when a voltage is applied. It consists of two conductors separated by an insulator called a dielectric.* CM 23

Cape Canaveral (Kennedy): SP 7, 17, 18, 40, 85

Capek, Karel: IC 10, RO 9

Card-sorter-aided diagnosis: HB 72

Cargo handling: *See* Marine terminals; Railroads

Cargo Selectivity System: TR 71

Carina nebula: CC *8-9*

Carlos, Walter: IO 101

Carmody, Liam: SO 75, 76

Carnegie Institute of Technology (Carnegie-Mellon University): AI 9, 77

Carnegie-Mellon University: AC 46, AI 77, PO 98, RO 46, 61, 62, 70, 74; Neptune, RO 74-75; Robotics Institute, RO 102; Rover 1, RO 102; Terregator, RO 75, *76;* Workhorse, RO 103

C

PLANKALKÜL, the first high-level language for computers, promised to simplify the writing of software by enabling a programmer to instruct the machine with notation that was easier to interpret than long strings of ones and zeros. The language was devised by Konrad Zuse, who, working alone in war-devastated Germany, formulated its syntax in part by writing a chess-playing program *(above).* Plankalkül was never used, and Zuse's achievement was not widely known until years later.

1946

INSPIRING LECTURES at the University of Pennsylvania's Moore School of Electrical Engineering stimulated post-World War II competition in stored-program computers. Delivered by J. Presper Eckert, John Mauchly, and seventeen other prominent scientists, the presentations would lead to a succession of computers, known in the late 1940s and the early 1950s as "electronic brains," with names such as EDSAC, BINAC, UNIVAC, and EDVAC.

1946

THE WILLIAMS TUBE won the post-World War II race for a practical random-access memory (RAM), making possible almost-instant retrieval of any item of stored data or program. To create the device, Fred Williams of England's Manchester University modified a cathode-ray tube. An electron beam inside the tube scanned successive lines across its face, "painting" dots and dashes of phosphorescent electrical charge on the screen to represent binary ones and zeros.

1947

Carpenter, Gail: AC 53
Carpenter, Scott: SP 7, 116
Carterphone: CO 21
Cartesian geometry: CI *10-11*
CARTOS (computer-aided reconstruction by tracing of serial sections): *a computer imaging system that translates two-dimensional photographs and video images of tissue slices into three-dimensional displays of features such as nerves.* HB 31-32
Cary, Frank: PC 11, 16
Case, Richard: SC 31, 38
CASE (computer-aided software engineering): SC 39, 51, 62-70; acceptance of, SC 66-67; costs of, SC 66-67; data dictionary, SC 41, 45; fully integrated, SC 64-66; function modules, SC 41, 42-47; languages for, SC 106; matrix, SC 44-45; process-oriented, SC 62; simulation, SC 48-49; states, SC 40; testing integration, SC 46-47; transitions, SC 41, 43

Case-control study: HB 67-68
Case Western Reserve University: HB 102
Casings: CM *112-113*
Cassidy, Frederic G.: PM 66
Cassiopeia A: CC *6-7*
Catalogs, star: CC 99, 100-101
Cathode-ray tube (CRT): *a television-like display device with a screen that lights up where it is struck from inside by a beam of electrons.* IO 12, *13*, 18, 32, *54-55*; memory, MS *11*, 12, 16; storage, SW 14; and word processor, IO 43

Catmull, Edwin: CI 89
CCITT (International Telegraph and Telephone Consultative Committee): CO 55, 56, 104
CDC: *See* Control Data Corporation
CD-I (compact disk-interactive): *a CD-ROM capable of storing together audio, video, textual, and graphics data.* MS 103
CD-ROM (compact disk read-only memory): *a type of compact disk used to store text or graphics in digital*

form and capable of storing together audio, video, textual, and graphics data. IC *113*, MS 102-103, 109; disk, MS *110*, 114-116; disk drives, MS 110, *111-116*; High Sierra format, MS 103
Cecula, Adolph: CS 29
Cedar system: IC *123*, PO 98, 102
Celestial mechanics: RV 7-12, SP *50-51*
Cell: *a single location in a computer's memory, capable of storing one bit of information. A group of cells forms a computer word. See* Magnetic recording: coding systems.
Center for Computer Research in Music and Acoustics (CCRMA): IO 101, 106, 107
Center for Computer Technology and Research in the Biomedical Sciences: RV 64
Centers for Disease Control: HB 66, 67, 68; computers, HB 66

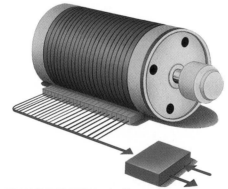

THE SEMICONDUCTOR REVOLUTION began with this point-contact transistor, invented by Bell Labs scientists William Shockley, Walter Brattain, and John Bardeen. Improved models would in time entirely supplant big, hot, power-hungry, and short-lived vacuum tubes used in ENIAC and other early machines.

THE MAGNETIC DRUM—the first random-access, magnetic storage device for computers—held far more data than did delay lines and Williams tubes. Invented in England, the drum registered information as magnetic pulses in tracks around a metal cylinder, by using a row of read/write heads to both record and recover the data. Because it was too slow to find many applications as a memory, it served mostly as a storage device. At the pinnacle of its development, the magnetic drum could store about 4,000 words and retrieve any one of them in as little as $5/1000$ of a second.

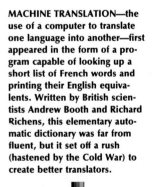

MACHINE TRANSLATION—the use of a computer to translate one language into another—first appeared in the form of a program capable of looking up a short list of French words and printing their English equivalents. Written by British scientists Andrew Booth and Richard Richens, this elementary automatic dictionary was far from fluent, but it set off a rush (hastened by the Cold War) to create better translators.

1947

1948

1948

Central processing unit (CPU): *the part of a computer that interprets and executes instructions. It is composed of an arithmetic logic unit, a control unit, and a small amount of memory.* CB *82-83,* 109, 110, IO *26, 27, 28, 29,* 30, LA *24,* PO *50-53,* SO 13, 14, 18, 19, 20, 41, 44, SW 21; and bootstrapping, CB 110, 112, 115, 117; coprocessor, PO *57;* IC, CB 77, 78, *82-83;* multiple functional units, PO *56-57;* pipelined, PO *58-59*
Centrella, Joan: CC 103-104, 105, 106, IC 107
Centronics: IO 46
Cen X-3: CC 69-70
Certainty factors: AI 50-51
Chaffee, Fred: CC 22, 28
Chaffee, Roger: SP 46, 117
Chaining, backward: AI 48-49
Chaining, forward: AI 48
Chalet satellite: MF 46
Challenger: SP 21, 70, 71, 120, 121

Channel: *an electronic communications path within a computer system or in telecommunications between systems. See* Computers: vulnerability.
Channel: *the region between the source and the drain of a field-effect transistor through which current flows. See* Switches.
Channel Navigation Information Service (CNIS): TR 91
Chaos (Gleick): PM 110
Chaos theory: HB 33, IC 52, PM 93, 108-112, 113, *114-121;* Lorenz attractor, PM 110, 111, 116, *117;* and meteorology, PM 108-110, *114-115;* period doubling, PM *120-121;* sensitive dependence on initial conditions, PM 110, *118-119*
Chaotic systems: SW 105-106
Character generator: IO *52*
Character recognition: IO 97-98; Kurzweil's software, HB 95-96; written, AC 62-63, 65

Charge-coupled device (CCD): *a three-layered semiconductor chip. Sensitive to electromagnetic radiation, it is useful for imaging systems, such as television cameras and telescopes.* CC 32, *33-35,* IC 67, MF 37, 38; in astronomy, CC *33,* 36, 37, 39; brightness recording range, CC 36; image, CC *33;* size, CC 33, 36
Charge-Coupled Device/Transit Instrument (CTI): CC 39-41
Charpentier, Al: CM 99, 101, 102
Charts: electronic, TR 55-56, *64-65*
Chase Econometric Associates: PM 97, 98, 99
Chebyshev, P. L.: RO 63
Checkers: AI 73-75, IC 28
Checksum: *an extra byte derived from a group of bytes and appended to them to*

enable a computer to detect errors after data has been transmitted or stored. MS 86, *87*
Chemicals: hazardous, CM 78
Chemical transport models: PO *82-83*
Chemical vapor deposition (CVD): *a method of depositing insulators, semiconductors, and metals in which a chemical reaction of gases causes the desired material to precipitate onto a wafer's surface.* CM 80-*81*
Chen, Peter: SC 63
Chen, Steve: PO 41, 98
Chess: AI 8, 9, IC 10
Chest: HB *49*
Chevron Geosciences Company: PO 7
Chicago: O'Hare Airport, TR 109; traffic control, TR 106-108

C

IBM'S SELECTIVE SEQUENCE ELECTRONIC CALCULATOR (SSEC), a hybrid machine with more than 20,000 relays and some 12,500 vacuum tubes, could handle larger problems more rapidly than any of its predecessors. Operation sequence was controlled by means of instructions stored in a hierarchy of memories that included some of the vacuum tubes and relays, as well as punched paper tape. The SSEC began its brief career calculating scientific data in public view near IBM's Manhattan headquarters. Before it was dismantled in 1952, it had produced moon-position tables that would be used for plotting the course of Apollo's 1969 flight to the moon.

1948

Chip: *an integrated circuit on a square of silicon or other semiconductor, made up of thousands of transistors and other electronic components. See* Integrated circuits.

Chipmakers: CM entire volume

Chipmaking industry: in 1980s, CM 73-74; and change, CM 56-57; chip yields, CM 55; customers, CM 54; geographic concentrations, CM 54; and government, CM 74; labor issues, CM 56; marketing by, CM 54-55; relationships among firms, CM 52-54; in Silicon Valley, CM 52-54; survival problems, CM 51-52, 73

CHIPS (Clearing House Interbank Payments System): SO 87

Chlorofluorocarbons (CFCs): and ozone layer, PM 105-108

Chomsky, Noam: AI 59

Choreography, computer-assisted: IO *94, 95, 107,* 110

Choropleth maps: PM 22-23

Chowning, John: IC *78,* IO 106, 110

Christiansen, Wilbur N.: CC 57

Chrysler: CI 104, RO 34, SO 13

Chu, Paul: CM 93

Chubb, Melvin: MF 109

Chubb, William: SP 61, 63, 64

Church, Alonzo: LA 69, SC 89, 91, 99

Churchill, Winston: MF 49

CICADA (Central Instrumentation, Control and Data Acquisition): RV 105-106

CICS (Customer Information Control System): SO 47

Cii Honeywell Bull: LA 81, 82

Cimino, Aldo: AI 41-42

Cincinnati Milacron T³ Robot: RO 34

Cipher: *an encryption system that arbitrarily represents each character by one or more other characters.* CS 103-104. *See also* Encryption of messages and data

Ciphertext: CS 104

Circuit: *a closed network through which current can flow. See* Logic circuits.

Circuit board: *an insulating board on which electronic components are mounted.* of PC, CM *8-13;* structure, CM 11, *114-117*

Circuit design: adder, CM 35, *36-49;* arrays in PC, CM *8-9;* computer-aided, CM 33-34, *100-101,* 102-104; criteria, CM 28; difficulties with LSI chips, CM 31; of high performance chips, CM 102-104; logic gates, CM 38,

39-47; mask making, CM *48-49;* networks of gates, CM *40-41, 46-47;* planning, CM *37;* rules, CM 31-32; table of combinations, CM *38;* training of designers, CM 31, 32

Circuit switching: CO 44, 65; virtual, CO *70-71*

CIS (Customer Information System): SO 47

CISC (Complex Instruction Set Computer): PC 99; architecture, PC *100;* and pipelining, PC *102-103*

Citibank, and fault-tolerant computer system: SO 74, 75

Clark, Barry: CC 60

Clark, David: CO 63

Clark, Wesley: RV 59-63, *64,* 65-67

Clarke, Arthur C.: CO 85-86

Clerman, Robert: AC 106

Climate: *See* Meteorology, computer modeling

Cliometrics: PM 19-23

Clock: *a device, usually based on a quartz crystal, that gives off regular pulses that are*

NORBERT WIENER published *Cybernetics,* a major influence on later research into artificial intelligence. In his book, the American intellectual contended that any machine with pretensions to intelligence must be able to learn or modify its behavior in response to feedback from its environment. Wiener drew this definition in part from his World War II experiments with antiaircraft systems that could anticipate the course of enemy planes by interpreting radar images. Wiener coined the term "cybernetics" from the Greek word for "steersman."

INFORMATION THEORY was first detailed in a treatise entitled "The Mathematical Theory of Communication." Author Claude Shannon's immediate purpose was to show communications engineers how to encode data so that it could be checked for accuracy following transmission between computers. His solution also shed light on the problem of conveying information so that it is not misinterpreted—a matter central to the field of artificial intelligence.

EDSAC, THE FIRST PRACTICAL STORED-PROGRAM COMPUTER, was designed by Maurice Wilkes according to ideas expounded in the Moore School lectures delivered three years earlier. Wilkes, a British computer pioneer, built the machine at Cambridge University, saving time by using readily available technology. For programming his machine, however, Wilkes established a library of short programs called subroutines stored on punched paper tapes.

1948

1948

1949

used to coordinate a computer's operations.
CB *83*, 111, 112, 115, 117; and speed, PO 51. *See also* Quartz crystal
Clock skew: AC 87
CLODO: CS 40
Clones, IBM PC: PC 23-25
CLOS (Common LISP Object System): SC 105
Closed-loop control: *a method of controlling robots and other devices in which the position of a moving member or the status of some other output is fed back to the control unit.*
RO *12-13*, 56-57
Cloud-in-cell method: CC 105, 107, 109, *112-114*, IC *107*
Clouds: PM *12-13*
Club of Rome: PM 104, 105
CMOS circuitry: CM 30-31, IC *62*; for logic gates, CM *42-45*
Coaxial cable: CO 82

Cobb, Ron: CI 83, 84, 88, 89
COBOL (Common Business Oriented Language): IC 47, LA 43-44, 67, 81, SC 19, SO 19, SW 29, 38, *39*; and microcomputers, LA 105; origins of, LA 41-43
Cochlea, artificial: AC 66
Cochlear implants: HB 97-99
Cocke, John: IC *82*, PC 98
Cockpit, computerized: TR *20-21*
CODASYL (Conference on Data Systems Languages): LA 42, 43-44
Codd, Edgar F.: IC 72, MS 73
Codebreaking: CB 55-59
Codec: *the abbreviation for coder/decoder, a device that is used in digital telephone systems to convert analog signals to digital ones and vice versa. See* Modems.

Code generator: LA *94-95*
Codes: *encryption systems whose components represent characters, words, or sentences.*
CS 103, SW 14; ASCII, CO 49, 54; Baudot, CO 9, 12; machine, SW 14; Short-Order, SW 16; simplifying writing, SW 16-18. *See also* Encryption of messages and data; Enigma; Schlüsselzusatz
Codes (formats), types: SW *22-23*
Cohen, Danny: MF 109
Cohen, Fred: CS 72, IC 113, SC 59
Cohen, Harold: IO 108
Colby, Kenneth: AI 59
Cold sites: CS 35
Cole, Edward: TR 8
Coleman, Dennis: PC 39
Collins, Michael: SP 47, 117
Collins Radio: TR 18

Collision avoidance: RO *58-59*
Colmerauer, Alain: IC *75*, LA 71
Color: and memory, CI *52-53*, 58; resolution of human eye, CI 52
Colorado State University: Natural Resource Ecology Laboratory, RV 96-98
Color analysis: AI 24-25
Color synthesis: MF *41*, 45
Colossus: CB *55*, 58, CS 92, IC *15*, IO 11, SW 13
Columbia: SP 70, 119, 120; software problems, SC 6
Columbia University: AI 68, RV 10-11; and astronomical computing, CC 87
Columbus, Christopher: landfall in America, PM 17, 23, *24-27*, 28-29
Columbus Project: CC 24
Columbus Research Tool: PM 17, 23, *24-27*, 28-29
Colvin, Neil: PC 24

C

MAGNETIC TAPE STORAGE was introduced by BINAC (Binary Automatic Computer), the first product of a company formed by Eckert and Mauchly. This innovation borrowed its technology from tape recorders, which were gaining popularity at the close of the 1940s. Like most computers of this era, BINAC was unreliable. To assure accuracy, the machine consisted of two complete computers, both performing the same calculations and comparing results.

SHORT CODE constituted an early step toward high-level programming languages. John Mauchly came up with the idea to simplify the writing of equations for BINAC. To represent mathematical symbols such as the plus sign and parentheses, Short Code substituted pairs of digits for the formidable strings of zeros and ones that are a computer's native dialect.

1949

1949

THE MANCHESTER MARK I boasted two innovations that would add impetus to the postwar boom in computer research—the first use of a magnetic drum for data storage and cathode-ray tubes for displaying output. Unfortunately, the two devices did not sit well together in this prototype machine. The magnetic drum created so much interference for the CRTs that it had to be kept in a separate room.

1949

Combinatorial explosion: AI 34, 37

Combinatory logic: SC 91

Comcor, Inc.: AC 27-28

Comets: SP *93*, 102

Command: *a statement, such as PRINT or COPY, that sets in motion a preprogrammed sequence of instructions to a computer. See* Instruction set.

Commercial Translator: LA 41, 42, 44

Commission of European Communities: and translation, PM 77

Commodore International: CB 103, 104, 107; PET, CB *99*, 103, IC *90*, PC 9

Commonwealth Edison: SO 46

Communications, computer: CO entire volume; incompatibilities, CO 40; services accessible through, CO 21, 26, 57; speed, CO 8, 15, 18. *See also* C3; Modems; Telecommunications networks

Communications and computers: *See* C3

Communications Biophysical Laboratory (CBL): RV 60; Digital Computer Laboratory, RV 60; and Linc, RV 59, 62, 64

Community Action Program: CS 62

ComNETco Virusafe: SC 59

Compact disk (CD): *a storage device for audio data that permanently records information in digital form as a series of pits, or depressions, etched by laser into the surface.* MS 101; CD-ROM, MS 102-103

Compaction: CS 104, *105*

Compander: MS 76, 77

Compaq Computer Corporation: IC 108, PC 22-23, 28, 68, 87; Deskpro 386, IC *120*; and 80386 machines, IC *120*, PC 87-88, 89

Compasses: TR 91

Compatibility: IO 62, PC 19, 22-25; plug, IO 63

Compiler: *a program that converts a program written in a high-level language into either machine code or assembly language, holding the instructions in memory without executing them. The compiled program is stored for use at any later time. See also* Interpreters. LA 21, 85, *86-97*, SC 107, 108-109, SW 18, 25, 37; CISC and RISC, PC *100-101*; development of, RV 40-41; FORTRAN, RV 41; paralleliz-ing, SC 107, 109-117

Complementary metal-oxide semiconductor (CMOS): *a logic circuit created by combining negative-channel and positive-channel metal-oxide semiconductor transistors. See* CMOS circuitry.

Complexity theory: SW 102

Complex Number Calculator (Model I): CB 37-38, CO 15, IC *13. See also* Bell Laboratories

Compressed-time simulation: *a computerized re-creation in*

THE ERA 1101 was the first commercially produced computer in America to offer drum-storage technology. Originally known as the Atlas, it was built by a Minnesota company called Engineering Research Associates for the U.S. Navy. Each of the computer's magnetic drums had a capacity of one million bits.

THE PILOT ACE computer, embodying Alan Turing's concept for a "universal machine," was tested by a trio of Turing's colleagues at the National Physical Laboratory. During 1945 and 1946, Turing had designed seven versions of the ACE (Automatic Computing Engine), but none of them were built. Finally, in 1950, Turing's associates constructed this scaled-down pilot model. The computer was unusually difficult to program, but it was several times faster than the landmark EDSAC machine completed at Cambridge the preceding year.

DSIR ACE PILOT MODEL 1950

1950

1950

and Index; IO Input/Output; LA Computer Languages; MF The Military Frontier; MS Memory and Storage; PC The Personal Computer; PM The Puzzle Master; PO Speed and Power; RO Robotics; RV Revolution in Science; SC The Software Challenge; SO The Computerized Society; SP Space; SW Software; TR Transportation

C

which events take place more quickly than they do in reality. *See* Simulations: using analog devices.

CompuServe: CO 21, 27

Computational chemistry: PO 20-21

Computed tomography (CT): *a medical imaging technique in which x-ray beams are passed through the body from many directions in a single plane to yield an image of tissues many times clearer than an ordinary x-ray picture.*
HB *50-51,* IC *74;* algebraic reconstruction, HB 21; heart, HB *12-13;* invention and development, HB 17, 19-23; speed, HB 19; three-dimensional, HB *103-105, 108-113;* views, HB 47; windowing, HB *48-49*

Computer: *a programmable machine that accepts, processes, and displays data.*
basic parts of, IO *26-27;* principal components, PO *50. See also* Computers

Computer-aided design (CAD): *the use of computers to shorten the design cycle by allowing manufacturers to shape new products on a computer screen without having to build physical prototypes.*
CI 91, *100-101,* 102-103, IO 78, RO 43, SW *84-85,* 113, *114-115;* in auto industry, CI 35, *36, 37,* 102, *103,* 104, 105-106; for integrated circuits, CM 33-34, 35, 99, *100-101,* 102-104; for interior design, PC 95-96; medical, CI 107; on micros, PC 88-89; for ship design, PC 93, *94,* 95; 3-D, PC 96, *97,* 98; for wiring paths within and between

chips, CM *94-97. See also* Architectural graphics

Computer-aided engineering (CAE): CI 102, SC 61-62; in auto industry, CI 103-105; finite element method (FEM), CI 104-105; medical, CI 107; on micros, PC 88-89, *97,* 98

Computer-aided manufacture (CAM): *the use of a computer in the manufacturing of a product.*
CI 32, 102, 105, 106, IO 78, 79; medical, CI 107. *See also* Computer-integrated manufacturing

Computer architecture: *the internal layout, or design, of a computer.*
parallel, AI 103, *106-107,* 108-110; and perception, AI 102-103, 108-109; serial, AI 102-103, *104-105*

Computer art: CI 115, *116-123,* IO *108-109;* and interactivity, CI 115

Computer Associates: SC 21

Computer basics: CB entire

volume

Computer bulletin boards: CS 10

Computer clubs: CB 99, 104, 106

Computer crime: CS 17-20, 27, 59-63; cost of, CS 19; data alteration, CS 18, 62-63, 67; and law, CS 19-20, 61; theft of computer time, CS 10, 61-62; theft of funds, CS 18, 19, 64, 66, 87; theft of information, CS 60-61, 65, 87, *94-95, 96-97;* theft of physical assets, CS 63-64; vandalism, CS 10

Computer-generated imagery (CGI): CI 76. *See also* Motion picture graphics

Computer graphics: *See* Graphics, computer

Computer images: CI entire volume

Computer-integrated manufacturing (CIM): *the use of computers to control the flow of information and materials through a factory. The term "computer-*

REAL-TIME COMPUTING was first possible with Whirlwind *(below),* a giant machine built at M.I.T. to the specifications of chief engineer Jay W. Forrester *(standing, left).* Begun more than six years earlier as part of a project to build a flight simulator, Whirlwind could perform a broad range of tasks, such as air-traffic control, that require direct interaction between operator and machine. The computer processed data and presented the results almost instantaneously on a video screen. An operator could then direct subsequent actions by touching a light gun to the screen.

1951

integrated" implies a more comprehensive role for computers than does "computer-aided."
CI 106, RO 42-43, *44-45*, 46; structure, RO 44

ComputerLand: PC 16, 25

Computer languages: LA entire volume

Computer malfunctions: MF 23-24

Computer Memory Project: CO 27

Computer modeling: RV 21; plant evolution, RV *22-29*. *See also* Computational chemistry; Finite-element analysis; Meteorology, computer modeling

Computer redundancy: *a system to protect against hardware failure by employing two or more identical computers to process identical software simultaneously. In cases of triple or quadruple redundancy, the computers may be able to compare data and results to identify a faulty computer. See Com-*

puters: redundant systems.

Computers: SO 9; accuracy of, RV *16-17*; alternative, AC entire volume; as appliances, SO 109; based on early microprocessors, SO 101-102; business users, SO 12; control by handicapped, HB 91-93; cost vs. speed, PC 91; critical functions, CS 7, 8; early programming, SO 9; electromechanical, RV 9-15, 18-20; fault-tolerant, CS 11, SO 65-67, 70-78; hierarchy of power, PC 89-91; linking different classes, PC 105; mainframe sales, PC 105; medical applications, HB entire volume; multiuser, CS *12-13*, 71, 73, *74-85*; personal, PC entire volume; pervasiveness, SO 8, 24; reclassifying, PC 98, 104; redundant systems, SO 65; RISC, PC 91, 98, 106; scientific users, SO 12; second generation, SO 20-22; structure and operations, CB 109, *110-121*;

vulnerability, CS 7, 8-10, *12-13*, *14-15*

Computers, analog: AC 8-27, CB 36, *54*, SP 10-11; difficulties with, AC 24, 26; electronic, AC 8-9, 11-16, *17-23*, 24-27; and microchips, AC 28; modular, AC 16, 24; nonelectrical, AC 9-11; optical, AC 89-91; for simulations, AC *17-23*, 24-26; vs. digital, AC 26-27, SP 10, 42; and weapons, AC 11, 13-15. *See also* Hybrid computers

Computers, digital: and 1952 U.S. election, CB 54, *57*; and binary number system, CB 36-38; development and World War II, CB 51-65; early program-storing, CB 60-61, 63, 64, *65*; first programmed operational, CB 53-54; and ICs, CB 74, 76-78; milestones of 1930-1944, CB *54-55*; milestones of 1946-1952, CB *56-57*; milestones of 1953-1981, CB *96-99*; non-von Neumann, CB *77*; precursors, CB 8-10,

11-13; single chip, CB *82-83*; structure and operation, CB 109, *110-121*; von Neumann architecture, CB *63*. *See also* Microprocessors

Computers, hybrid: AC 27-30; and microchips, AC 28; speed, AC 30

Computers, personal (PCs): CB *26-27*, *92*, PC entire volume; and Altair, CB 94-101; after Altair, CB 100-108; changes in industry, CB 101-103, 108; clubs, CB 99, 104, 106; first newsletter, CB 99; and graphics, CI 60, 114; growth of market, CB 93, 108; milestones, CB *98-99*; and networks, CO 56-57; portable, CB 101, 106, PC 22-23, 25, 26; structure and operations, CB 109, *110-121*

Computers and astronomy: CC *6-13*, 16, 17; beginnings, CC 86-89

Computers and brain: HB 24-25; cross-field research, HB 33; simulation, HB *24-25*, 26, *27-29*, 33

Computers and space flight:

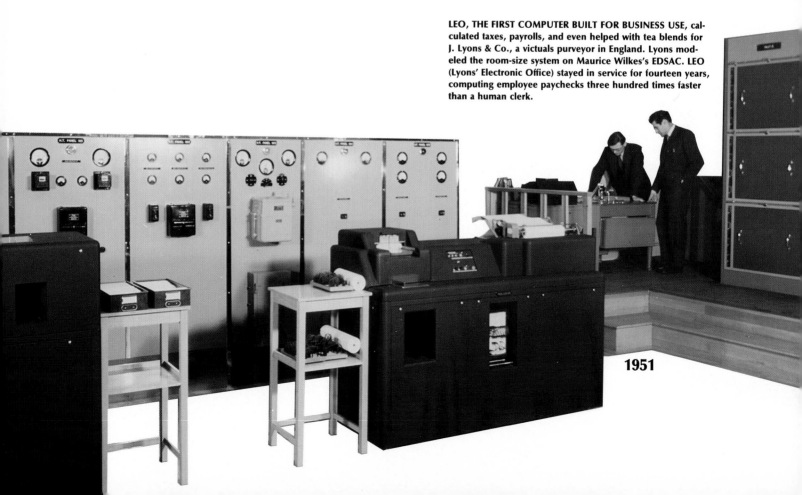

LEO, THE FIRST COMPUTER BUILT FOR BUSINESS USE, calculated taxes, payrolls, and even helped with tea blends for J. Lyons & Co., a victuals purveyor in England. Lyons modeled the room-size system on Maurice Wilkes's EDSAC. LEO (Lyons' Electronic Office) stayed in service for fourteen years, computing employee paychecks three hundred times faster than a human clerk.

1951

SP 8; early German work, SP 8-9, 11-13; early U.S. work, SP 13; testing equipment, SP 40-42; and unmanned spacecraft, SP 86. *See also* Milestones; Sequencer

Computer Sciences Corporation: SW 61

Computer security: CS entire volume, MF 103, *104-105*, 106; electromagnetic pulse, MF 106-107

Computer Security Evaluation Center (CSEC): MF 103

Computer simulation: *See* Simulation

Computer systems, redundant: SO 65; hot and cold switched backup, SO 66-67

Computer Technology Corporation (CTC): SO 101

Computing and communications, convergence: CO 48-49

Comrie, Leslie John: CC 86, 87, RV 9-10, 12

Comsat: CO 89, 96

Concatenation: LA 54

Concentrator: *a support computer in a supercomputer center that manages files and buffers high-speed supercomputer data for slower-working peripheral devices.* PO *46*

Conceptual dependency: AI 69

Concordances: PM 52-53, *54-57*, 58-60

Concurrency: *the simultaneous execution of different parts of a program. See Parallel architectures.*

Concurrent processing: SO 41

Conklin, Ned: LA 106

Connection Machine: AC 7, *56-59*, AI 109, IC *120*, PO 104-106

Connection weights: *the strengths of relationships between neurons in a neural-network computer. See Backward-error propagation algorithm.*

Connectivity map: AI *26-27*

Conner, Finis: MS 52

Connes, Pierre: CC 18

Conrad, Alfred: PM 21

Conrad, Charles, Jr. (Pete): SP 61, 116, 117, 118

Conrail: TR 77

Constructive solid geometry (CSG): CI *62-63*

Content addressability: AI 108

Control bus: *the wires that carry timing and control pulses to all parts of a computer. See Bus.*

Control Data Corporation (CDC): LA 99, PM 28, PO 11, 14-17, 31-32, 34, 45, 91, SO 20; 160G, SP 41; 1604, IC *43*, PO 11, 14, 16; 3600, PO *12*; 6400, CC 42; 6600, CC 96, IC *55*, PO 14, *15-17, 35*; 7600, PM 35, PO 18, *46*; Cyber 170/185, PM 17, 28; Cyber 175, RV 94; Cyber 203, PO 45, 89; Cyber 205, CC 85, PO 45, 98, RV 102; and IBM, PO 16, 18; Star-100, PO 33,

UNIVAC made Remington Rand the world's first large-scale seller of computers. The company, which bought out the UNIVAC's financially strapped inventors John Mauchly and J. Presper Eckert, sold forty-six of the general-purpose machines to government and industry. A year after the first UNIVAC installation, broadcast newsman Walter Cronkite *(standing, right)* reported on the use of the machine to predict 1952 presidential election results.

THE IAS COMPUTER, shown here with its developer John von Neumann, shattered computational speed records. Created at the Institute for Advanced Studies in Princeton, New Jersey, the new tool for science achieved its rapid pace by loading data one forty-bit "word" at a time, rather than bit by bit. This innovation required the simultaneous operation of forty Williams tubes, which were arranged as a row of cylinders jutting from the machine's base.

THE JUNCTION TRANSISTOR, invented by William Shockley, revolutionized electronics. Shown above in prototype form, this transistor was simpler to construct and more reliable than the earlier, point-contact variety. Even so, several more years of development would be needed before the junction transistor supplanted vacuum tubes.

1951

1951

1951

34, 39

Control decoder: CB 82

Control unit: *the circuitry within a computer that manages the flow of processing. In conventional computers, the control unit is part of the central processing unit and directs activity in a step-by-step sequence known as the instruction cycle; in parallel-processing computers, one or more control units govern multiple processors. See Central processing unit.*

Convair: SO 14-16

Conway, Lynn: AC 66, CM 31-32, IC 98

Cooley, James: RV 43, 44

Cooling systems: PO 35-37

Cooper, Gordon: SP 20, 116

Cooper, Leon: AC 62

Cooper, Thomas: SC 68

Copland, Aaron: IO 101

Copps, Ed: SP 66

Coprocessor: *a subsidiary processor, controlled by the main processor, designed to perform specific tasks much faster than a general-purpose processor.*
mathematical, PC 96, PO 57

Copy protection: CS 64-67; by bit ambiguity, CS 67; by checksum altering, CS 66; by directory shift, CS 65; by half tracks, CS 66; by hardware

key, CS 67

Corbató, Fernando J.: CO 40, IC 65, SC 35, 36

Core, magnetic: MS 8, 16-22; operation of, MS 13-15

Core memory: *an early type of computer memory that stores data on tiny magnetized rings suspended in a grid of current-carrying wires. See Memory: magnetic core.*

Cormack, Allan: HB 21, 22

Cornell Medical Center: HB 72

Cornell University: PO 74, 75, 97-98

Corning Glass Works: CO 102

Corona Data Systems: PC 23-24

Cortex Corporation: CorVision, SC 64, 66

Cortney, Robert: CI 35, 36

Cosmic Cube: IC 116, PO 102, 103, 105

Cosmology: CC 85, 89, 91, 94-95; bottom-up model, CC 96, 97, 106; and hidden mass, CC 97-98, 106; top-down model, CC 98, 102, 103, 105. See also Big Bang; Computer simulations; Steady State

Cosmos, computers and the: CC entire volume

Coughenour, Michael B.: RV 96

Coupleux, Edouard E.: IO 100

Courtney, Robert: CS 17, 19, 71

CP/M: IC 89, PC 16, SO 103, 108, SW 71, 73

CPU: See Central processing unit

Crash: SW 32

Cray, Seymour R.: CM 99, PO 14, 15, 17, 18, 31-33, 38-39, 41, 44, 45, 48, 96, 98

Cray computers: CI 83, 84, 85, 88, 90; Cray-1, CC 104, IC 88; Cray-2, IC 115, MS 7, PM 36; speed, CC 109, 119; time-sharing system, MS 78;

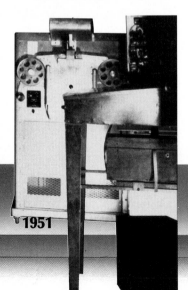

EDVAC, long-awaited successor to ENIAC, arrived at the Aberdeen Proving Grounds after a troubled seven-year gestation period. Intended to be the first computer to store programs internally, EDVAC encountered numerous production delays, including the departure of its creators, Mauchly and Eckert. By the time remaining team members completed EDVAC in 1951, British imitator EDSAC had long since claimed the title of the world's first fully functional, stored-program computer.

A PROGRAM THAT PLAYED CHECKERS—and could "learn" from its experience with the game—was tested on IBM's soon-to-be-released 701 computer. IBM employee Arthur Samuel began the checkers project in 1947 as a professor at the University of Illinois. He expected the program would take about a year to complete. Instead, he spent three decades refining it. Fifteen years into the project, the program won a master's rating in a 1962 tournament. It was not beaten by another checkers program until 1977.

1951

1951

X-MP, CC 107, IC *106*
Cray Research: PO 32-33, 39, 41, 45, 48, 91; Cray-1, PO *36,* 38-39, 42, *46,* 89; Cray-2, PO *37, 46, 48,* 96, 105; Quarter Horse, PO 45; X-MP, PO 7, 41, 44, *46,* 96, 98, 105; X-MP/48, PO 22, 23, 96
Credit-card checking: SO *68-69*
Crick, Francis: HB 42
Crippen, Robert: SP 67, 70, 119, 120
Crockett, Bruce: CM 99
Cromemco: PC 9
Crooks, Bill: MS 60
CRT: *See* Cathode-ray tube
Cruise missiles: MF *75-77, 78;* antiship, MF 95-96
Crutchfield, James: PM 111, 112, SW 105
Cryptography: *the encipher-ing and deciphering of mes-sages using secret ciphers or codes. See* Encryption of

messages and data.
Crystallography: x-ray, RV 81, *82-91*
CT scans: CI 90, 106-107. *See also* Computed tomography
CTSS (Compatible Time-Sharing System): IC 48, SO 44
Culler, Glen: PO 74
Curry, Haskell: SC 91
Cursor: *the movable spot of light that indicates a point of action or attention on a com-puter screen. See* Cursor control.
Cursor control: IO *68-71*
Curti, Merle: PM 19
Customs Service: *See* U.S. Customs Service
Cybernetics: *the science of control and communications systems founded on the the-ory that intelligent beings adapt to their environments and accomplish goals by re-*

acting to feedback from their surroundings. Cybernetic theories became the basis of neural-modeling, or bottom-up, artificial-intelligence research.
AI 11-14, 103, 108, IC 22
Cybernetics (Wiener): IC 22, RO 17
Cyc: AI 84
Cygnus A: CC 56, 61, *62, 63*
Cygnus X-1: CC 70, 73
Cylindrical-coordinate robot: RO 52
CYRUS: AI 70-71

C

THE A-0 COMPILER was the first example of a type of software that converts symbols from a high-level language into instruc-tions that a computer can exe-cute. It was developed by a team under former navy pro-grammer Grace Hopper *(left),* who coined the term "compiler" because the software combined, or compiled, instruction sequences to create a program. Written for the UNIVAC, the A-0 was intended as a preliminary effort only, and the A-1, A-2, and A-3 soon followed.

A REPLICA OF THE IAS COMPUTER, playfully dubbed MANIAC and attended by operators like the young woman shown here, went to work on hydrogen-bomb calculations at Los Alamos National Laboratory. Los Alamos was one of several American research sites that built IAS-like machines as scientific interest in high-speed computing grew. Within a few years, similar devices appeared in the Soviet Union, Western Europe, Israel, and Australia.

THE INTEGRATED CIRCUIT was first proposed by G. W. A. Dum-mer *(above)* at a Washington, D.C., electronics symposium. The British radar expert sug-gested that transistors, resistors, and other components could be combined into a single semicon-ductor block that would be smaller, faster, and more reli-able than separately wired parts.

1952

1952

1952

DAC-1: CI 35, *36-37*, IC *56*

Dahl, Ole-Johan: IC *58*, LA 78, SC 102-103, 104, 106

Daimler-Benz, driving simulator of: IO *80-81*

Dainichi-Sykes PT600 Robot: RO 34

Dark matter: CC 98, 102, 106; cold (CDM), CC 106-108. *See also* Hidden mass

DARPA (Defense Advanced Research Projects Agency): AI 100, IC 38, 114, MF 46-47, 80, 101, 110, PO 90, 105, 106; and neural networks, AC 46, 65, 66

Dartmouth College: CO 15, SW 25, 26-28; Summer Research Project on Artificial Intelligence, AI 31, 42, IC 35; time sharing, CO 20, 41

Darwin III: HB 26, *27-29*

Data: storage and vulnerability, CS 11, *14-15*, 27, 34-35; transfer and vulnerability, CS 7, *14-15*, 35, *94-95, 96-97. See also* Encryption of messages and data

Database: *a collection of facts about a particular subject or related subjects, divided into individual files and records that are organized for easy access.* CO 26, MS 72, SO 53; applications, MS 73, 76; attribute, SO 56; binary searches, SO *62-63;* fingerprint, MS 71-72; genetic, HB 43; hierarchical, SO 53; indexes, SO *63;* medical, HB 18, 59; network, SO 53; queries, SO *58-63. See also* Database, relational

Database, relational: IC 72, SO 53, *54-63;* attribute, SO 56; binary searches, SO *62-63;* indexes, SO *62-63;* occurrence, SO 56; queries, SO *58-61;* record, SO 56; table, SO 56

Database Design, Inc.: SC 64

Database management system (DBMS): *software that organizes and provides ready access to the information in a database.* MS 72, *79-81,* SW 70, *80-81;* hierarchical, MS 72-73, *79;* network, MS 72, 73, *80;* relational, MS 72, 73, 76, *81*

Database manager: SO 41

Database searching: PM *64-65*

Database structures: SC 63

Data bus: *the wires in a computer that carry data to and from memory locations.* See Buses.

Data compression: MS 76-77

Data dictionary: SO 54

Data diddling: CS 18, 62-64

Data Encryption Standard (DES): *a single-key system selected by the U.S. National Bureau of Standards for encryption of commercial data.* CS 92-93, 98, 102, 103, *106-111,* 112, IC *92* ; hardware implementation, CS 102, 106; Message Authentication Code (MAC), CS 93, 111, 112; and National Security Agency, CS 98

Dataflow architecture: IC 84, PO *99-101,* 102-103; Sigma 1, PO 106

Dataflow processing: *a parallel-processing technique in which data travels through the computer as packages encoded with information that controls the execution of the program. Individual packages activate processors*

THE AUTOCODE compiler was written in Britain by nuclear researcher Alick Glennie *(below)* to simplify the difficult task of programming the Manchester Mark I. The secrecy of Glennie's research passed to his compiler, however, and he was the only one ever to use it.

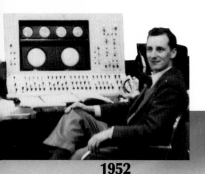

1952

IBM'S 701 made its debut as the company's first fully electronic computer. Organizations including aircraft companies, the U.S. Navy, and atomic research laboratories installed a total of nineteen 701s during the three years it was manufactured. Like previous IBM machines, the 701 relied primarily on punch cards for input and output, but it could also operate high-speed printers and store data on magnetic tape.

1952

to work either concurrently or in sequence, as the data allows. See Dataflow architecture.

Data General: PO 71; and microcomputers, PC 10

Datagram: CO *72-73*

Data leakage: CS 60-61

Datanet-30: SW 28

Data Resources, Inc. (DRI): PM 96-97, 98, 99

Data storage schemes: SW *50-53*

Data structure: *a collection of data in which related ele-*

ments are referred to by a common name in order to organize, store, and retrieve the information efficiently. arrays, LA *52, 53;* records, LA *53*

Data synchronizer: IO 18

Data transmission: SP 17; time to interplanetary craft, SP 86, 89; from Uranus, SP 100-101, 113

Data types: LA 51, *52-53;* checking, LA *92-93*

Datavue 25: HB 90

Davida, George: CS 102

Davies, Donald: CO 45

Davis, Marc: CC 106, 107, 108

Davis, Nan: IO 96-97

Dawkins, Oliver: TR 45

dBase II: IC 104, SW 70-71, 72

DCS (Defense Communications System): MF 101

D-Day: and navigation, TR 44-46

Deaf: computer aids for the, HB 96-99

Dean, Andrew: HB 68, 70

Dean, Jeff: HB 68

Debugging: SC 28-29, SW 17, 26, 32

DEC: *See* Digital Equipment Corporation

Decca Flight Log: TR 47

Decca Navigator: TR 44-45, 46, 47

Declaration statements: LA 53, 92, 93

DECtalk: AC 61, IC *110*

Deere & Co.: IO 79

Davies, Donald: CO 45

Defense Advanced Research Projects Agency: *See* DARPA

Defense Mapping Agency: Topographic Center, PM 32

De Forest, Lee: CM 17

Dell, Michael: and Dell Computer, PC 24-25, 89

Deltamatic: SO 41

Deltamax: MS 18

DeMaio, Harry: CS 8

DeMarco, Tom: SC 60-61

DeMars, Bruce: MF 32

Deming, W. Edwards: CM 67, 70-73

Demos, Chris: SO 110

Demos, Gary: CI 83, 85

Demultiplexer: *a circuit that separates one input signal from multiple accompanying signals and distributes it to an output line. See* Multiplexing.

DENDRAL: AI 39, IC 59, SW 111

Dendrochronology: PM *44-45*

Denning, Peter: MS 83

Dennis, Jack: IC *84,* PO 102

Depth migration: PO 27

Derick, Lincoln: CM 57

D

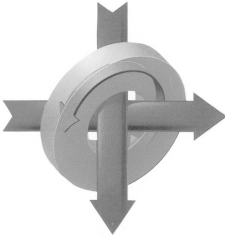

MAGNETIC CORE MEMORY made its first appearance, significantly improving the performance of the Whirlwind computer. Replacing an array of sensitive, failure-prone Williams tubes, the new 17,000-bit memory doubled the Whirlwind's computing speed, quadrupled its data-input rate, and cut memory-maintenance work from twenty-eight hours a week to two.

SPEEDCODING, an early high-level language, was written by IBM's John Backus *(above)* for the 701 computer. Though programs composed in Speedcoding occupied more memory and typically demanded fifteen times as much processing time as software coded in the 701's assembly language, Backus's creation could also trim weeks from a programming assignment.

A HIGH-LEVEL LANGUAGE written for Whirlwind by M.I.T. scientists Niel Zierler and J. Halcombe Laning, Jr. allowed programmers to issue commands with such ordinary words as "STOP" and "PRINT"—and even to enter mathematical formulas much as they were written with pencil and paper. This long-sought convenience, however, took the computer so long to convert to machine code that the language, though influential as a model, was little used and never even received a proper name.

1953

1953

1954

Descriptive languages: LA 111, *118-121*

Design of integrated circuits: *See* Circuit design

Desktop publishing: PC *50-51*, page-description language, PC *50-53*; printing by, PC *56-57*; and scanned images, PC *54-55*

Detector: area, RV *85*; Supercollider, RV *114-115*

Deutsch, Herbert: IO 100

De Valcouleurs, Gerard: CC 38

Devitt, Scott: PM 28

Devol, George C., Jr.: RO 33, 35-36, 37

DEWs (directed-energy weapons): MF 107, *108, 116-117*

Diabetic: computer aid for the, HB 101-102

Diablo Systems: IO 45-46

Diagnosis, computer-aided: HB 71-78; expert systems, HB 79, *80-87*; and mental illness, HB 30, 33, 75-78; precursors, HB 71-72

Diagnostic slide rule: HB *71*

Dial-back machines: CS 17

Dialect: *a variation of a programming language that tailors the language to a certain application or exploits the strengths of a particular computer.*

Dialect, language: LA 67

Dialog (France): CO 7

Dialog Information Services: CO 26

Dibble, Harold: PM 30

Dicing: CM *87*

Dicker, Richard: HB 68

Dickey, Frederick J.: SP 72

Dictionaries: PM 62-63, 66

Dictionary of American Regional English (DARE): PM 63, 66

Dietzel, David: SO 109

Difference Engine: CB 10-11, *12*, 13, SW 10

Differential analyzers: CB 36, *54*, 59, CC 87, IC *11, 14*, RO 15; electronic, AC 11; mechanical, AC 11, *12*

Differential equation: *a mathematical equation describing the interaction of a function and its rate of change. It is frequently used to model processes in the physical world. See Differential analyzers.*

Diffie, Whitfield: CS 99, 100, 101

DiFrancesco, David: CI 89

Digit: *a character position in a number (the number 344, for example, has three digits), or any one of the numerals from zero to nine. See Computers, digital.*

Digital: *pertaining to the representation, manipulation, or transmission of data by discrete signals. See Computers, digital.*

Digital computer: *a machine that operates on data expressed in discrete, or on-off, form, such as the ones and zeros of binary notation. See Computers, digital.*

Digital Effects, Inc.: CI 80

Digital Electronic Automation: RO 34

Digital Equipment Corporation

A SILICON-BASED JUNCTION TRANSISTOR improved on William Shockley's germanium version of the device. Perfected by Gordon Teal, it offered much greater reliability at high temperatures and cut the price of a transistor from $15.00 to $2.50. Teal's employer, an obscure electronics firm called Texas Instruments, made itself a household name by using the new transistors in rugged little portable radios.

1954

THE IBM 650 MAGNETIC DRUM CALCULATOR established itself as the first mass-produced computer, with 450 sold in its inaugural year. Spinning at 12,500 rpm, the 650's magnetic data-storage drum allowed much faster access to data than other drum-memory machines. Designed for easy programming and operation, this sturdy workhorse also incorporated error-checking procedures that halted the machine if data was incorrectly read from the drum.

1954

(DEC): CB *98*, IO 35-36, LA 100, PO 67-72, RV 60, 62, 67, SW 69; DEC 20, CC 103, 105; employees, PO *70*; and inexpensive computers, PO 67; and LINC, RV 67; and minicomputers, PC 90; PDP-1, IC *45*, PO 67, 70; PDP-5, RV 70; PDP-7, RV 78; PDP-8, IC *57*, PO 71, *73*, RV *65*, 67; PDP-9, CC 42; PDP-11, CC 68, PO 71, RV 78, 79; and personal computers, PC 10; production, PO *73*; strategy, PM 104; VAX, CC 16, 107; VAX 11/780, IC *93*, RV 66, 80, 102

Digital FM: IC 78, IO 106, 107, *118-119*

Digital Productions: CI 83, 84, 85, PO 44

Digital Research Inc.: SW 71

Digital scene-matching area correlation (DSMAC): RO 26, 27

Digital Scene-Matching Area Correlator (DSMAC): MF 75, 77, 79

Digital-to-analog conversion: IO *32*, 117

Digitize: *to represent data in digital, or discrete, form, or to convert an analog, or continuous, signal to such a form. See Digitizing.*

Digitizers: PM 32. *See also* Optical character readers

Digitizing: CB 39, *48-49*

Digitizing tablet: *a device that allows the user to enter drawings into the computer as a sequence of coordinates by moving a hand-held control over a flat tablet.* CI *16, 18-19,* SW 82, *83*

Dijkstra, Edsger W.: LA 37, 78, SC 60, 98-99, SW 30-31, 32

Dinosaur, robot *(Quetzalcoatlus northropi)*: RO 113-114

Diode: *an electronic device that allows current to flow in only one direction.*

CM 22; junction, PO *109*; molecular, AC 97, 104

DIP switch: *a series of toggle switches built into a dual in-line package (DIP) and used to encode various kinds of information, such as the amount of memory or the type of monitor in a computer system.* CB 110, 112, *113*

Direct access: *the ability to retrieve a specific piece of information directly from storage without having to search sequentially through data. See Memory: random-access.*

Direct Access Radar Channel (DARC): TR 103-104

Direct-mail applications: SW *92-93*

Direct memory access (DMA): *a mechanism that transmits data directly between a computer's input/output ports and its temporary memory. See DMA (direct-memory-access) controller.*

Disabled, computer assistance for: IO 95-98, *99. See also* Handicapped, computer aids for the; HB index

Disaster-recovery plan (DRP): CS 34-35

Discoverer satellites: MF 36-37

Discovery: SP 120, 121

Disk: *a round magnetized plate, usually made of plastic or metal, organized into concentric tracks and pie-shaped sectors for storing data.* SW *20*

Disk drive: *the mechanism that rotates a storage disk and reads or records data.* CB *27*, 109, *110,* SW 20

Disk farms: PC 104

Disk storage: SC 25

Disney Studios: CI 77, 80, 82

Distortion, correcting for: CO 18-19

Distributed processing: and WWMCCS, MF 102

D

TRADIC (TRAnsistor DIgital Computer) showed that transistors were suitable for computing devices. Built by Bell Labs for the U.S. Air Force as a prototype for an airborne bombing and navigation system, TRADIC underwent a two-year, round-the-clock reliability test. Only eight of the computer's 700 point-contact transistors and nine of its 10,000 germanium diodes had to be replaced, a failure rate dramatically lower than was usual with vacuum tubes.

1955

DIVAD (Division Air Defense): MF 64-65

DMA (direct-memory-access) controller: IO 26, 27, *30-31*

DNA: HB *8-9, 36-37*, RV 81, *90*, 91; modeling, HB 34; sequencing, HB *38-41, 42-43*

DOCTOR: AI 58-59

Doctor, Louis: CM 101

Domain knowledge: AI 85, 86-87

Dopant: *an impurity (most often boron or phosphorus) that is added to silicon for the purpose of enhancing certain electrical properties. See Doping.*

Doping: *deliberately introducing impurities into a semiconductor to alter its conductivity.* CM 19-20, 23, 80; dopants, CM 19-20, 57, 85; gallium arsenide, CM 99; process, CM 62, *84-85*; of semiconductors, CB 68, 69-70, 72-73, *86-87*

Doppler, Christian: MF 53

Doppler effect: CC 94

Doppler radar: MF 53, 64

Doppler shift: TR 49

Doriot, Georges: PO 69, 70

Dostert, Leon E.: PM 67, 74, 75

Drain: *in MOS transistors, the area toward which current flows when the switch is turned on; equivalent to the collector in a bipolar transistor. See Switches.*

DRAM (dynamic random-access memory) chip: *an integrated circuit that serves as a temporary memory for program data. Although DRAM chips can store more information than any other type of memory chip, their circuits preserve data for only a short time, so the data must be continually refreshed, or rewritten, onto the chip. See Dynamic random-access memory (DRAM).*

Draper, Charles Stark: SP 43-44

Dr. Dobb's Journal of Computer Calisthenics & Orthodontia—Running Light without Overbyte: LA 101-102

Drexler, Eric: AC 85, *107*, 108, 111, IC 125

Drexler, Jerome: MS 105-106

Dreyfus, Hubert: AI 10

Drones: MF *68-69*

Drug modeling: HB *10-11*, 35

DSA (Digital Subtraction Angiography): HB *62-65*, IC *99*

DSI (delivered source instructions): SC 52

Dummer, G. W. A.: CB 73, CM 19, 20-21, 22, 23, IC *29*

Dunwell, Stephen: PO 10, *11*

Duplex, full and half: CO 50

Du Pont: CI 112

Dvorak, August: IO 41; keyboard, IO *41*

DVST (Direct-View Storage Tube): CI 38

DXplain: HB 18, 74-75, 79, *82-83*

Dymax: LA 100

Dynabook: IO *72*, 73-74, 75, SC 104

Dynamic address allocation: SC 34

Dynamic legged systems: RO 61. *See also* Walking robots

Dynamic random-access memory (DRAM): PO 91

HERBERT SIMON AND ALLEN NEWELL unveiled Logic Theorist, software able to apply rules of reasoning and prove theorems in the branch of mathematics known as symbolic logic. The program, considered a milestone in the field of artificial intelligence, led Simon to predict that computers would soon tackle any problem addressed by the human mind.

THE ERA OF MAGNETIC-DISK STORAGE dawned with IBM's shipment of a 305 RAMAC computer *(below)* to San Francisco's Zellerbach Paper Company. The storage component of RAMAC (short for Random Access Method of Accounting and Control) was the IBM 350 disk file. Consisting of fifty magnetically coated metal platters, stacked one atop the other and rotated by a common drive shaft, the IBM 350 held the astonishing total of five million bytes of data.

1955

1956

E-3 aircraft: MF 97
Eagle Computer: PC 23, 24
EAI (Electronic Associates, Inc.): AC 25-26, 27, 28; 16-231R, AC 26; 16-31R, AC 25
Ear, human: and deafness, HB 98-99
Early Bird: CO 94
Earth-observation platform: SP *68-69*
Earthquakes: locating, RV *50-51. See also* Seismology
East Bay Municipal Utilities District: SC 51, 64
Eastwood, James: CC 107
EBCDIC: *the acronym for Extended Binary Coded Decimal Interchange Code, an IBM system for encoding letters, numerals, punctuation marks, and signs that accommodates twice as many symbols and functions as ASCII by using eight-place binary*

numbers instead of seven-place numbers. CO 54
Ebert, Jim: PM 30
EC-18 aircraft: MF 98
Echo, Project: SP 14; *Echo I,* CO 88
Echoes: CO 18-19
Eckert, J. Presper: CB *56,* 59-61, 62, 63, 64-65, IC 19, IO 15-16, LA 9, 11, 14, 20, MS 37, 43, RV 15, SW 12, 13, 14, 16
Eckert, Wallace: CC 87, RV 10-11, 12, 13, 15, 18
Eckert-Mauchly Computer Corporation: LA 11, 20, SW 13, 17
Eckstein, Otto: PM 96-97
Ecology: computer modeling, RV 95-98; data collection, RV 97-98
Econometrics: IC 56, PM 94-99; Brookings model, PM 96; commercialization, PM 96-97,

98-99; equations, PM 94; limitations, PM 97-98; on personal computers, PM 98-99; practitioners, PM 94-97; Wharton models, PM 95-96
Edelman, Gerald: HB 26
Edge detection: AI *18-19, 105, 106-107*
Edge recognition: AC 65-66
Editors, program: IO 38-39
EDSAC (Electronic Delay Storage Automatic Computer/Calculator): CB *65,* CI 8, IC 22, IO 10, 14, 38, LA 14-15, SW 14
EDVAC (Electronic Discrete Variable Computer): AC 7, CB 60-61, 62, 63, IC *28,* IO 15, LA 14, MS 10, RV 38, SW 12-13, 14
EEPROM (electrically erasable programmable read-only memory): MS 23, *29*
Efron, Bradley: PM 61

INFORMATION PROCESSING LANGUAGES (IPLs), a family of computer languages developed by AI pioneer Allen Newell and his colleagues, opened new frontiers for artificial intelligence. In addition to permitting the use of list processing, in which data is represented as lists of words, phrases, and other symbols, the languages also made possible a technique called associative memory. It allowed programmers to store concepts in a computer's memory as researchers believe they may be organized in the human brain.

THE TX-0 MAINFRAME, one of the first general-purpose, programmable computers to be built with transistors, was designed at M.I.T.'s Lincoln Lab in Lexington, Massachusetts. Two years later, the lab donated the TX-0 to the institute's Research Laboratory of Electronics, where it hosted some of the earliest "hacks"—imaginative feats of programming—by university students and computer enthusiasts. These ranged from a program that translated Arabic numbers into Roman numerals to one that simulated the inside of a cell nucleus.

FUTURE THEMES OF AI RESEARCH were set by an elite corps of computer scientists during a six-week colloquium known as the Dartmouth Summer Research Project on Artificial Intelligence. The conferees—who included the influential AI theorists Allen Newell and Herbert Simon *(far left),* as well as M.I.T. professors John McCarthy and Marvin Minsky—inspired a generation of AI programmers to apply their efforts to such real-world issues as optimizing the design of communications networks.

1956   **1956**   **1956**

Efstathiou, George: CC 107

EGABTR: CS 59

Egerton Hospital Equipment: RO 34

Eggebrecht, Lewis: PC 13, 14

EICAS (Engine Indication and Caution Advisory System): TR 18, 19

Einstein, Albert: CC 89

Einstein x-ray telescope: CC 71, 72, 73-74, IC *95;* Detailed Observing Program, CC 73; High Resolution Imager, CC 72; Imaging Proportional Counter, CC 72

EISA (Extended Industry Standard Architecture): PC 28

Eisenhower, Dwight D.: MF 98

Elbaum, Charles: AC 62, 63

Electrical computer circuits: early, CB 36, 37-38, 52, *58*

Electric Pencil: IC 88, SO 102, SW 68-69

Electroencephalograms (EEGs): HB 30, 76-78; automated, HB 77-78; and schizophrenia, HB *76*

Electromagnetic emissions: CC *6-13*

Electromagnetic pulse (EMP): *the surge of electromagnetic energy generated by a nuclear explosion, which can disable or destroy computers and other electronic devices.* CS 8, MF 104-105, 106-107

Electromagnetic radiation: *radiation associated with periodically varying electric and magnetic fields that vibrate perpendicularly to each other and travel through space at the speed of light, such as light waves, radio waves, and x-rays. See Electromagnetic emissions; Electromagnetic spectrum.*

Electromagnetic radiation leakage: CS 11

Electromagnetic spectrum: CO *10-11*

Electromechanical: *composed of both electrical and mechanical, or moving, parts. Most early computers were electromechanical devices. See Electromechanical relay.*

Electromechanical relay: *a type of switch consisting of a coil of wire wrapped around a small iron bar magnet. The magnetic field induced by current through the wire moves the bar and activates the switch.* MS 9

Electron: *a negatively charged particle revolving around the nucleus of an atom. See Switches.*

Electron-beam lithography: CM 107-108

Electron density map: RV *87-89*

Electronic bulletin boards: CO 27

Electronic circuit boards,

assembly of: RO 41, *44-45*

Electronic components: CB 67-78. *See also* Integrated Circuits; Relays; Transistors; Vacuum tubes

Electronic computers, early: SW 12

Electronic funds transfer: CS 7, 19, 64, 87; encryption, CS 87-88, 92, 102

Electronic keyboards: CM 100-101

Electronic libraries: PM 60-61

Electronic locks and keys: CS 30-31, 41

Electronic mail: CO 7, 26-27; and ARPANET, CO 47

Electronics: *the science or use of electron-flow devices, such as vacuum tubes and transistors, with no moving parts. See Electronic components.*

Electronic warfare, radar: MF 49, *50-59;* costs of preparation, MF 49

THE FIRST OPERATING SYSTEM was the joint creation of computer programmer Bob Patrick at General Motors and engineer Owen Mock at North American Aviation. Called the GM-NAA I/O system, it used a group of supervisory commands to syncopate—and accelerate—the processing of individual jobs in an IBM 704 mainframe by performing each task in three phases: input, execution, and output. Because the GM-NAA I/O system enabled a number of separate jobs to be carried out in a continuous sequence, it popularized the technique known as batch processing.

A LANGUAGE WITH LOOPS, FORTRAN (short for formula translator) enabled a computer to perform a repetitive task from a single set of instructions. Created by John Backus and a team of twelve other computer scientists under the auspices of IBM, FORTRAN would soon become the standard high-level programming language among scientists and engineers.

A COMMERCIAL COMPILER was released by Sperry Rand for its UNIVAC computer. Developed by Grace Hopper as a refinement of her earlier innovation, the A-0 compiler, this version was dubbed **MATH-MATIC** by the company's sales department.

GENERAL PROBLEM SOLVER (GPS), an elaboration of Logic Theorist, sparked two decades of research in the field of AI known as problem solving. As a strategy for computers, GPS emulated key aspects of the human approach to unraveling a puzzle—notably trial-and-error and means-ends analysis, which tests whether a step taken in pursuit of a goal appears to lead there.

1956

1957

1957

1957

Electronic warfare, simulated: MF *10-21*

Electrotechnical Labs: RO 79

Elephant Memory Systems: PC 24

Elin, Larry: CI 80

Eliza: AI 58-59, 71, HB 75-76, IC 60

Elliott, David: CM 107

Ellison, John W.: PM 59-60

Elston, Richard: CC 37

Em, David: CI 115, IO 108; images by, CI *120-121*

Embedded computer systems: LA 78-84

EMI Ltd.: HB 17; EMIDEC 1100,

HB 17, 19; ICL1900, HB 17, 22

Empirical induction: AI 38

Employee attacks on computer systems: CS 42, 44, 60, 71. *See also* Programmers

EMYCIN: AI 40

Encryption: *scrambling data or messages with a code or cipher so they are unreadable without a secret key.*

Encryption of messages and data: CS 87-90, 104; and computers, CS 92; implementation of, CS 102; key distribution, CS 98-99;

single-key, CS 92-93, 98, 102, 103, 104, *106-111*, 112; testing of, CS 93; two-key, CS 92, 99-102, 103, 104, *112-117*; unbreakable, CS 89, 102; during World War II, CS 91-92. *See also* Blocking; Compaction; Expansion; Permutation; Substitution

End-effectors: RO *34, 35, 38, 39, 42, 43*, 49

Engelbart, Douglas: IC 62, IO 64, *65*, 66-67, 75, PC 59

Engelberger, Joseph F.: RO 33, 37, 38, 41

Engelmann, Carl: RV 44

Engerman, Stanley: PM 21

Engineering Research Associates (ERA): MS 39, 43, PO 11-13, 31; Atlas, MS 43, PO 12; ERA 1101, IC *24*, MS 43, PO 12-13

English: use of in computer languages, LA *46-47*

English Channel: vessel traffic management, TR 91-92

Engstrom, Howard: PO 12

Enhanced Naval Warfare Gaming System (ENWGS): MF *18-19*

ENIAC (Electronic Numerical Integrator and Computer): CB *56*, 59-60, 65, 67, IC *18*, IO 11-12, *13*, LA 9, MF 46, MS 8, RV 15, 39, SO 8, SW *8-9*, 12, 58; and pi, PM 35

Enigma: CB 55-56, 58, CS 90-91

Ensoniq, Inc.: CM 100-101

Entry probes: SP *92-93*

Environmental problems: CS 29; and air conditioning, CS 29; electrical fluctuations, CS 29-32; fire, CS 33-34; lightning, CS 32; static electricity, CS 29-30

Environmental regulation systems: IO 82

Epaulard (ROV): RO 104-105

Epi Aid: HB 68

Epidemiology: HB 66-71; tracing an infection, HB 66-70

E

THE TX-2 at M.I.T. foreshadowed the era of word processing. Engineer Jack Gilmore and his colleagues outfitted the computer with unique text-handling utilities and devised a system that allowed software writers to "type" words into their programs by pointing a light pen at characters on a computer-generated display of the alphabet. The text handler also provided for setting tabs and margins, erasing characters, and moving words or entire paragraphs.

M.I.T.'S AI LAB was founded by John McCarthy and Marvin Minsky, two of the acknowledged fathers of artificial intelligence. The lab would be the birthplace of McCarthy's LISP programming language—a favorite of AI investigators—and the site of Minsky's most influential work, a description of how the human brain might organize knowledge.

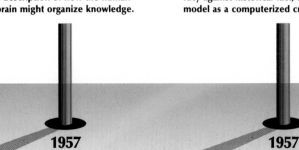

SYSTEM DYNAMICS, software brainchild of hardware designer Jay Forrester *(above)*, was a computer-modeling strategy that differed from its predecessors. Instead of predicting the future of a complex system from its historical performance, system dynamics seeks to build a model of the system, to test the model's accuracy against historical fact, and then to use the model as a computerized crystal ball.

1957

1957

1957

Epi Info: HB 68-69, 70

EPROM (erasable programmable read-only memory): IC *69*, MS 23, *29*; interior, CM *12-15*; in PC, CM *8-9, 10-11*

Epson Corporation: IO 46, PC 16; HX-20, PM 31

Equalizer, The: HB 90

Equatorial Earth Stations: CO 97, 100

Equity Funding Corporation: CS 18

ERA: *See* Engineering Research Associates

ERICA (Eyegaze Response Interface Computer Aid): HB 92-93

ERMA (Electronic Recording Method of Accounting): IC *42*, IO *14*

Error back propagation: *See* Backward-error-propagation algorithm.

Error correction: MS 85;

Hamming codes, MS *88-93*

Error detection: MS 26, 85; checksum, MS 86, *87*; and interleaving, MS *94-95*; parity, MS *86, 92-93*

Errors: arithmetic, RV *16-17*; burst, MS *94-95*; hard and soft, MS 85

Espinoza, Chris: PC 62

Estridge, Philip Donald: PC *11*, 14, 15, 16, 17, 27

ETA[10]: MS 7

Eta Carinae: CC *8, 9*

Etak, Inc.: IC *111*, TR 54-55

ETA Systems: PO 45, 91, 96

Etching silicon: CM 57, 62, *83*

Ethernet: CO 57, 62, IC 78

Euler, Leonhard: RV 8

Eurisko: AI 81-83, IC 99

European Centre for Medium Range Forecasts: SW 103-104

Europort: TR 92-93, 98

EUROTRA: PM 77

Evans, Bob O.: IO 62, SC 24, 34

Evans, David: CI 35, 37, IO 72

Evans, Michael: PM 95, 96, 97

Evans & Sutherland Computer Corporation: CI 37, 38; LDS-1, CI 37

Everett, Robert R.: CI 13, CO 18

Evolution: computer models, RV 21, *22-29*

Excel: PC 68

Exclusive-OR function: *a logic operation that yields a zero when combining two bits that are alike and a one when the bits are different.* See Data Encryption Standard; Error detection: parity.

Exhaustive search: AI 34, *37*

Exocet missile: MF 71-72, RO 110

Expansion: CS 104, *105*

Experimental Autonomous Vehicle-East (EAVE-East): RO 105

Expert system: *a computer program that mimics the reasoning powers of a human expert, drawing conclusions and generating advice through the manipulation of*

extensive data on a given subject. See also Inference engines; Knowledge base. AI 9, 38-42, 43, LA 71, 119, SW 110-112; biochemical, SW 111-112; certainty factors, AI 50-51; chaining, AI 48-49; chemical, AI 39; detective example, AI *44-53*; inductive, SW 111, 112; industrial, AI 41-42; limitations, AI 42, 75; medical, AI 40-41, HB 79 *80-87*; in space, AI 111, 113. See also Medical expert systems

Expert-system shell: *a general-purpose expert system containing reasoning mechanisms and a skeletal knowledge base into which a user can inject specialized knowledge.* See Expert system.

Explorer I: SP 13, 87, 116

Extension: *an expanded version of a language supplemented with features that increase the language's capabilities.*

Extension, language: LA 67

Eyescan Communicator: IO *99*

PROJECT LIGHTNING, a huge government-sponsored computer-research project, was a major stimulant for the commercial computer boom in the 1960s and 1970s. During the project, which lasted until 1962, the National Security Agency distributed $25 million for research in such areas as semiconductor properties and component-fabrication techniques. Then the normally secretive organization published the findings for the benefit of the burgeoning U.S. computer industry.

1957

THE SAGE AIR-DEFENSE system incorporated the first production-model computer with built-in interactive graphics. Operators had keyboards, light guns, and CRTs—a configuration proven effective by M.I.T.'s Whirlwind. SAGE—for Semi-Automatic Ground Environment—also broke new ground as the first large-scale communications network to serve computers, linking hundreds of radar stations in the U.S. and Canada to consoles in twenty-seven regional command centers.

1958

and Index; IO Input/Output; LA Computer Languages; MF The Military Frontier; MS Memory and Storage; PC The Personal Computer; PM The Puzzle Master; PO Speed and Power; RO Robotics; RV Revolution in Science; SC The Software Challenge; SO The Computerized Society; SP Space; SW Software; TR Transportation

F

F-16 aircraft: IC *98*, MF 66
Fabrication: building structure, CM *76-77*. *See also* Manufacturing of chips
Fabry-Perot resonator: AC 92
FACT (Fully Automatic Compiling Technique): LA 43, 44
Faggin, Federico: AC 67, CB 77
Fagin, Lawrence: HB 72
Fahlman, Scott: AI 64, 102-103, 109
Faint Object Classification and Analysis System (FOCAS): CC 33
Fair, Ray: PM 98

Fairchild Semiconductor Corporation: CB 74, 76, CM 18, 23, 26, 53-54, 74
Faith 7: SP 20
Falkland Islands War: MF 71-72
Falkoff, Adin: LA 72
False-color processing: CC 6-7. *See also* Image processing
Fanuc factory: RO 33, 34
Farhat, Nabil: AC 45, 67
Farman, Joseph: PM 106-107
Farmer, Doyne: PM 111
Farrior, James: SP 13

Fast Fourier transform: *a computational technique used to speed the resolution of complex phenomena into their simpler components, and vice versa. It makes possible computer models of the universe and the production of images from radio waves.* See Fourier transforms, fast.

Fault-tolerance: *the ability of a computer to continue processing despite the failure of any single hardware or software component.* See Fault-tolerant computers.

Fault-tolerant computers: SO 70-77
Faury, François: TR 24
FCC (Federal Communications Commission): CO 21; microwave transmission decisions, CO 83, 84; satellite decisions, CO 94, 96
Fearnot, Neal: HB 100-101
Feature extraction: AI 26-27
Federal Express: SO 109-112
Federalist Papers, The: PM 61
Fedwire: SO 86, 87

Feedback: *information sent to a mechanism's control unit from internal or external sensors to convey the mechanism's response to a command or the external effect of its action.*
RO *12-13*, 14, 17; automatic, AI 10-11; in humans, RO 17; with resolvers and optical sensors, RO *56-57*

Feedback loop: *a control system incorporating controller commands to a mechanism, the mechanism's response, measurement of the re-*

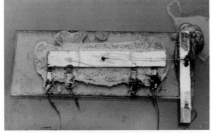

THE FIRST INTEGRATED CIRCUIT was built by Texas Instruments engineer Jack St. Clair Kilby to prove that resistors and capacitors could be made simultaneously on the same piece of semiconductor material. Kilby's homely prototype was a sliver of germanium with five such components linked by wires.

1958

IBM'S 7000-SERIES MAINFRAMES (the model 7090 is shown here) were the company's first transistorized computers. The new machines were at least five times faster than their vacuum-tube predecessors and many times more dependable. The 7090 became the workhorse of scientific computing throughout the early 1960s, with IBM selling or leasing more than 400 of the $3-million machines.

1958

sponse, and transmission of the measurement back to the controller for comparison with the original command. See Feedback.

Feet: analysis of pressures on, HB *73*

Feigenbaum, Edward: AI 38-39, 40, HB 72, IC *59*, SW 111, 112

Feigenbaum, Mitchell: PM 120-121

Felsenstein, Lee: CB 106, CO 27

Ferguson, Charles H.: CM 107

Ferranti Limited: MS 39

Fetus: HB *54-55*

Feynman, Richard: AC *106, 107*

Fiber optics: *the technology of encoding data as pulses of laser light beamed through ultrathin strands of glass. See Optical fibers.*
AC 86, IC *91*

Fiber-optic tactile sensors: RO 80

Field-effect transistor (FET): *a solid-state device in which current is controlled between source terminal and drain terminal by voltage applied to a nonconducting gate terminal. See Transistors: field-effect.*

FIFO storage: SW *52, 53*

Fifth-generation computer: *an experimental, parallel-processing computer. See Fifth Generation project.*

Fifth Generation project: IC 104, PO 89-90, 97

FIG (FORTH Interest Group): LA 107

File: *a collection of related data stored in a computer.*

Files, storage of: UNIX, RV 74-75

Fingerprint-identification system: CS *56-57*, MS 71-72

Finite-element analysis: PO *24-25*

Finite element method (FEM): CI 104, 105

Fire detection: IO 82

Fire-extinguishing systems: CS 33-34

Fire problems: CS 33-34

First National Bank of Chicago: SO 76

First National State Bank of New Jersey: SO 75-76

Fish Engineering & Construction, Inc.: PC 87, 88-89, 91

Fisher, David A.: LA 80, SC 20

Flat-panel displays: CI 15, IO 55

Fletcher, James: SP 65

Flex: IO 73

Flexowriter: IO 12, *13*, 35, 46

FL (functional level): SC 99-100

Flight-data acquisition: TR *12-13;* graphic reconstructions, TR *14-15*

Flight simulators: CI 51, 112, *113*, 114, SW 106; view from, SW *107*

Flip-flop: *an electrical circuit with two stable states—on or off; the basic component of a logic or memory terminal.*

Flip-flop circuit: MS *32-33*

INPUT/OUTPUT CAPABILITY LEAPED AHEAD with the commercial introduction of I/O channels on the IBM 709. First installed in SAGE computers, these small, special-purpose processors worked independently of a computer's central processing unit to store and retrieve data. IBM customers could add as many as six channels to a 709, speeding processing by relieving the CPU of most input/output chores.

ALGOL, a high-level computer language, pioneered the concept of block structure—the dividing of programs into self-contained units. Devised by a committee of computer scientists from Europe and the United States, ALGOL never caught on in America, where FORTRAN was already deeply entrenched. But it became popular in Europe and influenced the development of other languages.

FLOW-MATIC, a compiler tailored to the world of business computing and data processing, became available to Sperry Rand customers. Written by Grace Hopper to complement its predecessor MATH-MATIC, this improved compiler was able to translate into machine code programs written in English-like notation. FLOW-MATIC encouraged a number of nonscientists —businesspeople in particular— to write their own programs and thereby automate many data-intensive tasks in the world of commerce, notably inventory control and payroll processing.

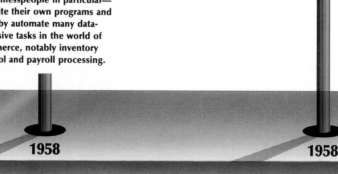

1958   **1958**   **1958**

Floating-point arithmetic: PO *40*

Floating-point notation: *a method of expressing a number as a product of a mantissa and a base number raised to a certain power; so named because the decimal point moves, or floats, depending on the size of the exponent: for instance 93,000,000 can become either .93 x 10^8 or .093 x 10^9. Floating-point notation allows computers to work with very large and very small figures by reducing the number of digits needed to represent them. See Floating-point arithmetic.*

Floating Point Systems: PO 72-74, *75-76*; AP-120B, IC *84*, PO 73-74; AP-190L, PO 74; scientific computers, PO 76

Floppy disk: *a small, flexible disk used to store information or instructions. See Magnetic disk storage.*

Flops: *floating-point operations per second; used as a measurement of processing speed in supercomputers. See* Floating-point arithmetic.

Flow chart: SW *48-49*

FLOW-MATIC: IC 40, LA 22, 41, 42

Fluid dynamics: PO 19, *22-23*, SW 105

Fly-by-wire systems: IC 98, 121, TR 21, 22-23; and maintenance, TR 22

FMCS (Flight Management Computer System): TR 18-19

FMS (flexible manufacturing systems): IO 78-79

Fogel, Robert: PM 22

Ford: CI 104-105, RO 41

Ford Aerospace Corporation: MF 27

Forrester, Jay W.: CB 96, CI 9, *12*, IC 31, *37*, IO 12, MS

18-19, 20, 21, 22, PM 99, 104

FORTH: IC 70, LA 7, 8, 9, 105-107, SC 36, SW 38, *39*

FORTRAN (Formula Translator): *a computer language used primarily for scientific or algebraic purposes.* IC 36, LA 37-41, 67, 81, 99, RV 41, 44, SC 19, 85, 86, 87, 90, 99, SO 18, SW 27, 29, 37, *39*; and ALGOL, LA 45, 48; FORTRANSIT, LA 40; and microcomputers, LA 105; and PL/I, LA 50

Forward Error Correction Algorithm: MF 99

Fourier, Jean-Baptiste: CC 109, IO 113

Fourier synthesis: RV *86-87*

Fourier transforms: CC 57; fast, CC 57, 109, 111, 113, 114, 117, RV 42-44

Fowler, Alan: AC 92

Fox, Geoffrey: PO 102

Foxboro Company: AC 12, 13

Fractal geometry: CI *66-67*, IC *86*, PM *100-103*

Frame buffer: *See* Buffer, frame

Frames: AI 65, *66-67*, 81

France: sailing ships, TR 24, 25

Frank, Andrew: RO 63

Frankston, Robert: IC *97*, PC 9, *11*, SW 69-70, *72*

Fredkin, Edward: RO 46

Freight distribution: TR 67, 73

Frenk, Carlos S.: CC 107

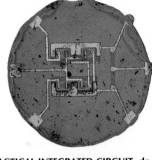

A PRACTICAL INTEGRATED CIRCUIT, designed by Robert Noyce, incorporated Jean Hoerni's planar transistor. Use of the flat transistor allowed Noyce to replace all the connecting wires in Kilby's integrated-circuit design with conducting channels printed directly on the silicon surface by accepted semiconductor manufacturing techniques.

JOHN McCARTHY PROPOSED TIME-SHARING in a New Year's Day memo to the artificial-intelligence center he had helped found at M.I.T. Time-sharing software, McCarthy said, would enable a mainframe computer to run several programs at once, attending to each one for a few milliseconds at a time in a rapidly repeated cycle. In this way, several programmers, time-sharing on individual terminals, would each have the illusion of sole possession of the mainframe.

THE PLANAR TRANSISTOR, more resistant than Jack Kilby's original IC to damage and dust-contamination during manufacture, led to the mass production of integrated circuits. Developed by Swiss physicist Jean Hoerni, this bull's-eye design relied on thin coatings of silicon dioxide to insulate and protect the device.

1958

1959

1959

Freon: PM 106

Frequency: *the number of times per second that a wave cycle (one peak and one trough) repeats. See Electromagnetic spectrum.*

Frequency-division multiplexing: *a technique used to transmit multiple communications simultaneously over a single circuit by dividing the transmission path's bandwidth into several narrower bands, each carrying a single communication. See Multiplexing: frequency division.*

Frequency hopping: MF *59,* 99-100

Frequency-shift keying: *a method of impressing binary data on a carrier signal by switching the carrier between two frequencies, one signifying zeros and the other representing ones. See Modems: frequency-shift keying.*

Friedman, Herbert: CC 63, 66, 67

Friedmann, Alexander: CC 89, 94

Friendship 7: SP 18, 19-20

Frito-Lay: CI 102

Fritz X bomb: MF 62

Front-end programs: AI 61

Frosch, Carl: CM 57

Fry, T. C.: CO 15

Fuel producers: RO 113

Fujitsu: PO 45, 90, 91; VP-400, PO 91

Full duplex: *describing a communications system that makes possible the simultaneous transmission of information by two participants engaged in an exchange of data. See Duplex, full and half.*

Fulton, James: SP 85

Function: *a type of subroutine that produces a single value and is frequently employed for mathematical operations such as square or square root. In most languages,*

more commonly used operations such as addition or subtraction are represented by operators.

Functional Neuromuscular Stimulation: HB 106

Functional programming: IC 93, SC 86, 88-89, 90-91, 98-101; and FL, SC 99-100; and ISWIM, SC 91, 98; and LISP, SC 89-90

Functional units: SC 108-109

Function modules: SC 41, 42-47

Function-point analysis: SC 53-54

Functions: LA *54,* 55

Fusion, nuclear: research, RV 103-106

Futureworld: CI 76

Fuzzy concepts: AI 103

Fuzzy data: *inexact information that is difficult to convert into the digital form required by conventional computers, but for which analog computers are often well suited. ''About 40'' is an example of fuzzy data. See Fuzzy concepts.*

COMPUTERS FIRST READ NUMBERS with the invention of ERMA (Electronic Recording Method of Accounting), a computerized bookkeeping system developed for the Bank of America. In addition to magnetic-drum and magnetic-tape storage, a check sorter, and a high-speed printer, ERMA included a special scanner to read account numbers preprinted on checks in magnetic ink.

COMPUTER-ASSISTED MANUFACTURING was first exhibited at M.I.T.'s Servomechanisms Laboratory. There was a milling machine operated by means of instructions written in APT, a language created by the institute's Automatically Programmed Tools project. In a demonstration run, the computer-controlled device, neatly labeled for the audience, produced an aluminum ashtray for each attendee.

THE BACKUS NORMAL FORM (BNF) was a set of rules and definitions set forth by IBM computer scientist John Backus for describing and analyzing high-level languages and for using such a language to write correct programs. Backus presented BNF at a June 1959 UNESCO conference aimed at creating some order in the babel of computer languages in use. Later, the BNF became known as the Backus Naur form in recognition of the role in its development played by Danish astronomer Peter Naur.

1959

1959

1959

Gagarin, Yuri: SP 13, 87, 116

Galaxies: CC *10-11;* active, CC 56, 74, 106; clustering of, CC 23, 95, 96, 97, 108, 109, *110-118;* radio, CC 58, *64-65, 76, 78, 80, 82*

Galileo Galilei: RV 7

Galileo mission: RO 112, SP 102

Gallium arsenide (GaAs): *a synthetic semiconductor used in the construction of high-speed transistors and integrated circuits; valued for its low power consumption and ability to withstand heat.* AC 95, CM 93, PO 48, 107, *112-113, 118-119;* doping, CM 99; fabrication, CM 98-99; gallium aluminum arsenide, AC 95; semiconductors, IC *113,* MF 107, 110

Gamma-ray imaging: HB *52-53*

GAP/R: AC 16, 24, 27

Garbage collection: MS 78, 82

Garrett, William: SC 54

Garvin, Paul: PM 74

Garwick, Jan Vaumund: SC 102

Garwin, Richard: RV 42-43, 44

Gate: *(a) a circuit that accepts one or more inputs and always produces a single predictable output; (b) the control terminal in a MOS transistor. See* Gates, logic.

Gate array: *an integrated circuit consisting of a regular arrangement of gates (a) that can be interconnected to perform specific functions. See* Integrated circuits: structure.

Gate electrode: *a metal contact that controls transistor current by creating an electric field. See* Switches.

Gates, logic: CM 38, *39-47;* AND, CM 39, *44-45;* arrays in PC, CM *8-9;* networks, CM *36-37, 40-41, 46-47;* NOT, CM 30, *39, 43;* OR, CM 39, 44; transistors in, CM *42-45*

Gates, William, III: CB 99, 100, IC *82,* 102, LA 102, PC *17,* 67, SC 106, SO 108, SW 62-63, *70,* 74

Gateway computer: *a support computer in a supercomputer center that performs security checks and protocol matching on incoming programs from remote sources. See* Supercomputers: centers for.

Gauss-Seidel technique: PM 96

GCA: CM 64-65

GE-635: PM 34

Gee: TR 46

Geiger counters: CC 63, 66

Geisberg, Samuel: PC 97

Gemini, Project: IC *57,* SP 20, 33, 35, 39; *Gemini 3,* SP 37, 116; *Gemini 4,* SP 37, 116; *Gemini 5,* SP 37, 116; *Gemini 6,* SP 38, 116; *Gemini 7,* SP 38, 116; *Gemini 8,* SP 38-39, 117; *Gemini 12,* SP 39, 117; guidance system, SP 33, 34-39; memory, MS 22

Genealogy: PM 20-21

General Dynamics Corporation: CI 35, RO 34

General Electric: CI 36, 103, 113, CO 41-42, IO 79, LA 42, RO 63, SO 20, 24, 77, SW 28; GE 645, RV 73, 78; Multics, SC 34-36

THE CDC 1604 established the Control Data Corporation as an important player in the computer industry. Designed by thirty-five-year-old Seymour R. Cray and priced at just under $1 million, the 1604 was, for a time, more powerful than any other computer on the market.

LISP made its debut as the first computer language designed expressly for writing programs in the field of artificial intelligence. Created by John McCarthy, LISP (short for list processing), offered programmers great flexibility in organizing their software, a boon in trying to make computers mimic the workings of the human mind.

1960

1960

General Motors: CI 35-36, CO 63, RO 38, 39, 40, 41, 43; early computerization of automobiles, TR 8; inertial navigation system, TR 54; and pollution control, TR 8-9; shipping, TR 77-78

General Motors Research: SO 16-18

General Theory of Relativity: CC 89

Genes: *See* DNA

Geographic Information System (GIS): PM 31-32

Geology: *See* Seismology

Georgetown Automatic Translation (GAT): PM 75

GEOS (Geostationary Operational Environmental Satellite): CI *44;* pictures from, CI *44-45*

Gerberg, Darcy: CI 101

Germanium: CB 67, 69, CM 19, 23, 57; cost, CB 72

Gezari, Daniel: CC 30

Giacconi, Riccardo: CC 66-67, 68, 69, 70, 71, 73

Gibson, Edward: IC 76

Gigachip: CM 89-90, 99, 104-108, IC 125; and superconductors, CM 90

Gigaflops: *one billion floating-point operations per second.*

See Supercomputers: speed comparisons.

Gigahertz (GHz): *one billion hertz. See* Electromagnetic spectrum; Hertz.

Gilmore, Jack: CO 39, IO 38-39

Giotto: SP 121

Giser, Samuel P.: AC 25, 27

Givelet, Joseph A.: IO 100

Gleick, James: PM 110

Glenn, John: SP 18, 19, 73, 116

Glennie, Alick E.: IC *30,* LA 20, SW 16

Glidden, Carlos: IO 36

Global Jewish Database/ Responsa Project: PM 60-61

Global Positioning System (GPS, Navstar): TR 51-52, *62-63*

GM-NAA I/O system: IC 36, SO 17-18

Goddard Space Flight Center: CC 90, SP 7-8, 17, 35, 70

Goeken, John: CO 83-84

Gold, Thomas: CC 94

Goldberger, Arthur: PM 95

Goldstine, Herman: CB 59, 62, 64, RV 43, SW 13

Good, I. J.: quoted, CB 58

Goodman, Joseph W.: AC 87

Gorin, Ralph: PC 39

Gorshkov, Sergei G.: MF 94

GOTO statement: SW 31, *40*

GPS (General Problem Solver): AI 35, 38, IC 36

GPS Instrument Company: AC 24-25, 27

GPS Navstar: *See* Global Positioning System

Graf, Hans Peter: AC 65, IC 121

Grand Trunk Western (GTW) Railroad: TR 77

Graphical interface: PC 59-60

Graphic database: CI *35,* 85, 92, 94

Graphics, computer: CB *6, 8,* MS 76, PM *6-15,* RV *96-97, 100-101,* 102, SW *56-57, 64-67, 82-83,* 102, *104-105, 107,* 110, 113, *114-123;* adoption by industry, CI 36; biomechanics, SW 113, *119;* biomolecular, SW 113, *120-121;* computer-aided design, SW *114-115;* data compression, MS 76, 77; medical, HB 6-15, SW 113, *114-115;* physics, SW 113, *122-123;* radio images, CC 61, 62, *63, 64-65;* tablets, SW 82, *83;* uses, CI 7, 15

Graphics, image-generation: IO 53

Graphics coprocessors: CI 58

Graphics software: CI 15, 17, 59. *See also* Modeling; Rendering

Graphics terminal: cost, CI 37; memory needed, CI 37-38, 50

Graphics work station: CI 15, *16-17*

Graphitext: SC 62

Graphs and charts: CI *105*

Graupe, Daniel: HB 96

Gravitational lenses: CC 43

Gravitinos: CC 106, 108

Gravitons: CC 106

Gray, Stephen E.: CB 94

Great American History Machine (GAHM): PM 22

Green, Mike: SO 70, 71, 72

Greene, Stephan: PM 23

Greenhouse Consultant: PM 30-31

Gregg, David: MS 98

THE LARC (Livermore Advanced Research Computer) provided unprecedented speed for nuclear-weapons research at Lawrence Livermore National Laboratory. Designed by Sperry Rand and built with 60,000 transistors, the machine was nearly 100 times as fast as any of its contemporaries. Instead of binary numbers, the LARC used decimal numbers in its computations and was the largest computer of its type ever built.

1960

DATAPHONE was the first commercial modem designed specifically for converting digital computer data to analog signals for transmission across the Bell System's long-distance telephone network. The high-speed data transmission techniques used in the Bell System device were originally developed for the SAGE air-defense network.

1960

Grenada invasion: MF 93
Grissom, Gus: SP 7, 18, 37, 46, 116, 117
Grolier's Electronic Encyclopedia: MS 102
Grossberg, Stephen: AC 53, 65
Grosser, Morton: HB 106-107
Grossman, Joel W.: PM 30-31
Groth, Edward: CC 96
Ground warfare: and Joint STARS, MF 98-99
Grumman Aerospace Corporation X-29: IO 7, 85, *86-93;* sensors, IO *88-89, 90-91*
GTE Laboratories: CM 101
Guardian Operating System: SO 74
Guggenheim Aeronautical Laboratory, California Institute of Technology (GALCIT): SP 86
Guidance systems: *See* Apollo, Project; Gemini, Project; Inertial guidance systems
Guide Star Catalog: preparation, CC 99, *100-101*
Guier, William H.: TR 49
Guilfoyle, Peter: AC 88
Gulfstream Aerospace Corporation: PO 44
Gyroscopes: TR 52; gyrocompass, TR 91

G

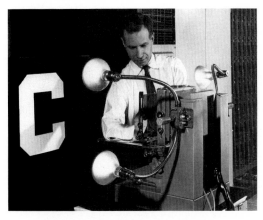

THE MARK I PERCEPTRON, the first neural network, could recognize letters of the alphabet, after instruction from a human. Invented by psychologist Frank Rosenblatt, the machine had a 400-cell photoelectric "eye" connected to circuitry that was meant to mimic the learning process of the human brain.

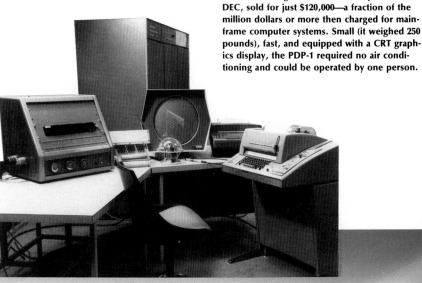

PRECURSOR TO THE MINICOMPUTER, the PDP-1 from Digital Electronics Corporation, or DEC, sold for just $120,000—a fraction of the million dollars or more then charged for mainframe computer systems. Small (it weighed 250 pounds), fast, and equipped with a CRT graphics display, the PDP-1 required no air conditioning and could be operated by one person.

1960

1960

Hacker Ethic: SW 61, 62

Hackers: CB 93, SW 58; attitude of, CS 10-11; development of programming by, SW 57-61, 63; entry to computer systems by, CS 8-11, 16-17

Hagopian, Jack: MS 50

Hale, Edward Everett: SP 71

Hale, George Ellery: CC 17

Half duplex: *describing a communications system in which the partners in an exchange of data must take turns transmitting. See Duplex, full and half.*

Hall, Eldon: SP 44

Hallock, Robert: PC 10

Hallquist, John: PO 44

Halon: CS 34

HAL/S: IC 70, SP 66

Halstead, Maurice: SC 53; metric, SC 53

Hamilton, Alexander: PM 61

Hamilton, Frank: MS 44, RV 18

Hamming, Richard: MS 88

Hamming codes: MS *88-93*

Hammond Organ: IO 100

Hand: HB *14-15*

Hand geometry-identification system: CS *54-55*

Handheld Products, Inc.: SO 109

Handicapped, computer aids for the: HB 18, 89-107

Hands, robot: RO *76, 78-79, 90-91*; grips, RO *92-93*; tactile sensing, RO *79-80, 90-91, 94-97*; temperature sensing, RO *98-99*

Hanley, Sam: RV 19

Hard disk: *a rigid metallic platter coated on both sides with a thin layer of magnetic material, where digital data is stored. Hard disks have more storage capacity than floppy disks but are usually permanently installed in a computer's disk drive and thus are less portable. See Magnetic disk storage.*

Hardware: *the physical apparatus of a computer system. See Computers.*

Hard-wired: *built in by the manufacturer and therefore incapable of being altered by programming.*

Hardy, Godfrey H.: PM 36

Haring, Keith: IO 108

Harker, Jack: MS 45

HARM (High-speed Anti-Radiation Missile): MF 70-71

Harpoon missiles: MF 95-96

Harris, Jim: PC 22

Harris, Kim: LA 106-107

Hartford Insurance Group: SC 55-56

Harvard College Observatory: CC 15

Harvard Mark I: IC 16, LA 8, 11, 21, SW 11, 16, 58

Harvard Medical School: HB 60, 74

Harvard-Smithsonian Center for Astrophysics: CC 71

Harvard University: MS 17

Haskell: SC 99

Haughton, Ken: MS 51

Hawking, Stephen: HB 89, *90, 91*

HD 93129A: CC *8, 9*

Head: HB *46-47, 48, 110-111, 114-115*

THE IBM 1401 brought data processing to small companies previously unable to afford a computer. Essentially a stripped-down version of other IBM offerings, the transistor-based 1401 was by far the most popular computer of its day. IBM leased more than 15,000 of these inexpensive office workhorses at prices as low as $2,500 a month.

1960

and Index; IO Input/Output; LA Computer Languages; MF The Military Frontier; MS Memory and Storage; PC The Personal Computer; PM The Puzzle Master; PO Speed and Power; RO Robotics; RV Revolution in Science; SC The Software Challenge; SO The Computerized Society; SP Space; SW Software; TR Transportation

H

Head crash: *a catastrophic malfunction in a hard-disk drive, during which the electronic read/write head touches the rapidly spinning disk, gouging its magnetic surface and destroying both its data and the head.* CS 31-32, MS *62-63*

Head-up display (HUD): MF 66

Hearing: and neural networks, AC 66

Hearing aids: conventional, HB 96; customized, HB 97; implanted, HB 97-99; zeta noise blocker, HB 96-97

Hearsay II: AI 100-102, IC 80

Heart: HB *12-13, 53*; computerized aids for, HB 99-101

Heat: generation, CM 27, 28, 30; and MOSFETs, CM 30; removal, CM 28; and superconductors, CM 90

Hebb, Donald: AC 48

Hecht-Nielsen, Robert: AC 65, 68; Hecht-Nielsen Neurocomputers (HNC), AC 65, 66

Heeschen, David: CC 58-59

Held, Michael: PM 33-34

Helicopters: Seahawk SH-60B LAMPS, MF 95

Helium, liquid: CM 90-91

Hellman, Martin E.: CS 99, 100

HELP: HB 61

Hemingway, Ernest: PM 51-52

Hemmes, David: LA 40, *43*

Herman, Neil: SP 95, 97, 98, 100

Herrick, Harlan: RV 40

Herschberg, I. S.: CS 71

Hersey, John: IO 45

Hertz: *a unit of frequency equal to one cycle per second. See* Electromagnetic spectrum.

Hertzfeld, Andy: PC 47-48, 62, 64

Herzog, Chaim: MF 67

Heuristics: *rules of thumb or good judgment, based on experience, that humans and computers use to narrow the search for the solution of a problem.* AI 34-35, 43, 74, 76, 85; search, AI 37

Hewlett, William: RV 67-68, 70, 71

Hewlett-Packard: CB 78, 106, CM 70, RV 67-68, 70-73, SO 65, 66, 70, 71, 109; electronic calculators, RV 71-73; HP-28C, RV *66*; HP-35, IC *71*, RV *66*, 72-73; HP-65, IC *79*, RV 73; and microcomputers, PC 10; Model 200A, RV 68; Model 2116A, RV *65*, 70; Model 9100A, RV *66*, 71; RISC machine, PC 98; Superchip, CB 102, *103*

Hexadecimal (Hex): *a number system, based on sixteen, in which a single digit represents four binary digits. See* Hexadecimal arithmetic.

Hexadecimal arithmetic: LA *12-13*

Hidden mass: CC 97-98, 106-108. *See also* Dark matter

High-electron-mobility transistor (HEMT): *a semiconductor switch that provides a swift passage for current-carrying electrons through a layer of undoped semiconductor material. See* Transistors: HEMT.

COBOL (COmmon Business Oriented Language), a prominent computer language designed specifically for commercial uses, was created by a team drawn from several computer makers and the Pentagon. COBOL excels at the most common kinds of data processing for business—simple arithmetic operations performed on huge files of data. The language endures because its syntax is very much like English and because a program written in COBOL for one kind of computer runs on many others without alteration.

COMPUTER-AIDED COMPOSITION was the goal of the MUSIC system, developed by a Bell Laboratories team under engineer and amateur violinist Max Mathews *(below, right)*. Composers using MUSIC manipulated a light pen to indicate the pitch, loudness, and length of notes for several instrumental voices. Within minutes, computerized sound synthesis allowed them to hear what they had written.

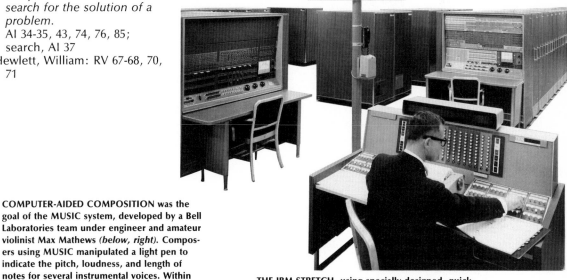

THE IBM STRETCH, using specially designed, quick-switching transistors and a new technique called multiprogramming, reigned briefly as the world's fastest computer, executing as many as a hundred billion calculations a day. Multiprogramming speeded the Stretch, officially named the 7030, by enabling it to perform calculations for one program while retrieving data for others. Though a technical success, the Stretch was a business disaster; IBM lost about $20 million on the machine because of cost overruns and schedule delays.

1960   1960   1961

High Energy Astronomy Observatory (HEAO): CC 71; High Energy Astronomy Observatory 2, CC 13

High-energy physics: IO *76, 77*, 82. *See also* Supercollider

High-level language: *a programming language that approximates human language more closely than does machine code or assembly language, and in which one statement may invoke several machine-code or assembly-language instructions. See* Languages, high-level computer.

High Sierra format: IC 116, MS 103

Hillis, Daniel: AI 109, PO *104*, 105

Hinton, Geoffrey: AC 55, AI 108, 109

Hirschler, Otto: SP 12

Historical investigations: PM 18. *See also* Artifacts; Cliometrics

Hitachi: PO 45, 90-91, RO 34; S810-20, PO 91; SMA hand, RO 76

Hoare, C. A. R. (Tony): LA 76-77, 78, 83, 103, SC 22

Hobday, Stephen: IO 41

Hockham, G. A.: CO 101

Hodgkin's disease: computer-aided diagnosis and treatment of, HB *82-87*

Hoehn-Saric, Christopher: MS 107

Hoelzer, Helmut: AC 15, IC 14, SP 9-13

Hoerni, Jean: CB 74, *97*, CM 23, *24*, IC 41

Hoff, Marcian Edward, Jr. (Ted): AC 50, 52, CB 76-77, *98*, SO 90, 91

Hoffman, Paul: PM 32

Hofstein, Steven: CB *97*, IC 49

Hohmann transfer ellipse: SP 54-55, 56-57

Hole: *the concept used to describe the movement of the absence of an electron through the crystal structure of a semiconductor. The movement of a hole is equivalent to the movement of a positive charge. See* Switches.

Holiday Corporation: and TPF system, Holidex, SO 51-52

Hollerbach, John M.: RO 78, 79

Hollerith, Herman: CB 13-14, IO 9, 10, RV 9, SW 11; tabulator, CB *13-14*, 51, 52, IC 9

Holographic image processing: AC 89

HOLWG (High Order Language Working Group): LA 79, 80-81

Homebrew Computer Club: CB 104, 106, LA 102, SW 63, 68

Honey, Stan: TR 54, 55

Honeywell Corporation: LA 42, 43, 81-82, 99, SC 36, SO 20

Honeywell 6000: MF 26-27, 102

Hood, Leroy: HB 43

Hooks and scars: AI 113

Hopfield, John: AC 36, *54*, 55, HB 33, IC *107*; Hopfield network, AC *36-39*

Hopfield net: *a type of neural network designed by physicist John Hopfield to solve optimization problems.*

Hopper, Grace Murray: IC *29*, 40, LA 10-11, 15, *21*, 22, 41-42, 44, 48, PO 96, SW 16-*17*, 18

Horton, David: CO 55

Hospital for Special Surgery: CI 107

Hot sites: CS 35

Houbolt, John: SP 34, 39

Hounsfield, Godfrey: HB 17, 19, 20, 21, 22, IC 74

Hounsfield numbers: HB 48-49

Houston Area Research Center (HARC): PO 91, 96

Howard, Richard: AC 65

Howe, Robert: AC 30

Hoyle, Fred: CC 94

Hs-293 bomb: MF 62

Hubble, Edwin: CC 15-16, 23, 29, 94

Hubble Space Telescope: CC 28-29, *90-93*; fine guidance sensors, CC 100, *101*; Guide Star Catalog, CC 99-101

THE FIRST INDUSTRIAL ROBOT, Unimate, started work at a General Motors factory in New Jersey. Obeying step-by-step commands stored on a magnetic drum, the 4,000-pound, one-armed automaton, built by Unimation, Inc., quenched and stacked hot pieces of die-cast metal using a specialized gripper.

TIME-SHARING ARRIVED with the Compatible Time-Sharing System (CTSS) at the Massachusetts Institute of Technology, the first practical demonstration of the time-sharing concept proposed by M.I.T. professor John McCarthy in 1959. Run by an IBM 709 computer, the CTSS handled processing requests from keyboard-equipped terminals in milliseconds.

MANNED SPACEFLIGHT got an assist from NASA's ground-based computers as Project Mercury astronaut John Glenn orbited the earth. The agency's IBM 7090 continuously calculated Glenn's position and speed—information that helped controllers decide whether to continue or abort his flight. The Mercury Monitor, a program that anticipated modern-day operating systems, juggled the tasks of data transmission, processing, and printing, assigning a sensible priority to each.

SPACEWAR!, the seminal computer game, made its first public appearance at M.I.T.'s spring open house. Displayed on the screen of a PDP-1, Spacewar! featured interactive, shoot-'em-up graphics that inspired many of the next decade's video games. Dueling players fired at one another's spaceships and wielded early computer joysticks *(below)* to steer away from a central black hole. In a typical hacker touch, stars in the game's background occupied shifting, astronomically correct positions.

1961   **1961**   **1962**   **1962**

and Index; IO Input/Output; LA Computer Languages; MF The Military Frontier; MS Memory and Storage;
PC The Personal Computer; PM The Puzzle Master; PO Speed and Power; RO Robotics; RV Revolution in Science; SC The Software Challenge; SO The Computerized Society; SP Space; SW Software; TR Transportation

Hudspeth, Thomas: CO 89
Huffman, David A.: MS 77
Huffman coding: MS 77
Hughes, David: CO 27-28
Hughes Aircraft Company: CO 89, 94, MF 72
Hughes Research Laboratories: CO 100
Hulbert, Edward: CC 63
Human body: HB entire volume
Humphrey, Watts: SC 33
Hump list: TR 86; as-humped list, TR 86
Hurd, Cuthbert C.: RV 40

Husky Hawk: PM 30
Hutchinson, Thomas: HB 92-93
Hybrid computers: *See* Computers, hybrid
Hybrids: CM *119*
HYDAC: AC 28
Hydraulic actuators: RO *50,* 51
Hydrogen bomb: CB 60, 64
Hydrophones: MF 31, 32
Hypercard: IC 123, PC 59
Hypermedia: PM *78-91;* browser, PM *88-89;* links, PM *84-87;* nodes, PM *80-81;* use, PM *90-91;* windows, PM *82-83*

H

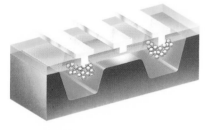

SIXTEEN MOS TRANSISTORS like the one above were combined into a single integrated circuit by an RCA team. The achievement quickened the pace of electronic integration, since MOS (for "metal-oxide semiconductor") transistors are smaller, less power hungry, and more easily manufactured than other transistor types.

1962

LINC (Laboratory INstrumentation Computer), designed and constructed by Wesley Clark at M.I.T.'s Lincoln Laboratory, was the first computer able to process data from laboratory experiments in real time. Initially used in biomedical studies, Linc was inexpensive—less than $25,000—and small enough to fit in crowded quarters.

1962

IAS computer: IC 27, MS 12, 16

IBM: CI 35, CM 54, 67, IO 9, 46, 61, LA 21, PM 33, PO 8, 16, 91, RO 34, RV 10-11, SC 21, 23, SO 20, 4Pi, SP 73; 4Pi TC-1, SP 60; 90, PO 16, 17-18; 305 RAMAC, IC 34, MS 44; 350, MS 44-45, 50; 360, TR 101; 370/168, PO 75; 650, CB 96, IC 32, LA 40, 99, MS 43, SO 13, SP 14; 701, AI 73-74, IC 30, IO 14, 18, LA 21, MS 20, RV 20, 40, SO 13, 14; 702, SO 13; 704, AI 13, LA 37, 39, MS 20, PM 35, PO 9, 10, 11, RV 40, SO 16, SW 26; 705, MS 20, SO 19; 709, IC 40, SO 18, 20, SP 16, 17, 19; 1301, MS 50; 1401, IC 46, SC 23, SO 21; 2250, CI 36; 3081, PO 76; 3083, TR 105; 3340, MS 51; 4341, PC 88, 91; 5100 series, PC 10; 7070, SO 22; 7074, SO 22; 7080, SO 21; 7090, IC 39, SO 21, 40, SP 16-17; 7094, CC 96, SP 35, 36; 9020, TR 101, 105; 9083, SO 50; and ALGOL, LA 48;

AP-101, SP 65; and APL, LA 72-73; and AT&T, CO 97; and COBOL, LA 42, 44; computer incompatibilities, SC 24; and concordance to Aquinas, PM 58, 59; and core memory, MS 20-22; data codes, CO 49, 54; and data encryption, CS 93; department of applied sciences, RV 40; Dirty Dozen, PC 11-13; and early microcomputers, PC 8, 10; entry into computer production, IO 17-18; Entry Level Systems unit, PC 10, 11-12, 25; and fast Fourier transform, RV 42, 43; and FORTRAN, LA 37-41, SW 27, 39; and Gemini, SP 33-38; growth, CB 65; launch vehicle digital and IMS, SO 45-46, SW 11; computer (LVDC), IC 59, SP 42; and machine translation, PM 74; and magnetic diskettes, MS 51; and magnetic disks, MS 44-45, 50; and magnetic drums, MS 43-44; Mark I, RV

15; and Mercury, SP 16, 18; and MS-DOS, SO 108; origins, CB 14; OS/360, SC 26, SO 23-24; pipelining, PO 33; and PL/I, LA 50; Pure Science Department, RV 15; and relational data base, MS 73; restructuring of microcomputer division, PC 25; and RISC technology, PC 98; and SABRE, SO 40; and SAGE, MS 20, PO 68; and satellite communications, CO 96-97; and Skylab, SP 60; SNA, CO 55; and SOS, SO 18; and space shuttle, SP 65; SPREAD, SC 24-26; SSEC, IC 21, RV 18-20; Stretch, IC 47, IO 15, MS 73, PO 9, 11; and superconductivity, CM 91, 92, 93; and synchrotron chipmaking, CM 107; System/360, IC 53, IO 61-63, LA 49, SC 23-27, 30-34, SO 23-24, 41; System/370, SO 49; Systems Application Architecture (SAA), PC 105; tabulating equipment of 1930s, RV 11; and tape

BRIAN JOSEPHSON won a British patent for his superconductive switch. Called a Josephson junction, the switch worked ten times as fast as an ordinary transistor, but because it operated only at a temperature near absolute zero, it generated little interest outside the laboratory.

NASA'S ACE system automated flight-readiness testing for the agency's Apollo spacecraft, making some 2,000 prelaunch checks of the moonbound vehicles. To handle the job, ACE (Acceptance Check-out Equipment) had two minicomputers that were linked through a shared memory. One computer gathered data from the ship, and the other evaluated it.

1962

1962

drives, MS 38-39; and time sharing, CO 42, SO 45, SW 88; TPF, SO 51; TTS, SO 45; typewriters, IO 42-43; vector processor experiment, PO 45; and virtual memory, MS 84; during World War II, CB 51-53, RV 14; Winchester disk, IC *77;* XT, IO 96. *See also* IBM PC; IBM PS/2

IBM PC: CB 93, *99,* 106, 108, IC *102,* PC *11,* SW 73; Acorn, PC 14; aftermarket, PC 18-19; approach to building and selling, PC 15-16; AT, IC *112,* PC *12,* 25; BIOS, PC 22, 23, 24; compatibles to, PC 19, 22-25; debut, PC 16-17; early planning, PC 11-14; microprocessor, PC 12-13; open architecture, PC 14, 15; operating system, PC 15; Project Chess, PC 14; RT PC, PC 98; software, PC 19

IBM PS/2: IC *122,* PC 27; 80386 models, PC 89; industry reaction to, PC 28; Micro Channel Architecture, PC 28; protection from clones, PC

27-28

IBSYS: SO 22; and Direct Couple, SO 22-23

ICBM (Intercontinental Ballistic Missile): guidance systems, MF 73-74, 78; MX, MF 74, 78; stages of flight, MF 107, 111. *See also* Strategic Defense Initiative

Ichbiah, Jean: LA 82-83

Icon: *a symbol that represents a command or an object on a display screen.* IO 74, PC 60, SW *82*

ICs: *See* Integrated circuits

Idahex: MF *14-15*

Identifiers: LA 53, 89; type checking, LA *92-93*

IFIP (International Federation for Information Processing): LA 76, 77

If-then rules: *simple statements of logic employed by AI programs such as expert systems and learning programs. See* Language comprehension, computer: if-then rules.

Ignition: automobile, TR *30-31*

ILLIAC IV (Illinois Automatic Computer): IC *73,* PO 34, 96

Illuminator: MF 95

Image analysis applications: PO 105-106

Image formation: AI *16-17*

Image processing: *computer techniques for creating or reassembling images from digitized data.* CC 37-38, 42, CI 39, *40-47, 56-57;* AIPS, CC 60-61; Clean, CC 61, 62; color, CI 39, 40; false color, CC *6-7,* 38; gray scale transformation, CI *41;* interactive, CC 42; Maximum Entropy, CC 62; radio images, CC *6-7,* 11, 13, 61, *62, 63, 64-65;* Voyager, SP *109, 110-111*

Image Reduction and Analysis Facility (IRAF): CC 42

Images, computer: CI entire volume

Imaging, medical: *See* Medical imaging

Imhof, Arthur: PM 20, 21

IMIS (Intelligent Management Information System): AI 113

IMP (Interface Message Processor): MF 101

Imperial Chemical Industries: CS 27-28

IMS (Information Management System): SO 46, 47

IMSAI Manufacturing (Information Management Science Associates, Incorporated): CB 101-103

Index of refraction: AC 92, *93,* 94

Indium antimonide: AC 94

Inductor: CM 23

Industrial espionage: CS 61. *See also* Computer crime

Inertial guidance systems: SP 11-12, 52; Gemini, SP 33-38; space shuttle, SP 74

Inertial Guidance Unit (IGU): MF 73

Inertial measurement unit: TR *58*

Inertial navigation system (INS): MF 75

Inference engine: *the section of an expert system that*

VIRTUAL MEMORY emerged from the computer-science department at England's University of Manchester. Developed by a team under Tom Kilburn, this technique permitted a computer to use its storage capacity as an extension of memory, allowing it to run outsize software and to switch rapidly between multiple programs.

SKETCHPAD, an interactive, real-time computer drawing system, was published by Ivan Sutherland (right) as his M.I.T. doctoral thesis. Using a light pen and Sutherland's software, a designer or engineer who knew nothing about programming could draw geometric figures on-screen, then manipulate them to solve complex engineering problems.

1962

1963

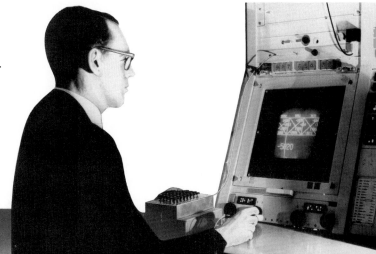

comprises the procedures for manipulating data.
AI 40, 43, HB 81

Influenza: modeling epidemic of, HB 70-71

Information Engineering Facility (IEF): SC 65-66

Information Engineering Workbench: SC 64

Information International, Inc.: *See* Triple I

Information theory: CB 37

Infrared: *a band of electromagnetic radiation having a lower frequency and a longer* wavelength than visible light. Most infrared radiation is absorbed by the earth's atmosphere, but certain wavelengths can be detected from earth. See Infrared emissions.

Infrared emissions: CC 7, *9, 11*

Infrared sensors: MF 63; for space-based defense, MF *114,* 115

Ingot: *in chip fabrication, a single large silicon crystal several inches in diameter* and up to six feet long, grown around a tiny seed crystal. The ingot is sliced into wafers, polished, and used to fabricate chips. See Silicon: wafer manufacture.

Input: *information fed into a computer or any part of a computer. See* Input/output.

Input and output methods: SO 14; slow early methods, SO 15

Input/output: IO entire volume; channel, SO 20; circuits, CB *83;* control system, SO 20; devices, CB *110,* CI 8, 14, 15, SW *20-21;* I/O controller, IO 26, 27, *28-29;* I/O technology, IO *7-8, 12-15,* 19, *20-33;* ports, CB *111, 120-121;* processor, PO *54;* and speed, PO 51

Input/output (I/O) port: *an outlet on a computer circuit board for attaching input or output devices such as keyboards or printers. See* Input/output: ports.

Institute for Advanced Study:

IAS computer, CC 88, IC 27, MS 12

Instruction: *an elementary machine-language order to the central processing unit of a computer. A sequence of such instructions forms a program. See* Instruction cycle.

Instruction cycle: *the series of activities a computer performs in order to read an instruction from memory, decode it, execute it, and prepare for the next instruction.* LA *28-29,* PO 51, *52-53*

Instruction set: SW 21, 23

Insurance rates, and computer security: CS 18, 42

Integer: *in computer science, a data type consisting of zero and both positive and negative whole numbers; also known as a whole number. See* Data types.

Integrated circuit (IC): *an electronic circuit all of whose components are formed on a single piece of semiconduc-*

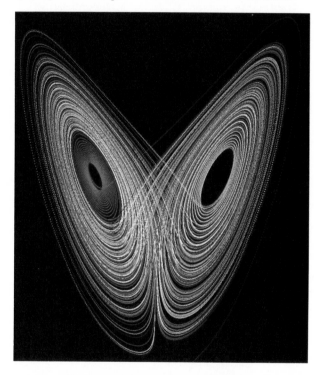

THE LORENZ ATTRACTOR revealed limits of disorder in seemingly random phenomena such as the weather. Studying a computer model of a simple convection system, M.I.T. meteorologist Edward Lorenz expected to discern no pattern among data points plotted on his computer screen. But where anarchy had been presumed, a tantalizing picture of orderliness emerged *(above),* leading to a new field of scientific investigation called chaos.

1963

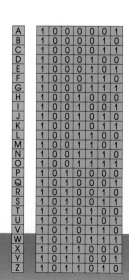

A	1	0	0	0	0	0	1
B	1	0	0	0	0	1	0
C	1	0	0	0	0	1	1
D	1	0	0	0	1	0	0
E	1	0	0	0	1	0	1
F	1	0	0	0	1	1	0
G	1	0	0	0	1	1	1
H	1	0	0	1	0	0	0
I	1	0	0	1	0	0	1
J	1	0	0	1	0	1	0
K	1	0	0	1	0	1	1
L	1	0	0	1	1	0	0
M	1	0	0	1	1	0	1
N	1	0	0	1	1	1	0
O	1	0	0	1	1	1	1
P	1	0	1	0	0	0	0
Q	1	0	1	0	0	0	1
R	1	0	1	0	0	1	0
S	1	0	1	0	0	1	1
T	1	0	1	0	1	0	0
U	1	0	1	0	1	0	1
V	1	0	1	0	1	1	0
W	1	0	1	0	1	1	1
X	1	0	1	1	0	0	0
Y	1	0	1	1	0	0	1
Z	1	0	1	1	0	1	0

ASCII (American Standard Code for Information Interchange) was developed to permit machines from different manufacturers to exchange data. Produced by a joint industry-government committee, ASCII was the first universal standard for computers. The code consists of 128 unique strings of seven ones and zeros. Each sequence stands for a letter of the English alphabet (either uppercase or lowercase), one of the Arabic numerals, one of an assortment of punctuation marks and symbols, or a special function such as the carriage return.

1963

and Index; IO Input/Output; LA Computer Languages; MF The Military Frontier; MS Memory and Storage; PC The Personal Computer; PM The Puzzle Master; PO Speed and Power; RO Robotics; RV Revolution in Science; SC The Software Challenge; SO The Computerized Society; SP Space; SW Software; TR Transportation

tor material, *usually silicon; also called a chip.*
CB *66-67,* 79, *80-91,* CM *64,* IC *39, 41, 62,* SC 23, SO 45; advantages over wired circuitry, CM 24; ASICs, CM 101-102; circuit design, CM 31-34, *100-101,* 102-104; on computer motherboard, CM 7, *8-15;* and computers, CB 74, 76-78; cost, CB 77-78, CM 18; density of components, CM 18, 19, 30; design, CB 78, *84-85;* development, CB 73-74, 76-78; early, SO 89; early proposal for, CM 19, 21, IC 29; execution time of, CM 18; fabrication, CB 72, 78, 79, *84-91;* feature size comparison, CM *104-105;* first, CM *21, 22-23;* first computers using, CB 98; flaws, CB 78, 87, 90; future, CM 108; gallium arsenide, CM 93, 98; gigachip, CM 89, 102, 104, 108; IBM conservatism with, SC 25; interconnecting, CM *94-97;* layers, CM *80-81;* manufacturing diffi-

culties, CM 25; megachip, CM 89, 108; miniaturization, CB 76, 78, 79; MOS, CB 77-78, 97, IC *49;* and MOS technology, CM 30; n-MOS, CB *88-89;* power consumption, CM 31; price, CM 25, 26; quality control, CM 65-67, 70; RAM, CB 80-81, 83, IC *60;* shift-register frame buffer, CI 51; significance, CM 7; single chip computer, CB *82-83;* and space program, SP 44; speed, CB 76, 79; structure, CM *8-15;* and superconductors, CM 90-93; surface, CM *27;* testing, CB *90-91;* and time-sharing services, SO 45; and transistors, CM 18; VLSI, CB 78; wires linking circuit to pins, CM *12-13. See also* Chipmaking Industry; Manufacturing of chips; Memory, semiconductor; Microprocessors; Transistors; VHSICs
Integrator: *a circuit or device in a computer essential to*

the solution of differential analyses.
TR 53
Intel: CM 51, 53, SO 102; 4004, CB 77, 98, *102,* CM *68,* IC *69,* SO 91, 100-101; 8008, CB 94, IC *75,* SO 101; 8080, CB 95, *102,* IC *79,* SO 102, 103; 8086, PC 12; 8088, PC 13; 80286, PC 25; 80386, IC *117,* PC 27, 87-88; 80387, PC 96; 80486, PC 104; iPSC, PO 102; and memory chips, CB 76-77; and microprocessors, SO 89, 90, 100-101; RISC processor, PC 98
Intelligence, artificial: *See* Artificial intelligence
Intellipath: HB 79, *84-85*
Interactive Picture Processing System (IPPS): CC 42, IC 94
Interactive system: *a computer system in which information and graphics are changed or manipulated in immediate response to a user's input. See* Imaging, medical.
Interconnection: *a communication channel that trans-*

mits data between computers or their components. See Optical computer: light transmission.
Interface: for expert systems, HB 81
Interferometry: *a process in which a source of electromagnetic radiation is viewed simultaneously from two or more points for the purpose of improving resolution.*
with radio telescopes, CC 55-62, *78-79,* 80-83
Interleaving: MS *94-95*
Intermetrics, Inc.: LA 81, 82, SP 66
International Business Machines Corporation: *See* IBM
International Species Inventory System (ISIS): PO 44-45
Interplanetary voyages: SP 49, *50-57;* computers, SP 86; future, SP *90-93,* 101-102; Jupiter, SP *92-93,* 99-101, 102; Mars, SP 87, 89, 95-97, 98-99, 101; Mercury, SP 97; Neptune, SP 99-101; and

PRIMITIVE INTEGRATED CIRCUITS APPEARED in IBM's System/360 *(below)*, **a family of six mutually compatible computers and forty peripherals that could work together. IBM invested $5 billion to build the machines and to write the operating system. The huge gamble paid off; within two years, orders for the /360s reached 1,000 a month.**

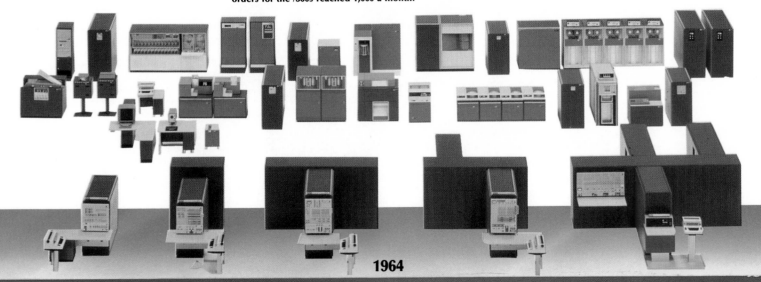

1964

Interplanetary voyages (continued)
Ranger, Project, SP 87-88; Saturn, SP 99-101; Uranus, SP 99-101; Venus, SP 87, 89, *90-91*, 97, 101. *See also* Voyager

Interpreter: *a program that translates a program written in a high-level language into machine code one line at a time, waits for the computer to perform the instructions, then goes on to the next line. See also* Compilers.

LA 14, 21, 85, *86-97*, SW 17, 25, 37

Interrupt: *a temporary halt in executing a program, or the signal that causes the temporary halt.*
IO *28-29;* nonmaskable, IO 28

Intersil: CM 53

Interuniversity Consortium for Political and Social Research (ICPSR): PM 19-20

Introduction to VLSI Systems (Mead and Conway): CM *31,* 32, IC 98

Inverter: *a logic element that receives a single input and changes it to its opposite state.*
CM 30, *39, 43*

I/O: *See* Input/output

Ion: *an atom that has either gained or lost electrons, making it either a positively or a negatively charged particle. See* Ion implantation.

Ion implantation: CM 62, *84-85*

IPARS: SO 44

IPL (Information Processing Languages): IC 35, LA *69,* SC 89

IRCAM (Institute for Research and Coordination of Acoustics and Music): IO 106

ISDN (Integrated Services Digital Network): CO 103-104

ISWIM (If you See What I Mean): SC 91, 98

Itek Corporation: IO 15

Iteration: LA *60-61*

ITT: CO 101

Iverson, Kenneth: LA 72

THOMAS KURTZ AND JOHN KEMENY CREATED BASIC, an easy-to-learn programming language derived from FORTRAN. Kurtz *(above, left)* and Kemeny, professors at Dartmouth College, wrote BASIC (Beginners All-Purpose Symbolic Instruction Code) to help their students program the school's General Electric 225 mainframe. In the next decade, BASIC would become hugely popular among users of personal computers.

OLTP (on-line transaction processing) made its debut in IBM's SABRE reservation system, set up for American Airlines. The first large commercial network to operate in real time, SABRE (Semi-Automated Business Research Environment) linked 2,000 terminals in sixty-five cities via telephone lines to a pair of IBM 7090 mainframes, one running full-time and one for backup. The system had a 500-megabyte magnetic-disk memory and delivered data on any flight in less than three seconds.

1964

1964

Jackel, Lawrence: AC 65, IC 121
Jacobsen, Stephen C.: RO 79
Jacquard, Joseph Marie: CB 9, CI 8, IO 8, RO 34, SW 9; loom, CB *12*, IC 7
Jacquet-Droz, Pierre: AI 8
Jaggies: *See* Aliasing
Jamming: radar, MF *53*, 97; self-jamming, MF 99
Jane's Defense Weekly: MF 38
Janesick, James: CC 36
Jansky, Karl: CC 53, *54*
JANUS: MF *12-13*, 15
Japan: CM 67, 70, 71-72;

interest in robots, RO 38-39; production, RO 40; and sailing ships, TR 24
Japanese characters: IO *44-45*
Japanese language: and speech recognition, AC 64; word processing, AC 63
Japanese supercomputers: PO 89-91; dataflow, PO 106; Fifth Generation project, PO 89-90; MIT, PO 89, 90; National Superspeed computer project, PO 89, 96; structure of industry, PO 90
Jason (ROV): RO 103

Jet Propulsion Laboratory (JPL): CC 36, CI 49, MF 43, SP 86-87, 89; policy, SP 87
Jimerson, Leroy: SP 33
J.J. (Jason Jr.) (ROV): RO 103
Job: *the unit in which a user submits work to the computer system. See* Operating systems: components.
Jobs, Steven: CB 104, 105, 106, 107, 108, IO 74, 75, PC 7, 46, 62-63, SC 106, SW 68, *71*; and Apple, PC 7, 45-46, 59, 60, 61-62, 65, 66, 67; and NeXT, IC *124*, PC 7, 67
Jodrell Bank: CC 55
Johannsen, David: IC *104*
John, E. Roy: HB 76, 77, 78
Johns Hopkins University: HB 101, RO 70
Johnson, Colin: AC 62
Johnson, Nicholas: CO 84
Johnson, Nicholas L.: MF 28
Johnson, Olin: PO 96

CONTROL DATA CORPORATION'S CDC 6600 super-computer, fastest computer in the world at the time of its delivery to the Lawrence Radiation Laboratory, fanned the rivalry among companies striving to build mainframes of ever-increasing speed and power. With ten smaller computers (called peripheral processors) funneling data to a CPU performing three million instructions per second, the CDC 6600 was three times faster than its closest competitor, IBM's Stretch. The 6600 retained its edge in speed until surpassed in 1968 by a successor from the same company, the CDC 7600.

1964

Johnson, Reynold B.: MS 45, 50

Johnston, John: RV 14

Joint STARS (Joint Surveillance Target Attack Radar System): MF 98-99

Jon, holding tapes for ransom by: CS 27-28

Jones, Fletcher: SW 61

Josephson, Brian: CB 78, CM 91

Josephson junction: *an experimental class of integrated circuit designed to operate at extremely high speeds (roughly one-billionth of a second per operation) and at temperatures only a few degrees above absolute zero (−459.7° F.).* CB 78, CM 91-92, IC 50, PO 114-115

Joystick: *a hand-held lever that can be tilted in various directions to control a cursor's movement on a screen.* IO 70-71, SW 60, 66

JTIDS (Joint Tactical Information Distribution System): MF 93, 98-100

Judge, Joseph: PM 23, 24, 28, 29

Jump instruction: LA 30-31; conditional, LA 31; and program clarity, LA 78

Jumpseat satellite: MF 46

Junction: *on a semiconductor, the boundary between a p-type region and an n-type one. See Switches.*

Junction diode: *a simple switch composed of two regions of semiconductor material abutting each other. The switch is turned on or off by the presence or absence of a flow of electrons and holes across the junction. See Diode: junction.*

Jupiter: SP 86, *92-93*, 99-101, 102

Jupiter C rocket: SP 13, 87

Juraszek, Steve: CI 49

Kahn, David: CS 98

Kahn, Philippe: IC *109*, LA 104-*105*

Kanada, Yasumasa: PM 36

Kao, Charles Kuen: CO 101

Kapor, Mitchell: IC *106*, PC 12, 67, 106, SW 72-73

Karp, Richard: PM 33-34

Karth, Joseph: SP 85

Kato, Ichiro: RO 69

Katzman, Jim: SO 70, 71, 72

Kawaguchi, Yoichiro: images by, CI *122-123*

Kawasaki Heavy Industries: RO 39

Kay, Alan: IC 71, IO 72-73, 75, PC 59, SC 104, 105

Keck telescope: CC *24-28*

Kelvin, Lord: AC 10

Kemeny, John: CO 41, IC *54*, LA 71, 103, SW 25-28, 31-32, 38

Kennedy, John F.: SP 13-14, 87

Kenzler, Gene: CM 91

Kepler, Johannes: RV 7, 8

Kernel: *the most basic section of the UNIX operating system. It manages the storage of data, organizes tasks, and handles peripheral devices.*

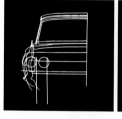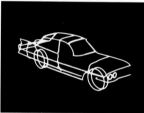

COMPUTER-AIDED DESIGN got its start with DAC-1 (Design Augmented by Computers), a project that was sponsored jointly by General Motors and IBM. Geared to the design of automobiles, the DAC-1 system featured an interactive mode of operation that revolutionized the field of computer graphics. To enlarge, rotate, or alter the shape of an entire car body or its parts, automobile designers simply touched an electronic stylus to the contours displayed on a computer screen. The first of DAC-1's designs to enter production was the trunk lid for GM's line of 1965 Cadillacs *(above)*.

LAWRENCE KLEIN, dean of modern econometrics, helped create the Wharton model, an influential tool for economic forecasting. Devised in collaboration with Michael Evans, a fellow professor at the Wharton School of Business, the Wharton model predicted quarterly performance of the U.S. economy two years into the future.

A UNIVERSAL LANGUAGE was the goal of the IBM programmers and corporate clients who joined forces to produce PL/I, or Programming Language One. By incorporating the best features of FORTRAN, COBOL, and ALGOL, PL/I could perform both analytical tasks for scientists and data processing for businesspeople.

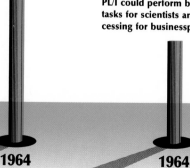

1964   **1964**   **1964**

K

RV *74-75*
Kernighan, Brian: PM 34
Kertesz, François: PM 75
Kerwin, Joseph P.: SP 61, 118
KEWs (kinetic-energy weapons): MF 107, 108
Key: *a sequence of symbols used to encrypt and decrypt data. See* Encryption of messages and data.
Keyboards: CB 26-27, 109, *110,* IO 12, 13, 16, 47, SW *20;* arrangement, IO *40-41;* interpretation of signals, IO *50-51;* mechanisms, IO *48-49*
Keydata Corporation: CO 39, SO *45*
Keywords: LA 51, 57, 89
KH-11 satellite: MF 37, 45, 46; image, MF *38-39*
KH-12 satellite: MF *38-39,* 48
Khang, Dawon: CM 30
Kilburn, Tom: MS 12, 82, 83
Kilby, Jack St. Clair: CB 73, 74, *97,* CM *21,* 22-23, 25, IC 39
Kildall, Gary: IC *89,* PC *16,* SO 102-103, 108, SW *71,* 73
Kilobit: CB 76
Kilobyte (K byte): *1,024 bytes (1,024 being one K, or two to the tenth power); often used as a measure of memory capacity. See* Kilobit.
King, Martin: IO 99
Kircher, Donald: SO 91
Kitt Peak: CC 38, *39-41*
Kjetsaa, Geir: PM 62
KLA Instruments: CM 66
Klatt, Dennis: AC 61, 62
Klein, Lawrence: IC *56,* PM 95-96, 97, 99
Kleiner, Eugene: SO 70, 71
Klein-Goldberger model: PM 95
Klypin, Anatoli: CC 102
Knaus, Friedrich von: AI 8
Knee: HB *57*
Knorr: LA 7, *8*
Knowledge base: *the database of an expert system, consisting of the facts and inferences from which conclusions are drawn.* AI 43, HB *80,* 81
Knowledge engineer: AI 41, 43
Knowledge representation: AI *62-63,* 64-65, *66-67,* 68-71; frames, AI 65, *66-67,* 81; MOPs, AI 70-71; scripts, AI 69; semantic network, AI *62-63,* 64-65
KnowledgeWare: SC 64
Knox, Dillwyn: CS 91
Knuth, Donald: SC 85
Kocak, Huseyin: CI 111
Koch, Christof: AC 66
Koenig, William: PM 51
Kohonen, Teuvo: AC 63, IC *123*
Kompfner, Rudi: CO 87
Kotok, Alan: IO 36
Kowalski, Thaddeus: CM 102, 104
Krum, Charles: IO 10
Krum, Howard: IO 10
Kryukov, Fyodor: PM 62
Krüger, Johannes: HB 102
Kuck, David: IC *123,* PO 98, 103, 106
Kuiper, Gerard: CC 18
Kurtz, Thomas: CO 41, IC *54,* LA 71, 103, SW 25-28, 31-32, 38
Kurzweil, Raymond: HB *94-95,* IC 87, *110,* IO 97-98, *106,* 107
Kushner, Donald: CI 77, 80
Kvamme, Kenneth: PM 32
Kwoh, Yik San: RO 106, 110

DEC UNVEILED THE PDP-8, the first commercially successful minicomputer. Small enough to sit on a desktop, the PDP-8 sold for $18,000—one-sixth the price of Digital's PDP-1 and one-fifth that of the IBM 360 mainframe. The combination of speed, smallness, and reasonable cost enabled the PDP-8 and other minicomputers to win a place in thousands of manufacturing plants, small businesses, and scientific laboratories.

THE GEMINI COMPUTER was the first general-purpose digital computer in space. Contoured for a snug fit against the Gemini capsule's curved wall, the nineteen-inch-long IBM machine orbited the earth three times aboard *Gemini 3.* It guided the astronauts in maneuvers that, on later missions, would make possible a rendezvous with another spacecraft.

1965

1965

57

Labels: LA *32*

Labeyrie, Antoine: CC 29, 30

Laboratory use of computers: RV 59-68, 70-71, *74-77*

LADAR (laser radar): MF *65*

Lake, Clair: RV 11, 15

Lambda calculus: SC 89, 91

Lamont Geological Observatory: RV 43

Land: MS 99, *110*

Landauer, Paul: AC 30

Landin, Peter: SC 91, 98, 99

Landsat: CI *40*, MF 40, PM 32; pictures, CI *41-43;* thematic mapper, CI 40

Langley, Patrick: AI 77, SW 111

Langley Research Center: SP 34, 39

Langmuir-Blodgett technique: AC 99

Language: *a set of rules or conventions to describe a process to a computer. See* Languages, computer.

Language, programming, for AI: AI 56-57

Language comprehension, computer: AI 56-61, 64-65, 68-71; if-then rules, AI 71; knowledge representation, AI 64-65, 68-71; and semantics, AI 60-61, 64-65, 68-71; syntax approach, AI 56, 60-61

Languages, computer: LA entire volume; assembly, SO 12; compiled versus interpreted, LA 21; dissatisfaction with standard, SC 87-88; early progress, LA 8-11, 14-16, 20-22; functionally programmed, SC 85-86, 88-91, 98-101; hexadecimal code, LA 10, *12-13;* imperative approach, SC 87; machine code, LA 8, 10, 23; object-oriented, SC 89, 101-106; octal code, LA 10, 11, *12-13;* rate of software production, SC 19, 20; and scheduling tasks, SP 66; and von Neumann model, SC 88. *See also* Languages, high-level computer

Languages, high-level computer: LA 7, 20-22, 51, 50, 13, RV 40-41, SO 13; C, RV 79; dates of release, LA *80-82;* early commercial, LA 37-40; European versus U.S.

COMPUTERS HONED THE HEARING of radio telescopes with the development of a technique known as Very Long Baseline Interferometry (VLBI), which lets two or more small antennas act as a single telescope having a diameter equal to the largest distance between them—the so-called baseline. The longer the baseline, the greater the accuracy with which radio signals emanating from deep space can be pinpointed. The signals are collected by the widely separated telescopes and recorded on magnetic tapes, which are then fed into a central computer for collation and interpretation.

OBJECT-ORIENTED LANGUAGES got an early boost with Simula, the creation of Norwegian computer programmers Kristen Nygaard *(right)* and Ole-Johan Dahl *(left).* In his work designing airports and weapons systems, Nygaard had been frustrated by the lack of a computer language adept at simulating complex phenomena. He and Dahl therefore invented a new kind of language that groups data and instructions into modular building blocks called objects, each representing one facet of a system intended for simulation.

1965

1965

scientific, LA 45, 48-49; example of program, LA *62-65*; features, LA 51, *52-65*; FORTRAN, RV 41-42; and microcomputers, LA 99-100; military, LA 78-84; natural-language use in, LA *46-47*; portability, LA 41-42; procedural and nonprocedural, LA 71, 111; program flow, LA *56-61*; special-purpose, LA 68-69, 78-79; translation, LA 85, *86-97*. See also Machine translation; *specific languages*

Language translation, computer: AI 55-56
Laning, J. Halcombe, Jr.: IC 31, LA 21, SP 66
LANs (local area networks): CO 57, *58-61*, 62, IC *78*; bus topology, CO *58-59*; MAP, CO 63-64; nonstandardization, CO 62-63; and optical fibers, CO 102; ring topology, CO *60*; star topology, CO *61*
LANTIRN (Low-Altitude Navigation and Targeting Infrared for Night): MF 66-67; shortcoming, MF 66
La Quina, France: PM 32, *33*
LARC (Livermore Advanced Research Computer): IC *44*, PO 8-9, 11
Large-scale integration (LSI): *the placement of 100 to 5,000 gate equivalents, or 1,000 to 16,000 bits of memory, on one chip. See LSI.*

Laser: *the acronym for Light Amplification by Stimulated Emission of Radiation; a light source that produces intense monochromatic, coherent light in a very directional beam.*
AC 86, CO *98*, 100, 102; and optical storage, MS 99. *See also* Optical fibers
Laser diode: *a diode that acts as a laser.*
AC 86, IC *71*
Laser printer: *a printer that uses particles of dry ink, which cling in the desired pattern to electrically charged paper.*
IC *83*, IO 46, *59*
Laser radar: MF *65*
Laser weapons: MF *108*, 116-117
Lasher, Gordon: AC 92
Lashlee, Hal: SW 71
Last, Jay: CM *53*
Last Starfighter, The: CI 83, *84*, 85, 88-89
Latency: CI 51, 54
Latham, Donald: MF 101, 109

L

EXPERT SYSTEMS—programs designed to apply the accumulated expertise of human specialists—began with DENDRAL. Devised by a Stanford team that included the noted computer scientist Edward Feigenbaum *(above),* the program applied a battery of "if-then" rules about chemistry and physics to identify the molecular structure of organic compounds.

1965

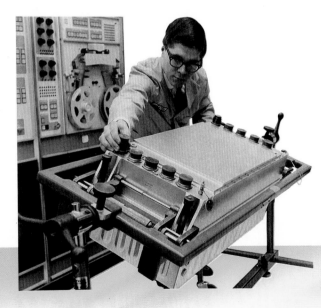

THE LVDC (Launch Vehicle Digital Computer) provided on-board digital guidance for NASA's Saturn rocket booster, which would loft Apollo spacecraft toward the moon. IBM designed and built the machine not only to control the Saturn in flight, but also to direct the complicated procedure of testing the rockets prior to launch.

1966

Latter Day Saints Hospital (Salt Lake City): HB 61

Lawrence Livermore National Laboratory: CI 112, PO 8, 14, 41, 44, 48, SW 108

Layering process: CM 57, *80-81*

Leading Edge Products: PC 24

Learning: AI *78-79;* computer model of, HB 26, *27-29;* by reading machine, HB 95-96

Learning by discovery: AI 76-77, 80-84, 97

Learning by example: AI 75-76, 85, *86-97;* domain knowledge, AI 85, 86-87; learning task, AI 85, 86-87; overgeneralization, AI 94; overspecialization, AI 94; performance task, AI 85, 86-87

Learson, T. Vincent: IO 61, *63,* SC 23, 24, 26; quoted, CB 65

Leavitt, Henrietta: CC 15

Lederberg, Joshua: AI 38-39, SW 111, 112

Leeuwenhoek, Anton van:

HB 25

Lehovec, Kurt: CB 74, *97*

Leibniz, Gottfried Wilhelm: CB 8, 9, 30-31; calculator, CB *12,* IC *7*

Leininger, Steven: CB 103-104, 106

Lemaître, Georges: CC 94, 97

Lenat, Douglas: AI 77, 80-84, IC *83,* 99

Lenz, John: SP 33

LEO (Lyons' Electronic Office): CB *57,* 65, IC 26

LES (Liquid Oxygen Expert System): AI 111

Levinthal, Cyrus: HB 30-*31,* 32, 34-35

Levy, Steven: SW 61

Lexicography: PM 62-63, 66

Lexitron Corporation: IO 43

Li, Tien-Yien: PM 110

Libraries, software: SC 55

Library of Congress: optical storage, MS 104

LifeCards: MS 107

LIFO storage: SW 52, *53*

Light, and optical fibers: CO *98-99,* 101

Light emissions: CC 7

Light-emitting diode (LED): *a semiconductor device that emits light when a current passes through it. See* Calculators: electronic.

Lightning: CS 32

Light pen: *a photosensitive input device used to direct the computer or to draw and modify images by touching the screen or terminal.*

CI 15, 16, 18, *20,* IO *15,* 39, SO *104*

Lille, France: automated commuter train, TR *102-103*

Lillestrand, Robert: PM 28-29

Limited access highways: TR 106-108

Limits to Growth, The (Meadows): PM 105

Lin, Shen: PM 34

LINC (Laboratory instrumentation computer): IC *49,* RV 64-67, 70

Lincoln Laboratory: Linc computer, RV 59-*63,* 64

MORE THAN 1,000 TRANSISTORS were squeezed onto a random-access memory (RAM) chip manufactured by the Fairchild Semiconductor Corporation. Using four transistors per bit, the integrated circuit had a capacity of 256 bits. It was also ten times smaller and much faster than the equivalent amount of magnetic core memory. At twice the price, however, the new chip was slow to become a commercial success.

A PROGRAM CALLED ELIZA, created by M.I.T. computer scientist Joseph Weizenbaum (*above*) to explore the feasibility of conducting a dialogue with a computer, played psychotherapist to "patients" at the keyboard. Inspired by the nondirective school of therapy, in which the analyst speaks only to draw out the patient, Eliza was convincing to many who tried the program. But its apparent intelligence was largely illusion. Eliza did little more than recognize key words and language patterns and respond with appropriate canned phrases.

THE ACOUSTICALLY COUPLED MODEM, invented in the early 1960s to connect computers to the telephone network by means of the standard telephone handset of the day, was vastly improved by John Van Geen of the Stanford Research Institute. Into his device he built a type of receiver that could reliably detect bits of data amid the hiss heard over long-distance telephone connections.

1966

1966

1967

and Index; IO Input/Output; LA Computer Languages; MF The Military Frontier; MS Memory and Storage; PC The Personal Computer; PM The Puzzle Master; PO Speed and Power; RO Robotics; RV Revolution in Science; SC The Software Challenge; SO The Computerized Society; SP Space; SW Software; TR Transportation

Lindquist, Mark: CI 72
Linked list: SW *50-51*
Links: AI *62-63;* hypermedia, PM *84-85;* types, PM *86-87*
Lippman, Andrew: MS 101
Lipton, Richard J.: MS 84
Liquid crystal (LC): *a liquid with optical properties similar to those of a crystal. For example, one type of LC can be switched from opaque to transparent by an electric current, making it useful in computer displays and as a memory unit in optical computers.*
Liquid crystal display (LCD): *a digital display mechanism made up of character-forming segments of a liquid crystal material sandwiched between polarizing and reflecting pieces of glass.* CB *16-17, 19*
Lisberger, Steven: CI 77, 80, 82

LIS *(Langage d'Implementation de Systèmes):* LA *83*
LISP: *(for List Processing) a widely used AI-programming language that manipulates nonnumerical symbols, particularly English words and phrases, which it can then link into complex hierarchies of thought.* AI 57-58, 81, IC 43, LA 49, 69, 71, SC 89-91, SW *38;* and memory use, MS 78, 82; and microcomputers, LA 105
List-processing language: *a*

type of programming language that represents data in lists of words and other symbols to link concepts in a manner roughly analogous to the way they may be linked in the human brain. Programs in a list-processing language may consist simply of lists. See LISP.
Literary investigations: PM 18, 51-77; authorship, PM 61-62; dictionaries, PM 62-63, 66; style and date analysis, PM 51-52; translation, PM 66-67

Lithium niobate: AC 92, 94
Lithography: *the transfer of a design from one medium to another, for example, from a mask to a silicon wafer. If light is used to perform the transfer, the process is called photolithography. See Photolithography.*
Litton Industries: LTN-51, TR 54
Llinas, Rodolfo: HB 33
Local area network (LAN): *a system of computer hardware and software that links computers, printers, and*

L

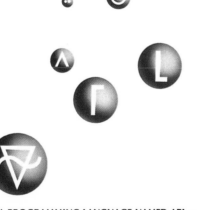

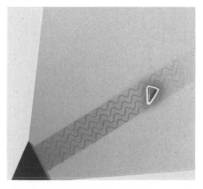

LOGO was designed by Seymour Papert as a computer language for children. No more than a drawing language at the outset, LOGO controlled actions of a "turtle." A mechanical version (*above*) traced its path with pen on paper; electronic turtles drew designs on a video display.

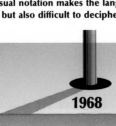

A PROGRAMMING LANGUAGE NAMED APL saw its grammar published after more than a decade of refinement. The work of IBM researcher Kenneth Iverson, APL is a general-purpose language that is particularly well suited for manipulating large tables of numbers. It is distinguished by its unique set of characters—ninety-five in all, including Greek and Roman letters, Arabic numerals, and fifty-five original symbols. APL's unusual notation makes the language very concise but also difficult to decipher.

THE FIRST PHASED-ARRAY RADAR came on line at Eglin Air Force Base, Florida. This remarkable radar relied on a computer to coordinate the transmissions of radar signals from thousands of stationary antennas arranged on a flat surface angled skyward. By precisely controlling the timing of the signals, the computer created a narrow and powerful radar beam and swept it across the sky many times a second, permitting the tracking of multiple targets.

1967   1968   1968

other peripherals into a network suitable for transmission of data between offices in a building, for example, or between buildings situated near one another. See LANs (local area networks).
Lockheed: LA 50, SO 13
Lockheed-Georgia: CI 36
Logic: See Boolean algebra
Logic bombs: CS 18, 19, 67-69. See also Trojan horses
Logic circuits, IC: CB 75, 76
Logic gate: a circuit that accepts one or more inputs and produces a single, predictable output.
CB 31, 36, 42, 43, 75; and binary adders, CB 44-47; molecular, AC 100-101, 105
Logic Theorist: AI 31-33, 34,

35, IC 34
LOGO: IC 61, IO 73, LA 107, 108-109, 110, SW 29
Log-on procedure: CS 74-75
Logos Development Corporation: PM 77
Look-up table: an area of memory set aside for a table of values that is referred to when necessary for a program.
CI 39, 58
Loop: a technique that allows a program to repeat a series of instructions a number of times.
LA 30, 34-35, SW 11; high-level language, LA 60-61; testing, SC 14-15
Loran: TR 46, 47, 60-61

Lorenz, Edward N.: IC 52, PM 108, 109-110, 116, 118, SW 105; attractor, PM 110, 111, 117, 118-119; model, PM 114-115
Lorimar, Inc.: CI 83, 84
Los Alamos: RV 33-34, 35
Los Alamos Scientific Laboratory: PO 8, 9, 41
Lotus 1-2-3: IC 106, PC 12, 19, SC 21, SW 72-73
Lou Gehrig's disease: HB 89-90
Loustanou, Jack: SO 70
Lovelace, Countess of: CB 11, 12, IC 8, IO 8-9, 111, SW 9-10, 11
Lovell, Bernard: CC 55
Lovell, Clarence A.: RO 10
Lovell, James: SP 38, 116, 117
Low, Frank: CC 17-18
Lowe, William: PC 8, 10-14,

18, 25
Low Level Windshear Alert System (LLWAS): TR 120-121
Lozano-Perez, Thomas: RO 78
LSE (Langage Symbolique d'Enseignement): LA 46, 47
LSI (large-scale integration): CM 18; design of circuits, CM 31-32
Lucas, Edouard: PO 7
Lucas, George: CI 89
Lucasfilm: CI 89-90, IO 108
Lucky, Robert W.: CO 19
Lukoff, Herman: MS 10, 12, PO 9
Lunar ephemeris: RV 8
Lupo, Jasper: AC 46
Luse, Duane: SC 69
Lutus, Paul: SW 74
Lyubimov, Victor Andreevich: CC 98

A PROTOTYPE MOUSE was part of an input console demonstrated by Douglas Engelbart at the Fall Joint Computer Conference in San Francisco. In addition to the mouse *(right in the photograph)*, Engelbart's console had a keyboard and a device with five piano-like keys that he called a chord keyset. Mouse and keyset were fruits of more than fifteen years devoted to exploring ways to make communicating with computers simpler and more flexible. While the chord keyset would have little impact on computing, the mouse would be popularized in 1984 by the Macintosh from Apple Computer.

COMPLEMENTARY MOS (CMOS) TECHNOLOGY, a variation of the highly efficient metal-oxide-semiconductor (MOS) transistor, earned patents for several corporations. In a MOS chip, the semiconductor material is treated to produce either of two varieties of transistors, called n-type and p-type. CMOS chips incorporate both kinds, a feature that reduced power consumption, but that also made such chips expensive to make. As manufacturing techniques improved, CMOS chips became less expensive and would eventually make possible portable, battery-powered personal computers.

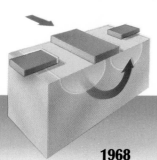

1968

1968

M3 (Massive Memory Machine): MS 84
M-9 gun director: AC 13, *14*
MAC (language): SP 66
MAC (Message Authentication Code): CS 93, *110-111*
MAC (Multi-Access Compiler; Machine-Aided Cognition): CO 40
McAlear, James: AC 105, 106
McAlister, Harold: CC 31
McCarter, Oliver: TR 8
McCarthy, John: AI 56-57, 65, 67, CO 40-41, IC *41*, LA *49*, 69, 71, MS 78, 82, RO 75, 78, SC 85, 89, 90, 91, 106, SO 24, 44, SW 38
McCarthy, Joseph: PM 95
McClure, Frank T.: TR 49
MacCready, Paul: RO 113-114
McCulloch, Warren: AC 47,

AI 11, 12
McDivitt, James: SP 37, 116, 117
McDonnell Aircraft: SP 33, 34
McDonnell Douglas: CI 106-107
McEvoy, Dennis: SO 71, 73
McGhee, Robert B.: RO 63, 68, 70
McGinley, John E.: TR 75
McGowan, William: CO 84
McGraw-Hill: PM 97, 99

Machine code: *a set of binary digits that can be directly understood by a computer without translation. See Languages, computer: machine code.* RV 40

Machine language: *a set of binary-code instructions capable of being understood by a computer without translation. See Machine code.*

Machine learning: *the process by which a computer increases its knowledge and changes its own behavior as the result of its experience and past performance.* AI 73-84, 97; by discovery, AI 76-77, 80-84, 97; by example, AI 75-76, 85, *86-97*
Machine-readable texts: collections, PM 60
Machines: nanotechnology, AC 108, *114-115*
Machine translation (MT): IC 20, PM 66-67, 74-77; automatic dictionary, PM 67, 74; program cutbacks, PM 75-76

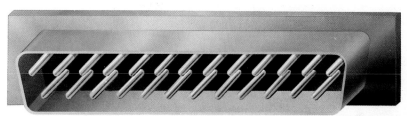

THE RS-232-C STANDARD for serial communication permitted computers and peripheral devices such as printers and modems to transfer information serially—one bit at a time. Proposed by a group that included Bell Laboratories and the Electronics Industries Association, the RS-232-C protocol spelled out, among other details, a purpose for a serial plug's twenty-five connector pins *(above)*.

THE APOLLO GUIDANCE COMPUTER, which would steer *Apollo 11* to the lunar surface on July 20, 1969, made its debut nine months earlier, orbiting the earth aboard *Apollo 7*. The AGC *(below, right)* was the first navigational device built for NASA that included integrated circuits and magnetic core-rope memory for permanent program stage. Astronauts communicated with the computer by punching two-digit codes into the display and keyboard (DSKY) unit *(below, left)*.

1968

1969

Machover, Carl: CI 36, 54
McLeod, John: AC 24
McMillan, Malcolm: RV 71
McNabb, Michael: IO *101*
McNees, Stephen: PM 93
McNulty, Kathleen: SW 9
MacPaint: PC 59, 65
MACSYMA: IC 68, RV 45-46
McVeigh, John: CB 97
MacWrite: PC 65
Madison, James: PM 61
Madry, Scott: PM 32
Magazines, personal computer: CB 94, *101*
Magellan mission: SP 101
Magic missile: MF 72
MAGI (Mathematical Applications Group, Inc.): CI 80-81
Magleby, Kay: RV *65*, 68-69
Magnetic cards: IO 43
Magnetic core memory: CI 50, IC *31*
Magnetic disks: IO 18, 43; vulnerability, CS 8, 31-32, 35

Magnetic disk storage: MS 35, 44-45, 50-52, 53; antecedents, MS 44; disk structures, MS *54-55;* floppy, IC *70, 94, 111,* MS 51; floppy drives, MS *56-57;* format, MS *48-49;* hard-disk drives, MS *58-63;* head crashes, MS *62-63;* miniature Winchester, IC *99,* MS 52; multiple-platter drives, MS *60-61;* read/write heads, MS *56-59, 62-63*
Magnetic drum: *a metallic cylinder on which electronic pulses representing data are stored magnetically.* CI 50, IC *20,* SO 14
Magnetic drum storage: MS *11,* 35, 39-44; revolvers, MS 43
Magnetic fields, planetary: Uranus, PM *14-15*
Magnetic ink: IO *14,* 98, SW 88
Magnetic recording: MS *40-41;*

coding systems, MS 42
Magnetic resonance imaging (MRI): *a medical-imaging technique that relies on the response of hydrogen atoms to a magnetic field to distinguish between various types of soft tissue.* HB 22, 23, *56-57;* three-dimensional, HB 103-105, *114-115;* views, HB 47, IC *91*
Magnetic tape: *plastic tape that is coated with a magnetic material on which information is stored in the*

form of magnetized spots. CB 64, 104, IO *14,* 16, 17, 18, SO 13-14, 15, 16-17; improved management, SO 19; and typewriter, IO 43; vulnerability, CS 27, 28, 35
Magnetic tape storage: MS 35, 53; audiotape, MS 36-37; cartridges, MS 66-69; drives, MS 38-39, 64-65; formats, MS *46-47;* materials, MS 37-38; read/write heads, MS 65; reel, MS *64*
Magneto-optic disk: *an optical disk that combines principles*

THE BOOK *PERCEPTRONS,* written by Marvin Minsky *(above)* in collaboration with Seymour Papert, attacked neural networks of the same name. The two artificial-intelligence researchers argued mathematically that perceptrons had debilitating limitations. Minsky's and Papert's seemingly devastating analysis proved, for example, that a perceptron could not distinguish a continuous line from one made of two or three segments. Minsky's and Papert's criticisms would later be overcome, but not until the book had nearly halted neural-network research for more than a decade.

THE FIRST FULLY MOBILE ROBOT navigated through the laboratories of the Stanford Research Institute. Known as Shakey for the wobble in its movements, the wheeled device assessed its surroundings with a video camera, obstacle detectors, and sensors to measure distance. Although Shakey demonstrated machine vision, problem solving, and other forms of artificial intelligence, the robot also showed how far AI still had to go. Even in a nearly empty room, the ungainly automaton could take an hour to find an object in plain view.

1969

1969

and Index; IO Input/Output; LA Computer Languages; MF The Military Frontier; MS Memory and Storage; PC The Personal Computer; PM The Puzzle Master; PO Speed and Power; RO Robotics; RV Revolution in Science; SC The Software Challenge; SO The Computerized Society; SP Space; SW Software; TR Transportation

of both magnetic and optical storage, permitting the erasure and rewriting of data. IC *105*, MS 104-105, *120-121*

Magneto-optic spatial light modulator: *a device in which a magnetic field modulates, or alters, the characteristics of a beam of light. See* Spatial light modulator.

Magnetophon: MS 36

Magnum satellite: MF 46

Magó, Gyula: PO 103-104

Mainframe: *the largest type of computer, usually capable of* serving many users simultaneously, with a processing speed about 100 times faster than that of a microcomputer. *See also* Computers.

SW 27; lull in sales, PC 105; redefined, PC 98, 104

Maintenance, software: SC 22-23; and CASE software, SC 63

Malt, Lillian: IO 41

Manchester Mark I: IC *23*, IO 13, 15, LA 15, 20, MS 35, 39, SW 14, 16

Manchester University: MS 82

Mandel, Alfred: PC 67

Mandelbrot, Benoit: CI 67, IC 86, PM 100

Manhattan Project: RV 13-14, 33-34

MANIAC (Mathematical Analyzer, Numerator, Integrator, and Computer): CB 64, IC *29*

Manley, John: SC 62

Manned Space Flight Center: SP 34

Mansell, Darrel: PM 51

Mantissa: *the fractional part of a number expressed in floating-point notation. See* Floating-point arithmetic.

Mantrap: CS 41-42, *43*

Manufacturing automation, and MAP: CO 6364

Manufacturing of chips: CM 75, 76-87; advantages of small size, CM 26, 55; basic process, CM 57, *58-61*, 62; chemical handling, CM 78, *79*; creating masks, CM *48-49*, 63; difficulties, CM 25, 55; doping, CM 62, 80, *84-85*; and dust, CM 26, *78-79*; electron-beam lithography, CM 107-108; etching, CM 57, 62, *83*; fabrication building structure, CM *76-77*; gigachip technology, CM 104, 106-108; NMOS and PMOS transistors, CM 29; photolithography, CM 62-65, *82-83*, 104, *106*; quality control, CM 65-67, 70-73, *86-87*; silicon wafers, CM *58-61*; testing, CM *86-87*; vibration isolation, CM *76-77*; x-ray lithography, CM *106*, 107. *See also* Packaging

MAP (Manufacturing Automation Protocol): CO 63-64

Mapping Venus's surface: SP *90-91*

Maps, computer-generated: PM 23, 28; choropleth, PM 22-23

Marden, Luis and Ethel: PM 28

Marince, Gary: IO 95, 96

Marince, Rob: IO 95-96

Mariner, Project: SP 89; *Mariner 1*, SP 85, 89; *Mariner 2*, SP 89, 94, 115, 116; *Mariner 4*, SP 96, 115, 116;

M

MULTICS, the first time-sharing operating system, appeared in preliminary form a decade after John McCarthy suggested the idea. M.I.T. professor Fernando Corbató *(above)* headed the Multics team, whose members came from General Electric and Bell Labs as well as M.I.T. Writing in the high-level language PL/I freed programmers from the minutiae of machine code. Even so, the project took five years to complete instead of the two originally estimated.

MACHINE TRANSLATION became practical with SYSTRAN, a program developed for the U.S. Air Force by multilingual researcher Peter Toma. The first version of SYSTRAN translated Russian to English; later editions handled English-to-Russian, English-to-French, and other language pairs. Best for technical literature, SYSTRAN used linguistic rules and a voluminous database linking words and idioms in different languages to produce results that were rough but comprehensible.

THE UNIX OPERATING SYSTEM was developed by Bell Laboratories programmers Kenneth Thompson *(above, left)* and Dennis Ritchie *(above, right)* on a spare DEC minicomputer. UNIX combined many of the time-sharing and file-management features offered by Multics, but in a simpler, more consistent way. As a result, the operating system won a wide following, particularly among scientists.

1969   **1969**   **1969**

The letter codes that follow represent the titles of Understanding Computers volumes: AC Alternative Computers; AI Artificial Intelligence; CB Computer Basics; CC Computers and the Cosmos; CI Computer Images; CM The Chipmakers; CO Communications; CS Computer Security; HB The Human Body; IC Illustrated Chronology

Mariner, Project (continued)
  Mariner 6, CI 50; *Mariners 6 and 7* (Mariner Mars 69), SP 95; *Mariners 8* and *9* (Mariner Mars 71), SP 96-97, 118; *Mariner 9,* CI 51; *Mariner 10,* SP 97, 115, 118; sequencers, SP 89, 95-97; software, SP 85
Mariner Mark II: SP 102
Marine terminals: computerized, TR 73-75
Mark-8: CB 94, 96, SO 101
Mark 46 torpedo: MF 95
Mark I (Harvard): CB *50-51,* 52, *53, 55,* IC *16,* LA 8, 11, 21, SW 11, 16, 58

Mark I (Manchester): CI 9, IC *23,* IO 13, 15, LA 15, 20, MS 35, 39, SW 14, 16
Marketing of chips: CM 54, 57
Markkula, A. C. (Mike): CB 107-108, PC 18, 46, 47, 60, 61, 63
Marron, Donald: PM 96
Mars, missions to: SP 49, *50-51,* 56-57, 86, 87, 95-97, 98-99, 101
Mars 2: SP 97
Marsh, James G.: RV 99, 102, 103
Marsh, Jeffrey: CI 106, 107
Marshall Space Flight Center: SP 33-34, 41

COMPUTERS MONITORED FREIGHT TRAINS for the first time with the TeleRail Automated Information Network (TRAIN). Continuously updated with reports from American railroads, the TRAIN database held the location of every freight car in the United States—more than a million cars. TRAIN was replaced five years later by TRAIN II, which recorded cargo and destinations as well.

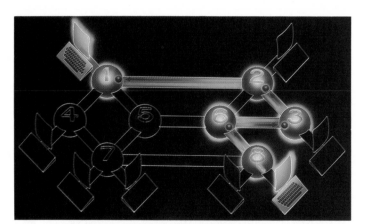

THE FIRST PACKET-SWITCHED NETWORK, known as ARPANET, was established to link computers in research facilities engaged in work for the Defense Department. Packet switching replaced the telephone network's inefficient circuit-switching approach, in which a separate circuit was set aside for each two-party exchange. In packet switching, information is divided into small parcels that travel any of several possible circuits between a sending computer and a receiving one, which reassembles packets into a coherent message.

1969

1970

Mars Observer: SP 101

Marsolais, E. Byron: HB 102

Martin, Bill: RV 44

Martin, James: SC 63-64, 65, 66

Martin Marietta: SP 34

Masers: CO 87, 100

Maskelyne, Nevil: RV 8, 9

Mask: *a patterned plate used to shield sections of the silicon chip surface during the manufacture of integrated circuits.* CM *48-49;* 63, 65

Mason, Clesson: AC 12

Mason, David: HB 90, 91

Massachusetts General Hospital: HB 74, 79

Massachusetts Institute of Technology: *See* M.I.T.

Master Control Program: SO 23

Master-slave devices: RO *118-119*

Masterson, Earl: IO 16-17

Mathematical processors: PO 72, 74; advantages, PO 67

Mathematical research: CI *110-111*

Mathematics: complexity theory, PM 35; computer, RV 32, 35, 38-40; computer, Monte Carlo method, RV 32, 35, 38-40; computer, symbolic manipulators, RV 44-45; fractal geometry, PM *100-103;* learning program, AI 80-81, 85, *86-97;* pi, PM 35-36; traveling-salesman problem, PM 32-34

Mathews, Max: IC *47,* IO 101, 106, 110

MATHLAB: RV 44-45

MATH-MATIC: IC 36, LA 21

Matsushita: and erasable optical disk, MS 105; and videodisk, MS 99, 100

Mauchly, John W.: CB *56,* 64-65, CO 15, IC 19, IO 15-16, LA 9, 11, 14, 20, MS 37, 43, RV 15, SW 12, 13, 14, 16; and EDVAC, CB 60-61, 62, 63; and ENIAC CB 59-60, 65; and UNIVAC, CB 64

Maxfield, John: CS 16-17

Mayer, Tobias: RV 8

Mayo Clinic: HB 22

Mazor, Stanley: CB 77

MC 1331+170: CC *51*

MCA: and videodisk, MS 98-100

MCC (Microelectronics and Computer Technology Corporation): AI 84

MCI: CO 84, 96

Mead, Carver: AC 66, 67, CM 31, *32,* IC *98*

Meadows, Dennis and Donella: PM 105

Medical applications: HB entire volume

Medical databases: HB 18, 59; genetic, HB 43

Medical expert systems: AI 40-41, HB 79, *80-87. See also* DXplain; Intellipath;

ONCOCIN

Medical graphics: CI 7, *46-47,* 90, *106,* 107; and biochemistry, CI 108, *109,* 112; and biomechanics, CI 107-108; and prostheses, CI *106,* 107; simulated surgery, CI 101, 107

Medical imaging: HB 7, *12-15,* 17-24, 45, *46-57;* brain maps, HB *76;* DSA, HB *62-65;* PET, HB 22; possible views, HB *46-47;* three-dimensional, HB *103-105, 108-115;* voxels, HB *48-49;* windowing, HB *49*

PASCAL, a computer language developed by Swiss computer scientist Niklaus Wirth, facilitated an approach to writing software called structured programming. In this method, a program is divided into small, logically arranged tasks that are easy to understand and to write.

THE FIRST AUTOMATIC TELLER MACHINE, or ATM, was installed at a bank in Valdosta, Georgia. The device dispensed cash to customers presenting it with magnetized cards, then recorded transactions on the cards to enforce a daily withdrawal limit. Although ATMs would later become a popular adjunct to the traditional bank, early efforts met with an unenthusiastic response, in part because of the machines' inflexibility and erratic performance.

LIGHT-SENSITIVE CHIPS called charge-coupled devices (CCDs) were invented by Bell Laboratories researchers Willard Boyle and George Smith, who intended their tiny creations to serve as computer-memory components. CCDs proved ill-suited for use as memory circuits, but they have served well in numerous optical applications, including instruments that have virtually revolutionized astronomy. A hundred times more sensitive than film, CCDs replaced conventional, almost featureless, deep-space photographs with richly detailed images.

1970

1970

1970

Medical information management: HB 59-61

Medical literature: database, HB 59

Medical robots: RO 105-106, 110, 113

Medical software: HB 18, SW 110, 113, *114-115*

Medication: computer-controlled release, HB 101-102

Medicine and computers: HB 17

Medicine and nanotechnology, AC 110, *112-113*

MEDINET: SO 45

MEDLARS (Medical Literature Analysis and Retrieval System): HB 59

MEDLINE: HB 18, 59, 67

Meetze, Henry W.: TR 78

Megaflops: *one million floating-point operations per second. See* Supercomputers: speed comparisons.

Megahertz (MHz): *one million hertz. See* Electromagnetic spectrum; Hertz.

Meindl, James D.: CM 104, 108

Meinel, Aden: CC 18

Melott, Adrian: CC 85; 102-103, 104, 105, 106, 108, IC 107

Memorex Corporation: MS 52

Memory: *the principal area within a computer for storage of instructions and data. The term is applied only to internal storage as opposed to external storage, such as disks or tapes.* CB 109, MS 7; addresses, MS 26-27; addressing, PC 20-21; auxiliary tape (ATM), SP 38, 60, 62, *76-77;* banks, PO 54, 55; cache, MS 25, PO 54, 55; characteristics, MS 9, 24-25; content addressability, AI 108; core, SC 30, SP 36; core-rope, SP 44-45; delay line, CB 61; distributed, AI 108; dumps, SW 26; of early commercial computers, SO 13; electronic vs. mechanical, SW 12; before integrated circuits, MS 7-22; and knowledge representation, AI *62-63,* 66-67; magnetic core, CB 76, 96, PO 10, 68; mass memory unit (MMU), SP 76; operation of, LA 24, 25; ordering data in, SW *50-51;* purging and garbage collection, MS 78, 82; random access, MS 16; raster scan requirements, CI 50, 58; registers on RISC processor, PC 99; secondary, SO 13-14; semiconductor, MS 23, *24-33;* speed, MS 7, PO 51, 97, 98; and storage, MS entire volume; types, CI 50, 51, 54; vector scan requirements, CI 37-38; virtual, MS *74-75,* 82-84. *See also* RAM; ROM

Memory, magnetic core: CB 76, 96, PO 10; and Whirlwind, PO 68

Memory, semiconductor: CB 76; address decoder, CB *80-81,* 110, CB 118; development, CB 76. *See also* RAM; ROM

Memory address: *a numerically coded location in a computer's memory. In a program, data is usually referred to by its memory address. See* Memory: addresses.

Memory chip: *a chip whose components form thousands of cells, each holding a single bit of information.* improvements in density, CM 27, IC *118;* interior of EPROM, CM *14-15;* mounting of, CM *10-11;* in PC, CM *8-9;* surface, CM 27

MemoryMate: HB 97

UHURU, an orbiting observatory launched from a converted oil rig off Kenya, monitored x-ray emissions of celestial objects and beamed the data to earth at the rate of 1,000 bits per second. Speedy PDP-11 minicomputers from DEC processed the information so quickly that astronomers could view the x-ray images almost instantaneously.

MACSYMA permitted computers to rescue scientists from the drudgery of complicated algebra. This collection of programs could solve complex equations for any variable far more quickly than the best of algebraists. MACSYMA was the work of Joel Moses, Bill Martin, and Carl Engelmann, researchers at the M.I.T. computer laboratory, who pooled the results of their earlier work in calculus, algebra, and computerized problem solving.

1970

1971

Memory Test Computer (MTC): PO 68

Menkus, Belden: CS 42

Mental illness: computer approaches, HB 30, 33, 75-78

Menu: *a list of commands, functions, or graphic symbols shown on a display screen.*

Mercury: SC 102, SP 97

Mercury, Project: IC 48, SP 7, 13, 15-20; hardware, SP 15-17, 19; software, SP 15, 18; testing, SP 40

Mercury delay lines: SW 12, 14

Merkle, Ralph: CS 99, 100

Message Authentication Code (MAC): *a component of the Data Encryption Standard (DES) used to ensure that a message has not been altered.*
CS 93, *110-111*

Messerschmitt-Bölkow-Blohm: AC 28

Metal-oxide semiconductor (MOS): *a technology for constructing integrated circuits with layers of conducting metal, semiconductor material, and silicon dioxide as an insulator.*
CB 77-78, 97, CM 29-30; n-MOS, CB *88-89*; types and varieties of, CM 29-30, 31

Metcalfe, Robert: CO 57, 62

Meteorology: RV 35, 39; and chaos theory, PM 108, *109*, 110. *See also* Ozone layer

Meteorology, computer modeling: PO *77*, *78-87*; and acid rain, PO *82-83*; general circulation models (GCMs), PO *78-79*; simulation of climate changes, PO *80-81*; thunderstorms and tornadoes, PO *84-85*

Meyer, Carl: CS 93

Meyer, John: PM 21

Meyers, Jack: AI 41, HB 74

Mica missile: MF 72

Michalski, Ryszard: AI 76

Michelson, Albert: CC 30

Microchip: *a popular nickname for the integrated circuit chip. See* Integrated circuits.
and analog circuits, AC 28; for neural networks, AC 65-67; optical circuits, AC 86-87, 96. *See also* Biochips; Integrated Circuits; Microprocessors

Microcode: PC 99, 100

Microcomputer: *a desktop or portable computer, based on a microprocessor and intended for use by an individual; also called a personal computer.*
CB 77, CI 114, PC 7-8; and early microprocessors, SO 101-102; growth of market, PC 18; and languages, LA 99-110; organizations using,

PC 88, 91-96; power of, PC 20-21. *See also* Computers, personal

Micromodule Plan: CM 22

Microprocessor: *a single chip containing all the elements of a computer's central processing unit; sometimes called a computer on a chip.*
CB 7, 15, 77-78, *82-83*, CM *68-69*; applications, CB 15, *16-27*; and calculators, SO 89; CISC, PC 99; clock speed, PC 20-21, 88, 98; eight-bit, CB 102; first, CM 68; four-bit, CB 102; Hewlett-Packard Superchip, CB 102, *103*; Intel, PC 12-13, 25, 27, 87-88, 96; Intel 4004, CB 77, 98, *102*, SO 91, 98; Intel 8008, CB 94, SO 101; Intel 8080, CB 95, *102*, 104, SO 102, 103; invention of, SO 90, 91; math coprocessors, PC 96; memory capacity, PC

M

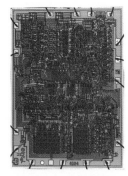

THE FIRST MICROPROCESSOR, the Intel 4004, was advertised for sale in *Electronic News*. An IC designed by Ted Hoff as a custom chip for Busicom, a Japanese calculator maker, the 4004 packed 2,250 transistors onto a silicon sliver the size of the head of a tack. It handled data in four-bit chunks, performed 60,000 operations per second, and had all the functions of a computer's central processing unit.

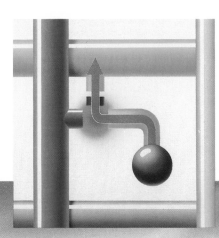

PERMANENT MEMORY CHIPS for long-term storage of computer programs were available in three varieties. ROM (read-only memory) chips are permanently programmed during manufacture. Programmable ROM (PROM), sold blank, is programmed by the purchaser but can never be altered. Erasable PROM, or EPROM *(left),* can be purged and reprogrammed thousands of times.

1971

1971

Microprocesssor (continued) 20, 21, 88; and microchip technology, PC 98; milestones, CB *102-103;* MOS Technology 6502, CB *102,* 107, SO 102; Motorola, PC 60-61, 68, 89, 96; Motorola 68000, CB *102;* and operating systems, SO 91, 102-103, 108; in personal computers, CB 26, *27,* 94, CM *8-9;* proliferation, SO 99; recent advances, PC 106; RISC, PC 91, 98, 106; sixteen-bit, CB *102;* speed, CB 78, 102-103; thirty-two-bit, CB 102, *103;* used in sewing machines, SO 91, 98-99; word size, PC 12-13, 20-21, 87-88; Zilog Z-80, CB 104, SO 102, 103. *See also* Integrated circuit

Microsoft: CB 100, IC 82, LA 102, 105, SC 21, SO 108, SW 63, 70, 74

MicroSoft: and Apple Macintosh, PC 68; and IBM PC, PC 15

Microwave: *any electromagnetic wave in the radio fre-quency spectrum above one gigahertz.*
CO 80, 81, 90; and communications, CO 81-89, 94-97, 100; land networks, CO 82-84; masers, CO 87; and radar, CO 81; and raindrops, RV 93, 94-95; satellite antennas, CO 79, 88-89, 97, 100; and satellites, CO 79, 85-89, *90-93,* 94-97, 100; and weather, CO 100

Middle East War, 1973: MF 67

MIDI (Musical Instrument Digital Interface): IC 108, IO 107

Milestones: of computers in the space program, SP *14-16;* in personal computers, PC 11-13

Military applications: PO 8, 43, *44,* 105-106; of neural networks, AC *66-67,* 68

Military computer applications: CI 9, 12-14, MF entire volume

Military computer systems: SW 108-110

Military electronics: as early market for chips, CM 27, 53; and soldered circuitry, CM 22

Military frontier: MF entire volume

Military robots: RO 26-27, 110-111

Military software: LA 78-79

Mill, Henry: IO 36

Millard, William: CB 101-103

Miller, David: AC 94-95, 96, PM 20-21, 22

Miller, Steve: RO 46

Mills, Harlan: SW 31

MIMD (multiple instruction/multiple data): PO 105

Mims, Forrest: CB 95, 97

Mingolla, Ennio: AC 65

Miniaturization of circuits: CM 18, 26, 55, 104, 106-108, *118-119*

Minicomputer: *a mid-size computer smaller than a mainframe and usually with much more memory than a microcomputer.*
CB 94, 97, *98,* RV 67, 80; advantages, PO 67; and communication networks, CO 45; inexpensive, PO 67, 70,

THE EIGHT-INCH FLOPPY DISKETTE was invented by an IBM team under Alan Shugart. Intended to simplify the maintenance of IBM's System/370 mainframe, it quickly won wide acceptance as a program- and data-storage medium. A disk of the same oxide-coated flexible plastic from which magnetic tape is made, the floppy offered inexpensive, reusable, high-density storage. It also boasted portability, an advantage over the fourteen-inch metal "hard" disks built into some machines. Within its protective jacket, a floppy was easily popped out of one drive and into another.

HAL/S, a programming language, was devised to speed the writing of software for the first flight of the space shuttle *Columbia*. Developed by a team of former M.I.T. programmers and named for J. Halcombe Laning, one of that institution's trailblazing computer scientists, HAL/S allowed the programmer to assign priorities to the computer's tasks, ensuring that they were performed in order of urgency; and it used time-sharing tactics to let the hardware run several programs concurrently.

FORTH TOOK ITS PLACE alongside other high-level languages. Very terse (some commands are punctuation marks) it requires little memory but is difficult to learn and to read. Invented by Charles H. Moore as a language for controlling processes and machinery, FORTH was first used to aim the Kitt Peak radio telescope in Arizona.

1971

1971

1971

and Index; IO Input/Output; LA Computer Languages; MF The Military Frontier; MS Memory and Storage; PC The Personal Computer; PM The Puzzle Master; PO Speed and Power; RO Robotics; RV Revolution in Science; SC The Software Challenge; SO The Computerized Society; SP Space; SW Software; TR Transportation

75; minisupers, PO 76; PDP, PO 70, 71; superminis, PO 76; uses, PO 71-72

Ministry of International Trade and Industry (MITI), Japanese: PO 89-90; Fifth Generation project, PO 89, 97; National Superspeed computer project, PO 89, 91, 96

Minitel: CO 7, IC *102*

Minsky, Marvin: AC 48, 50, *51, 52*, 55, 60, 68, AI 14, 42, 57, 65, 67-68, 99, 110, IC *64*, SW 60

MIPS: *millions of instructions per second; used as a measure of processing speed for conventional computers and for supercomputers performing scalar processing. See Supercomputers: speed comparisons.*

RISC machine, PC 98

Mirrors, large: CC 17, *18;* focal length, CC 24; polishing, CC 24, 29; for space telescope, CC 28-29, *92-93;* spin casting, CC *23-24*

Missiles: air-to-air, radar-

guided, MF 72-73; antiradar, MF 70-71; ballistic and SDI, MF 107; cruise, MF *75-77,* 78; ICBM, MF 73-74, 78, 107, 111; sea-skimming, MF 71-72; sea-to-air, MF 95; snap-launch point-defense, MF 72. *See also* Strategic Defense Initiative

M.I.T. (Massachusetts Institute of Technology): AI 9, 57, 65, CI 8-9, 12-13, 14, CO 18, 40, IC 37, IO 12, 35-36, 38-39, 79, 97, 98, MS 18, 78, PO 67-69, RO 14, 15, 40, 62, 78, 79, SC

34; Architecture Machine Group, MS 100-101; development of programming at, SW 58-61; Digital Computer Laboratory, PO 67-68; Tech Model Railroad Club, SW 58, *59;* Utah/M.I.T. hand, RO *76*, 79; X Window, PC 107, *108-119*

M.I.T. (Massachusetts Institute of Technology), and Apollo guidance systems: SP 43-47, 48; Block I, SP 44; Block II, SP 44-45

Mitchell, Dana: RV 13

MITS (Micro Instrumentation and Telemetry Systems): CB 95-101, LA 100, 101, 102, SO 101-102, SW 57, 62

Mitsubishi: RO 34

Miyakoda, Kiku: SW 106

Mnemonic: *a short term or symbol used to designate an instruction or operation. See Languages, computer.*

Mobility, human: computer-aided, HB 102, 106-107

Mock, Owen: IC 36, SO 17

Model: *a computer program that simulates complex phys-*

THE LASER DIODE, shown here in prototype form, advanced the cause of optical computing. Invented at Bell Labs, this source of the coherent light needed for processing data optically offered two major advantages. It was compact (it eventually shrank to one millimeter across) and it generated little heat, a bane of computer designers.

THE HP-35 ELECTRONIC SLIDE RULE marked the demise of the "slipstick" long used by engineers and scientists to make quick calculations. With thirty-five keys controlling five integrated circuits, three ROM chips containing mathematical routines and other circuits crammed into its pocket-size dimensions, the HP-35 took only sixty-five seconds to solve a navigation problem that required five minutes of slide-rule work. This marvel of miniaturization was an instant success; its maker, Hewlett-Packard, sold 100,000 in the first year.

WINDOWS BECAME A REALITY with Smalltalk, developed by Alan Kay at Xerox's Palo Alto Research Center (PARC). Smalltalk permitted the partitioning of a screen to display files, menus of commands, and icons. All could be manipulated by a mouse, a feature that would make the Macintosh computer so engaging. A version of Smalltalk introduced in 1981 was the first successful object-oriented language.

1971

1972

1972

ical phenomena through the manipulation of mathematical equations. See Modeling, computer.

Modeling: CI 61, *76*, 80-81, 84-85; constructive solid geometry, CI 61, *62-63*, 80; procedural, CI *64-65*, CI 89; solid, CI 62, 65, *76*

Modeling, computer: econometric, PM 93-99; physical systems, PM 105-112; system dynamics, PM 99, 104-105; uses, PM 93

Modem: *a device (modulator/ demodulator) that enables data to be transmitted between computers, generally over telephone lines but sometimes on fiberoptic cable or radio frequencies.* CB *110*, CO 8-9, 14, 15, 18, 19-21, 34-35, CS 9, *12*, IC *44*; amplitude-shift keying, CO *34-35*; asynchronous transmission, CO *52-53*; connect-

ing to phone system, CO 21; differential phase-shift keying, CO 52, *53*; early high-speed, CO 18; frequency-shift keying, CO *34-35*, *52*; Hayes protocol, CO 63; portable, CO 20; and RS-232-C, CO *50-51*; synchronous transmission, CO 52

Modulation: *the process of encoding one signal with information contained in another signal.* See Modems.

Modula-2: IC 105, LA 104

Modules: CM *8-9*; mounting

of, CM *10-11*

Moffett, Thurber: CI 35, 36

Molecular biology: HB 34. *See also* DNA; Proteins

Molecular computer: *a computer whose functioning components are either individual or small groups of molecules.* AC 7, 85, 97, *98-103*, 104, IC 125; construction, AC *98-99*; diode, AC 97, 104-105; logic elements, AC *100-101*, 105; memory, AC *102-103*, 105

Molecular modeling: CI 109,

112

Molecular rectifier: AC 97

Molecular studies: PO *20-21*

Molecule: *the smallest unit of a chemical compound that can exist independently. Molecules are usually made up of many atoms bound together.* See Molecular modeling; Molecular studies.

Moll, Kenneth: MF 94

Molnar, Charles: RV 60-64, 66

Mona Lisa: PM *42-43*

Monitor: *a television-like output device for displaying data.* CB *27*, 110, *111*, CI 15, *16*, IO *54-55*; CRT, CI *22-23*; DVST, CI 38; film recorder, CI *28-29*; flat-panel display, CI *24-25*; raster, CI *23*, 50; vector, CI *23*, *30-31*, 92. *See also* CRT

Monoclonal antibodies: AC

THE VIDEO GAME CRAZE TOOK OFF with the introduction of Pong, Atari's coin-operated version of table tennis. Created by Atari founder Nolan Bushnell, shown above with a game circuit board, Pong was such a hit that Bushnell eventually sold his company for $15 million.

SHRDLU, an experimental AI program devised by M.I.T. graduate student Terry Winograd, was the first software to integrate grammar rules, word definitions, and logical reasoning. It controlled an arm that played with blocks on a table, all simulated on a computer screen. If directed to "Put the green pyramid on top of the red block," SHRDLU moved the arm to do so. Asked "Had you touched any pyramid before you put the green one on the little cube?" SHRDLU might respond with "Yes, the green one."

THE RELATIONAL DATABASE, conceived by IBM's Edgar F. Codd, spawned thousands of electronic libraries. Such databases make facts easy to find by storing them in tables like this one, with rows of entries—college students, for example—crossed by columns of information about each one—grades, courses, birth dates. An intersection between a column and a row gives a characteristic for an entry. The same column appearing in several tables serves to link them, revealing interrelationships.

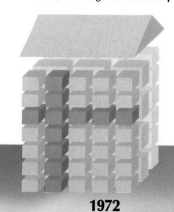

1972   1972   1972

98-99, 105

Monolithic Memories: CM 56, 74

Monsanto Chemical: SO 13

Monte Carlo method: *a procedure that uses random sampling in order to approximate the solution of a problem. The Monte Carlo method is employed when the problem is too complex for a mathematical solution.* IC 17, RV 32, 35, 38-40, SC 102

Montgomery County library system: CS 68-69

Moog, Robert: IO 100-101, 107

Moon, missions to: SP 87-89, 95, 97; surface, SP 87. *See also* Apollo, Project; Ranger, Project; Surveyor, Project

Moon, research and development on: AI *114-115*

Moore, Charles H.: LA 106, SW 39

Moore, Gordon: CM 18, *53*,

66; and Moore's Law, CM 18

Moravec, Hans: AI 110, RO 70, 74, 75

Morison, Samuel Eliot: PM 17, 23, 24

Morphemics: AI 101

Morris, Robert: CS 17, 18

Morrow, George: CB *100*, PC 10

Morse, Samuel F. B.: CO 9

Morton, John: SP 19

MOS: *See* Metal-oxide semiconductor

Moses, Joel: RV 44

MOSFET (metal-oxide semiconductor, field-effect transistor): *a semiconductor switch consisting of three regions of semiconductor material called the source, the channel, and the drain, with an electric field between source and drain controlling the flow of current. See* Transistors: MOSFET.

Mosher, Ralph S.: RO 63

MOS Technology 6502: CB *102*, 103, 107, IC *82*, SO 102

Mosteller, Frederick: PM 61

Motherboard, of PC: CM 7, *8-15*

Motion detection: AC 66

Motion picture graphics: CI 8, 59, 61, *64*, 75, 76, 77, 80-*81*, *82*, 83, *84*, *85*, 88, *89*, 90; computer-assisted animation, CI *78-79*

Motion pictures and computer control: CI 75-76

Moto-oka, Tohru: PO 89

Motor, brushless electric: RO *51*

Motor-generator: CS 32

Motorola: CM 27; 6800, SO 102; 68000, CB *102*, IC 95, PC 61-62; 68020, PC 68, 89; 68030, CM 68, *69*; 68881, PC 68, 96; RISC processor, PC 98

Mount Palomar telescope: CC 17, *18*

Mouse: *a hand-held input device that, when rolled across a flat surface, causes a cursor to move in a corresponding way on a display screen.* CI 15, 16, 18, *21*, IC *62*, IO 67, *68-69*, SO 108-109

Mouse interface: PC 59

Movie (language): LA 68

MP/M: SO 108

MRJ, Inc.: PO 105

MS-DOS: IC 102, SO 108, SW 74

Mullard Radio Astronomy Laboratory: CC 37

Mullin, John T.: MS 36

Multicomputer: *a computer architecture that incorporates more than one processor and both global and local memories.* PO *65*

Multics (Multiplexed Information and Computing Service): IC 65, RV 73, 78, SC 34-36

M

PARALLEL PROCESSING appeared in the huge ILLIAC IV, the first computer to abandon the classic one-step-at-a-time scheme of John von Neumann. ILLIAC IV had sixty-four processors, each with its own memory, all operating simultaneously on separate parts of one problem. Designed at the University of Illinois and built by Burroughs, the computer took six years to complete at a cost of $40 million. It was the fastest machine then in use, but ahead of its time. Plagued by technical ills and very difficult to program, ILLIAC IV was one of a kind.

1972

Multiple Integrated Laser Engagement System (MILES): MF 8

Multiple-Mirror Telescope (MMT): CC 19, 23, 43, *44-51*, IC *96*; alignment, CC *48-49*; mount, CC 46, *47*; optics, CC *44*; spectrograph, CC *50-51*

Multiple quantum well (MQW) device: AC 95-97

Multiplexer: *a circuit that transmits several signals simultaneously on a single output channel or wire. See Multiplexing.*

Multiplexing: *a technique that allows multiple transmissions of data to share a single communications link.* CS 96; frequency division, CO 13-14, *32-33*, IC 10; time division, CO *32-33*

Multiplication: LA *32-35*

Multiprocessor: *a computer architecture incorporating multiple processors that must share access to a central, global memory.* PO 64-65

Multiprogramming: *the apparently simultaneous operation of several programs that are loaded together into a computer's memory.* IC 47, MS 73, 83-84, SO 23

Multitasking: *the ability of an operating system to perform several functions in such quick succession that they seem to occur at the same time.*

SC 92-97, SO 110

Murphy, Ian: CS 72

Murray, Donald: CO 12

Murrow, Edward R.: CI 9

Murto, Bill: PC 22

MUSIC: IC 47, IO 101

Music, digitizing: CB 39, *48-49*

Music, synthesized: IC 47, IO 98, 100-101, 106-107, 111; additive and subtractive techniques, IO *114-117*; analog, IO 98, 100-101; digital, IO 101, 106-107; digital FM, IO 106, 107, *118-119*; and mathematical models of instruments, IO *120-121*; and sound characteristics, IO *112-117*

Müller, Karl Alex: CM *92*

MYCIN: AI 40, HB 72, IC 74

GODFREY HOUNSFIELD *(above)* of England's EMI, Ltd., invented computerized tomography (CT). This technique records multiple images electronically as an x-ray camera circles the body. A computer converts the array of pictures into an image of a cross section. The example *(inset)* reveals cysts (dark areas) in the brain.

A LANGUAGE CALLED C was developed by Dennis Ritchie of Bell Labs, coauthor of UNIX. Though cryptic, C expresses complex instructions economically and produces programs that work almost as fast as those written in assembly language.

1972

1972

MYCIN transformed the computer into a savvy consultant. Created by Edward Shortliffe *(below)*, this pioneering expert system was programmed with 500 "if-then" rules to help physicians diagnose blood infections and select antibiotics. MYCIN's success led to so-called knowledge shells—problem-solving programs empty of specific advice—that could be filled in by human experts in any field, from finance to car repair.

1972

NAND gate: *a logic gate whose output is TRUE (one), unless all its inputs are TRUE. See Logic gates.*

Nano: *from the Greek word for dwarf; a prefix denoting the one-billionth part.*

Nanocomputer: *a hypothetical computer constructed by assembling individual atoms and molecules, each of which would be a functional component.*

Nanosecond: *a billionth of a second; a common unit*

of measure of computer operating speed. See Computers, digital: structure and operation.

Nanotechnology: *theoretical processes and techniques based on the manipulation of individual atoms and molecules.*

AC 7-8, 107-108, 110, 111, *112-119,* IC 125; and fabrics, AC 110, *116-117;* and machines, AC 108, *114-115;* and medicine, AC 110, *112-113;* and space stations, AC 110, 117, *118-119*

Napier, John: CB 8, IC 6; bones, CB 8, *11,* IC *6*

NASA (National Aeronautics and Space Administration): AC 28, 30, PO 34, 105, SO 24, SP 13; criteria for choice of equipment, SP 16, 17, 60; and data compression, MS 77; as early market for chips, CM 27; and JPL, SP 87; and raster graphics, CI 50-51; and spacecraft independence, SP 43, 45-46; space

program images, CC 38

Nash, Firmin A.: HB 71

Nastec Corporation: SC 62

National Advisory Committee for Aeronautics (NACA): AC 16, 25

National Aeronautics and Space Administration: *See* NASA

National Air Space System: TR 109, *110-115;* Advanced Automation System, TR 105, 109; approach controllers, TR 115; Central Flow-Control Computer, TR 109, *115;* collision avoidance, TR *116-117;* control to takeoff, TR *112-113;* departure controllers, TR *113;* en route centers, TR *111,* 114-155; flight delays, TR 109, 115; structured airspace, TR *110-111;* Terminal Control Areas, TR *110-111*

National Bureau of Standards: CS 35, RO 33, 62, 112; and data encryption, CS 92-93, 98

National Cash Register: LA 42, SO 20

PROLOG, a nonprocedural language and brainchild of Frenchman Alain Colmerauer *(above),* offered an alternative to writing step-by-step instructions for a computer. A programmer working in Prolog (for Programming in Logic) provides sets of facts and relations between them. For example, supplying the information that a hawk is a bird and that a bird has wings permits the computer to conclude that a hawk has wings. Nonprocedural languages facilitate the writing of expert systems, which emulate human powers of deduction.

INTEL'S 8008 microprocessor made its debut. The chip's eight-bit word, called a byte, afforded 256 unique arrangements of ones and zeros. This was a vast improvement over the sixteen combinations of its predecessor, the four-bit 4004. For the first time, a microprocessor could handle all the letters of the alphabet—both uppercase and lowercase—all ten numerals, punctuation marks, and a host of other symbols. The 8008 quickly found its way into primitive home-built computers, precursors of the PC.

1972

1972

National Center for Atmospheric Research (NCAR): PO 80

National Command Authority (NCA): MF 100, 101

National Defense Research Committee (NDRC): RO 11

National Emergency Airborne Command Post (NEACP): MF 100

National Institutes of Health (NIH): RV 59, 63

National New Technology Telescope: CC 24

National Optical Astronomy Laboratory: CC 42

National Photographic Interpretation Center (NPIC): MF 37

National Radio Astronomy Observatory (NRAO): CC 58

National Science Foundation: supercomputing centers, PO 90, 97-98

National Security Agency: CS

98, 99, MF 46; and computer development, MF 47-48

National Semiconductor: CM 74

National Test Bed facility: MF 110

National Training Center (NTC), U.S. Army: war games, MF 8-9

Natural language: *ordinary human language; unlike precisely defined computer languages, it is often ambiguous and is interpreted differently by different hearers.* AI 55, 56, 61

Naur, Peter: LA 48, *49*

Nautical Almanac (Great Britain): CC 86, RV 8-10

Nautical Almanac (United States): RV 12-13

Nautilus, USS: TR 53

Naval Research Laboratory (NRL): CC 63

Navigating robots: RO 70,

74-75, *76-77;* self-guided cars, RO 75, 78. *See also* Vision, machine

Navigation: RV 8-11, 12-13

Navigation in space: SP 49; and celestial mechanics, SP *50-51;* changing orbital planes, SP 50, *56-57;* changing orbits, SP *54-55;* inertial measurement unit (IMU), SP 36, 52, *53*

Navigation systems; for automobiles, TR 54; and aviation needs, TR 47; dead reckoning, TR 43, 52, 57, 58; external fixes, TR 43, 57; in invasion of Normandy, TR 44-46

Navigation systems, inertial: TR 17, 52, 57, *58-59;* in aviation, TR 54; components, TR 52-53, *58;* computers for, TR 53; and *Nautilus,* TR 53; and ship control, TR 56; and V-2 rocket, TR 53

Navigation systems, radio: TR

57, *64-65;* coverage of ground-based, TR 48-49; Decca Flight Log, TR 47; Decca Navigator, TR 44-46; and electronic charts, TR 55-56; Gee, TR 46; Loran, TR 46, 47, *60-61;* and microprocessors, TR 48; Navstar (GPS), TR 51-52, *62-63;* satellite-based, TR 49-52, *62-63;* Transit, TR 49-50

Navstar (GPS): TR 51-52, *62-63*

Nealey, Robert W.: AI 75

Nebulae: CC *8-9*

NEC (Nippon Electric Company): MS 71, PO 45, 90, 91; SX-2, PO 91, 96

THE ATM (APOLLO TELESCOPE MOUNT) console aboard the Skylab space station—here seen with astronaut Edward Gibson on duty—incorporated two off-the-shelf, IBM TC-1 computers, descendants of System/360 machines. Intended primarily for positioning the craft to study the Sun and the comet Kohoutek, the computers represented NASA's first use of machines not designed expressly for the space program.

WORD PROCESSING TOOK OFF with the Wang Word-Processing System (WPS), introduced by Wang Laboratories. Equipped with a standard typewriter that served both as keyboard and printer, and magnetic-tape cassettes to store documents, WPS was easy to use by anyone who knew how to type. Within five years, the system had a CRT screen for text display and controls to prevent accidental deletion, and it could handle material in most European languages, as well as English.

1972

1973

Nelson, George: SP 70

Neptune: SP 99-101, 102

Nerve connections: computer-aided, HB 106-107

Nestor: AC 62-63

NETtalk: AC *32-35, 61-62*, IC *119*

Networks: local vs. global, PC 108-109; X Window, PC 107, *108-119*

Neural network: *a computer or a program modeled after the interaction of neurons in the brain, including their ability to improve performance through experience.* AC 7, 8, 31, 45-55, 60, *61*, 62-68, AI 12-13, 103, 108-110, HB 33, IC 107; ADALINE, AC 50-51; advantages and disadvantages, AC 45-46; aircraft recognition, AC *66-67*; ART 2, AC 53; associative memory, AC *40-43*, 53, 64; back propagation, AC 32, 55, 60; early research, AC 47-52; edge recognition, AC 65-66; hardware for, AC 65-67, IC 121; learning by example, AC *32-35*, 61-62; military applications, AC *66-67*, 68; motion detection, AC 66; NETtalk, AC *32-35*, 61-62; optimization problems, AC 31, *36-39*; perceptrons, AC 48-50, 51, 52; revival of interest, AC 54-55, 60; simulations, AC 48, 54, 62, 64; speech recognition, AC 63-64; speech synthesis, AC *32-35*, 61-62; synapses, AC 31; three-layer, AC 55, 60; and vision, AC 66

Neurons: *nerve cells; the circuits in a computer that mimic the operation of nerve cells. See Neural networks.*

Neurons, electronic modeling of: *See* Neural network

Neuroscience: *See* Brain: and mind

Neurosurgery: and 3-D imaging, HB *114-115*

Neutrinos: CC 98, 102, 103, 105-106; mass, CC 98, 106

Neutron activation analysis: PM *48-49*

New connectionists: AI 109

Newell, Allen: AI 31, 32-33, 35, 39, 57, 100, IC *34, 36*, LA 69, SC 89

Newman, Max: SW 14

Newman, Mike: CI 115; images by, CI *118-119*

Newton, Isaac: CC 86, PM 35, RV 8

New York City: emergency services, SPRINT, SO 39, 47-49; excavation, PM 30-31

New York Institute of Technology: CI 80, 89

NeXT: IC *124*, PC 7, 67

NGC 326: CC *64-65, 76, 78, 80, 82*

NGC 5195: CC *10-11*

Nibble, definition: CB 36

Nichols, Herman: SC 51

Nicks, Oran W.: SP 85

Niklas, Karl J.: RV 22

Nilsson, Nils: AI 71

Nimbus 7: PM 107

Nippon Electric Company: *See* NEC

Nishibori, E. E.: CM 72

Nissan Motor Company: RO 42

IBM'S WINCHESTER DISK, housed in a component called the IBM 3340, redefined high-speed magnetic storage. This unit contained four magnetic disks. Skilike read/write heads, floating on an air cushion just twenty millionths of an inch thick, packed thirty megabytes of data onto the platters. The 3340's capacity reminded Ken Haughton, an engineer on the project, of his .30-caliber Winchester rifle and suggested the name—since applied to all hard disks.

THE UNIVERSAL PRODUCT CODE (UPC) automated supermarket operations. Each product has printed on it a unique code consisting of wide and narrow bars. They are read by a laser scanner, which informs a central computer of the code. The computer looks up the item in a database, signals the price to the cash register, and deducts the item from inventory. Such codes now are used to keep track of all kinds of goods in government and industry.

0 12345 67890 4

1973

1973

Nitrogen, liquid: CM 91
NMR (nuclear magnetic resonance) scans: CI 46, *47*
Noble, David: MS 51
Nodes: AI *62-63;* hypermedia, PM *80-81;* packet-switching, CO *66-67, 68-69, 114-115*
Nomads: pastoral, RV 93, 95-98
Nonlinearity: *behavior whereby a property of a material (its transparency, for example) changes abruptly at some threshold level of stimulation, rather than changing continuously in proportion to changes in the stimulus.*
Nonlinear material: AC 94
NON-VON: PO 103-104, 105, 106
NORAD (North American Aerospace Defense Command): CS *36-39,* MF 23, 26; computers, MF 26-28; phased-array radars, MF *26-27, 28-29,* 30
NOR gate: *a logic circuit whose output is FALSE (zero) if any input is TRUE (one).* See Logic gates.
Norris, William: PO *12,* 13-14,

16-17, 18, 31, 32
North American Aerospace Defense Command: *See* NORAD
North American Aviation: SO 17
North American Rockwell: on-line inventory system, SO 46
Northrop Aircraft Company: IO 16
North Star: PC 9
Norwegian Computer Center (NCC): SC 102, 103
Norwegian Defense Research Establishment (NDRE): SC 102
Norwest Bank: CS 34
NOT gate: *an inverter; a single-input logic circuit whose output is always the opposite of the input. That is, a TRUE (one) yields a FALSE (zero), and vice versa.* See Logic gates.
Nova (rocket): SP 33
Noyce, Robert: CB 74, 76, 97, CM 24, *25, 53,* 73, IC 41
Nuclear imaging: *a medical imaging technique in which a natural substance, such as*

glucose, is tagged with a radioactive marker and then injected into the patient. Radiation, emitted as the substance is absorbed by organs or tissues, is detected and analyzed by a computer to produce an image. See Imaging, medical.
Nuclear physics: RV 13-14, 31, 32-34, 35, 38, 39; and FORTRAN, RV 41; fusion, RV 103-106
Nuclear processes: PO 8, *20-21,* 42
Nutt, Roy: SW 61
N-version programming: SC 16
Nybble: *half a byte, or four bits. See* Bit; Byte.
Nygaard, Kristen: IC *58,* SC *102-103,* 104, 106
Nyquist, Harry: CO 37

ETHERNET linked minicomputers, becoming the first local area network (LAN). Conceived at Xerox PARC by Robert Metcalfe and later extended to personal computers, Ethernet permits machines to share software, data, and peripherals such as printers. Metcalfe's LAN and others use the so-called bus topology, with a central cable *(above)*. Alternative networking schemes include a ring topology, in which the ends of the central cable are joined, and a star topology, in which each computer is linked by its own cable to a central switching device.

1973

JOHN CHOWNING MADE COMPUTERS MORE MUSICAL with a process called digital frequency modulation (FM). Earlier methods of producing music resulted in dead, electronic-sounding tones. Chowning's scheme permits tones to evolve. This feature allows computerized music synthesizers to accurately reproduce the sound made by a sharply struck piano key, for example, from its percussive beginning to its mellow decay.

1973

A TRENDSETTER NAMED ALTO emerged from Xerox PARC. Providing near-mainframe speed, the computer embodied many of the ideas pioneered by the imaginative researchers at Palo Alto. With programs written in Smalltalk, Alto displayed several files simultaneously in windows, offered menus and icons, responded to commands from a mouse, and could be linked to a local area network. Although the Alto was never sold to individuals, its features eventually found their way into personal computers.

1974

O

Oak Ridge National Laboratory: and machine translation, PM 75

Object code: *the machine-code output of a compiler.* LA 87

Objective C: SC 89, 105

Object-oriented language: *a type of programming language that represents information in units called objects, each containing data and a set of operations to manipulate that data.* LA 111, *112-117*

Object-oriented programming: SC 71, 72-83, 89-90, 101-106; and Smalltalk, SC 101, 103-104

Object Pascal: SC 105

Observational Cosmology: CC 16

Oceanography: PO 19; radar altimetry, RV 98-99, *100-101*, 102; TOPEX , RV 103

Octal: *a number system, based on eight, in which a single digit represents three binary digits. See Octal arithmetic.*

Octal arithmetic: LA *13*

Oettinger, Anthony G.: AI 55

Ohio Scientific: PC 9

Ohio State University: RO 68; Adaptive Suspension Vehicle, RO 68, 70, 77; OSU Hexapod, IC *89*, RO 68

Oil exploration: PO 7, *26-27*, 43-44, 73-74

Okada, Tokuji: RO 79

Okun, Arthur: PM 98

Old Man and the Sea, The (Hemingway): PM 51-52

Oldsmobiles: shipment of, TR 77-78

Ole (robot): RO 105, 106

O'Leary, George: PO 74

Olsen, Kenneth: IO 36, PM 104, PO 67-69, *70, 71*, RV 60, SW 59-60

Olsen, Sven: RO 106

OLTP: *See* On-line transaction processing

ONCOCIN: HB 18, 72-73, 74, 79, *86-87*

Onera: TR 24-25

One-time pad: CS 89

On-line: *immediately accessible by a computer's CPU. The term refers to the technique of entering data and instructions directly into a computer.*

On-line processing: SO 39

On-line transaction processing (OLTP): *the term commonly*

THE INTEL 8080 MICROPROCESSOR performed calculations five times faster than its predecessor, the 8008, a speed difference that made it the chip of choice for many early microcomputers. Like the earlier chip, the 8080 worked with data in bytes. But the new microprocessor could address more than 64,000 bytes (64K) of memory, four times as much as the simpler 8008 could handle.

A PROGRAMMABLE CALCULATOR, the pocket-size HP-65 from Hewlett-Packard weighed eleven ounces—battery pack included—and cost $795. The HP-65 incorporated a tiny magnetic-card reader that could record and play back mathematical routines written by a user or supplied by the company.

THE Z-80 MICROPROCESSOR, a variation on the theme of Intel's 8080, was introduced by Zilog, a company founded by former Intel employees. Capable of running any program written for the 8080, the Z-80 offered several advantages over its competitor, including twice as many built-in machine instructions.

1974   **1974**   **1974**

used to describe a technique in which a common database is available to multiple users for retrieval and updates.
SO 39-40, 45, 46, 47, 52, SW 86-87, 88; and computer failures, SO 65-67, 70; development and minicomputers, SO 49-50; fault-tolerant systems, SO 65-67, 70-78

Onnes, Heike Kamerlingh: CM 90

Op-amp (stabilized operational amplifier): AC 24; K2W, AC 24

Opcode: LA 26, 32

Open architecture: PC 14

Open Systems Interconnections (OSI): *standardized communications procedures that make it possible to link diverse data-processing systems by means of networks.*

CO 105, *106-107*, IC 94; application layer, CO *108, 120*; data-link layer, CO *113, 115, 116-117*; host, CO *106-113, 116-120*; network layer, CO *106, 107, 112, 115, 116*; node, CO *107, 114-115*; physical layer, CO *106-107, 113, 114-115, 117*; presentation layer, CO *108-109, 120-121*; session layer, CO *106-107, 110, 118*; transport layer, CO *106-107, 110-111, 118*

Operand: *the part of an assembly-language instruction that gives the computer the address of the data to be operated on.*
LA 26, 32

Operating system: *a complex program used to control, assist, or supervise all other programs that run on a computer system.*
LA 73, RV 73, SC 26, SO 8,

25, SW 19, 73, 88; components, SO 26-27; controller, SO 28-29; CPU manager, SO 36-37; file manager, SO 32-33; first, SO 16-18; first comprehensive, SO 23; input/output manager, SO 30-31; limitations of MS-DOS, PC 105; memory manager, SO 34-35; for microprocessors, SO 91, 102-103, 108; MS-DOS vs. UNIX, PC 96-97; Multics, SC 34-36; OS/360, SC 26-27, 30-34; protection of files by, CS 11, 71, 73, *74-75*; and redundant computer systems, SO 67, 73; three-phase, SO 17-18; in transistorized computers, SO 22-33; UNIX, RV 73, *74-77*, 78-80. See also Access-Control List; Reference monitor; *specific systems*

Operator: *a word or symbol in a high-level language that*

HEARSAY II, a program created at Carnegie-Mellon University under Raj Reddy *(above),* made spoken English intelligible to a computer. The software employed twelve subprograms, from phonetics to syntactical analysis, to interpret oral questions about a database of computer-science abstracts. Within this limited context, the program correctly interpreted about 90 percent of the queries.

1974

A COMPUTER ON A CHIP, the Texas Instruments TMS 1000 was the first integrated circuit to include, along with a microprocessor, such essential components as permanent read-only memory (ROM), temporary memory (RAM), and input/output circuitry. Designed to handle data four bits at a time and incapable of further memory expansion, the TMS 1000 became a popular controller chip, embedded in devices ranging from microwave ovens to hand-held video games.

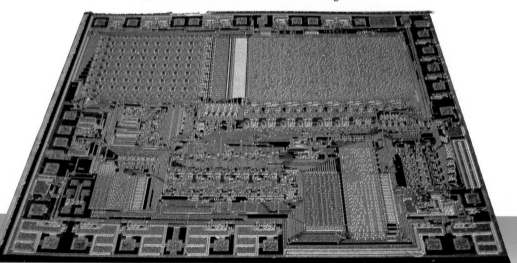

1974

represents mathematical operations, logical comparisons, or other operations on data; for example, + is commonly used as the operator for addition.
LA 54-55, 89; relational, LA 55, 59

Oppenheimer, Robert: RV 34

Optical amplifiers: AC 91-92, 94-96

Optical character reader (OCR): *a unit that can recognize ordinary print or characters in a special typeface, such as those on a check.*
IC *87*, PM *68-73;* expert systems, PM *73;* feature analysis, PM *71-72*, *73;* matrix matching, PM *70*, *71*, *73*

Optical computer: AC 7, 69, 70-83, IC 124; adding, AC 76-79; analog, AC 89-91; components, AC 74-83; digital, AC 91-92; index of refraction, AC 92, 93, 94; light transmission, AC 86-87; memory, AC 80-83; optical transistor, AC 91; parallel processing, AC 69, 71, 73, 85, 96-97; SAOBiC, AC 88; spatial light modulator, AC 74-75; speed, AC 85; symbolic recognition, AC 76-77; symbolic substitution, AC 78-79, 97

Optical computing: *an experimental technology in which information travels as a beam of light and the computer's switches are triggered by a flow of photons rather than electrons. See* Optical computer; Optical switch.

Optical disk: *a storage medium that holds information in the form of a pattern of marks on a rigid platter. An optical disk drive reads, erases, or writes data on the disk with a laser beam.*
MS 99-100; coding, MS 116-117; erasable, MS 104-105, 120-121; ROM, MS 110-116; tracks, MS 114-115

Optical disk drives: MS 110-113, 120; CAV and CLV, MS 114-115; erasable, MS 120

Optical fiber: *a fine thread of glass that carries light pulses in optical communications systems.*
CO 80, 81, 98-99, 100-104; data transmission rates, CO 102-103; and LANs, CO 102; low loss, CO 101-102; multimode, CO 102-103; single-mode, CO 99, 102; structure, CO 98

Optical memory card: CS 30-31

Optical Recording Corporation: MS 107

Optical scanners: SO 104-107

Optical storage: MS 97, 109; CD-I, MS 103; CD-ROM, MS 101-103; digital, MS 101-108; disk, MS 99-100, 110, 114-115; disk drives, MS 110-115; erasable, MS 104-105; High Sierra format, MS 103; magneto-optic disks, MS 104-105, 120-121; optical-memory cards, MS 106-108, 119; optical tapes, MS 108; precursors, MS 97-98; silver halide based, MS 105-106, 119; spectral-hole burning, MS 108; WORM, MS 103-104, 118-119, 121. See also Videodisk

Optical switch: *a semiconductor switch that is turned on*

O

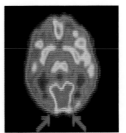

BRAIN ACTIVITY was revealed through a technique called positron emission tomography, or PET. Computer-controlled PET systems show concentrations of radioactively tagged substances, which indicate areas of chemical activity. Here, high levels of glucose (red) in the front of the cerebral cortex indicate the subject is looking at something. Costly and time-consuming, PET is employed primarily for research rather than for clinical diagnosis.

THE ALTAIR 8800 MICROCOMPUTER, vanguard of the personal-computer revolution, was unveiled on the January cover of *Popular Electronics*. Within months, its manufacturer—a New Mexico company called MITS—was inundated by thousands of orders for the 8080-based machine. Purchasers were seemingly unintimidated by the machine's serious limitations: virtually no software; a memory capacity of just 256 bits; switches instead of a keyboard to enter programs and data; and to display output, rows of lights instead of a monitor.

1974

1975

or off by beams of light. AC 92, 94-96, PO *116-119*

Optimization: with neural networks, AC *36-39*

Optimization problem: *a mathematical problem in which the best of many possible solutions is sought. The classic example is a salesman seeking the shortest route to every city on an itinerary.*

Optimizers: LA *96-97*

Optoelectronic: *combining optical and electronic devices. See* Optical computer: index of refraction.

OR gate: *a logic circuit whose output is TRUE (one) if any input is true. See* Logic gates.

Orthopedics: and 3-D imaging, HB *108-109*

OS/360: SO 23-24

Osborne, Adam: IC *101*, PC 8, 22; Osborne I, IC *101*, PC 23

Osborne, Tom: RV 71

Osborne I: CB 106, IC *101*, PC 23

OSI: *See* Open Systems Interconnections

Ostriker, Jeremiah: CC 97, 98

Output: *the data returned by a computer either directly to the user or to some form of storage. See* Input/output.

Output buffer: IO 57

Overgeneralization: AI 94

Overhead, parallel processing: PO 93

Overlaying: MS 82

Overspecialization: AI 94

Ovshinsky, Stanford: MS 105

Owechko, Yuri: AC 91

Oxford Computing Service: PM 60

Oxford English Dictionary: PM 63

Ozone layer: PM *8-9,* 106-108; modeling, PM 107-108

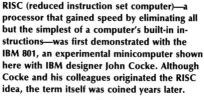

MICROSOFT WAS FOUNDED by Bill Gates *(below, left)* and Paul Allen to market a program they had written that enabled the MITS Altair to understand the computer language BASIC. The first software produced for a personal computer, BASIC for the Altair faded with the machine, but Microsoft went on to become the largest developer of personal-computer software in the United States, supplying programs for Apple, Commodore, Tandy Radio Shack, and IBM, among others.

THE 6502 microprocessor produced by MOS Technology was a fast, powerful eight-bit chip that could be purchased for as little as twenty-five dollars, a fraction of the cost of other microprocessors. Attracted by the new chip's bargain price, Steven Wozniak chose to design the Apple I and II computers around the 6502 rather than the better-known Intel 8080.

RISC (reduced instruction set computer)—a processor that gained speed by eliminating all but the simplest of a computer's built-in instructions—was first demonstrated with the IBM 801, an experimental minicomputer shown here with IBM designer John Cocke. Although Cocke and his colleagues originated the RISC idea, the term itself was coined years later.

1975

1975

1975

Paans, Ronald: CS 71
PABX: CM 101
Pacemakers: HB 99-101
Pacer 2000: AC 28
Package: *a case used for physically protecting and securing a chip and electrically connecting it to other electronic components. See* Packaging.
Packaging: CM 109; bonding, CM *110-111;* casings, CM *112-113;* lead arrangements, CM *112-113*
Packard, David: RV 67-68
Packard, Norman: PM 111
Packet switching: *the process of dividing a digitized message into packets and transmitting them independently to their destination on a network, where they are reassembled.*
CO 44-46, 48, 65, *66-77,* IC 66; adaptive routing, CO *74-75;* datagram transmission,

CO *72-73;* nodes, CO 66-67, *68-69;* protocols, CO 54-56; static routing, CO *76-77;* virtual circuit switching, CO *70-71,* 72; and WWMCCS, MF 101. *See also* Open Systems Interconnections
Page, Homer: IO 97
Page-description language (PDL): PC *51-53;* and printing, PC *56-57;* and scanned images, PC *54-55*
Pagels, Heinz: AC 61
PageMaker: PC 68
Page swapping: MS 82-83
Paint systems: CI *72-73*
Palo Alto Research Center: *See* Xerox PARC
PANAMAC: SO 41
Pancreas: computer aid for, HB 101-102
Papajohn, Ted: PC 22
Papert, Seymour: AC 51, 52, 55, 68, AI 14, IC *61,* 64, IO 73, LA *110*

Paper tape: *a continuous strip of paper about one inch wide on which data is recorded in the form of punched holes; used either for input or for output.*
CO 12, IO 10-11, 13, 15, 78, 100, LA 8
Papian, Bill: RV 62, 63, 64, 65
Paracelsus (Theophrastus Bombastus von Hohenheim): AI 8
Parafrase: PO 98
Parallel: *referring to the handling of data as instructions in groups of several bits rather than one bit at a time. See* Parallel architectures; Parallel processing.
Parallel architectures: PO 33-34, 49, 96-97; binary tree network, PO 103-104; Cedar, PO 98, 102; coordinating, PO *92-95;* dataflow, PO *99-101,* 102-103; hypercube,

DOUGLAS LENAT wrote the artificial-intelligence program Automated Mathematician (AM) at Stanford University. Supplied with the tenets of number theory and strategies of investigation followed by theoretical mathematicians, AM evolved, in just a few hours of operation, some 200 of the most significant concepts in the field, including division and prime numbers.

1975

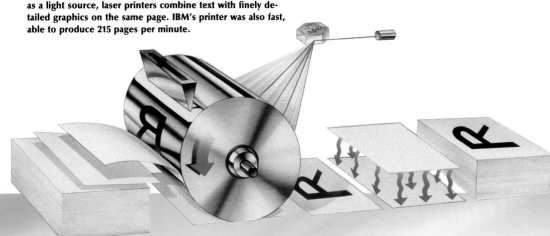

THE LASER PRINTER, introduced commercially by IBM, radically improved the quality of computer printout. Essentially a photocopying machine with a microprocessor-controlled laser as a light source, laser printers combine text with finely detailed graphics on the same page. IBM's printer was also fast, able to produce 215 pages per minute.

1975

Parallel architectures (continued)
PO 102; incorporation of, PO 96; large and small grain, PO 97, 103, 106; massively, PO 96, 98, 102, 103-104, 105-106; overhead, PO 93; programming, PO 97; reduction, PO 102, 103

Parallelizing compilers: SC 107, 109-117

Parallel Models of Associative Memory (Hinton and Anderson): AI 103-108

Parallel processing: *any of several techniques, such as pipelining and vector processing, that involve the execution of more than one instruction or part of an instruction at the same time. In so-called massively parallel systems, multiple-processing units work simultaneously to solve a* problem. *See also* Parallel architectures.
AC 7, *56-59*, AI 103, *106-107*, 108-110, CB 77, MF 47-48; and new languages, SC 87, 89, 100; and optical computers, AC 69, 71, 73, 85, 96-97; and target recognition, MF 66

Parametric Technology Corporation: PC 97

Parity: *a bit that indicates whether the number of ones in a bit string is odd or even.* MS 26, *86, 92-93*

Parity check: *an error-detection method that appends either a one or a zero to a group of bits to make the total number of ones even. After transmission or storage, a change from even to odd indicates an error. Some parity-check systems establish an odd number of ones and watch for an even number as a sign of an error. See* Parity.

Parker, Donn: CS 17

Parker, Edwin: CO 97

Parker, John E.: PO 12

Parkinson, David B.: RO 10

Parnas, David L.: MF 109, SC 37, 38

PARS (Program Airline Reservation System): SO 41

Parser: AI 60, LA 87, *90-91*

Particle beams: MF 107-108, *115*

Particle-mesh method: CC 105

Particle physics: *See* Supercollider

Pascal: IC 67, LA 77-78, 81, SC 20, 36, SW 29, 31, 38, *39*; and microcomputers, LA 103, 104-105

Pascal, Blaise: CB 8

Pascaline (adding machine): CB 8, *11*, IC 6

Passwords: CS 9, 21, 22-25, 69;

THE AP-120B, first commercial array processor, was an add-on system that could turn an ordinary minicomputer into a lightning calculator nearly as fast as a supercomputer. Array processing, originally developed for use in speech synthesis, achieves its speed by performing different operations on many pieces of data simultaneously. It is well suited for repetitive, number-intensive tasks such as weather analysis or the processing of wind-tunnel data.

1975

AIR-TRAFFIC CONTROL became fully computerized in the United States. An IBM 9020 mainframe in each of the twenty en route control centers across the country automated the radar tracking of aircraft, a chore that was formerly handled with wooden markers and handwritten data strips. To guard against computer failures, the system was supplemented within a few years by the Direct Access Radar Channel (DARC), a backup computer at each en route center, independent of the 9020.

1975

JACK DENNIS PIONEERED DATAFLOW, a strategy to simplify parallel processing. The M.I.T. researcher proposed constructing languages for parallel computers that would let such machines automatically assign tasks to their multiple processors, relieving programmers from specifying such details in advance.

1975

circumventing, CS 69

Patch panel: *a plugboard, resembling an old-fashioned telephone switchboard, in which interconnections are changed by moving the position of jumper wires; used to change the programming of early computers. See* Analog computers: electronic.

Patient medical records: HB 59-61

Patrick, Bob: IC 36, SO 14-17

Patterning process: CM 57, 82-83

Pattern recognition: IO 98, SW 112

Pavelle, Richard: RV 45-46

PAVE PAWS (Perimeter-Acquisition Vehicle Entry/Phased-Array Warning System): MF 26, 27, 30

Paveway II: MF 61-62

Paynter, Henry: AC 24

P.C.D.-Maltron keyboard: IO 40-41

PDP-1: IO 35-36, SW 59-60

PDP-5: RV 70

PDP-7: RV 78

PDP-8: CB 98, LA 100, RV 65, 67, SW 61

PDP-11: RV 78, 79

PDQ: HB 18

Peal, Dick: TR 17

PECo (Power Equipment Company): RV 18-19

Pecorella, Ed: SO 7

Peddle, Chuck: CB 103, 107

Peebles, James: CC 95-97, 98, 105, 106, 108

Peirce, Charles Sanders: CB 36

Pellionisz, Andras: HB 33

Pensak, David A.: CI 112

Penzias, Arno: CC 95

People's Computer Company: CB 101

People's Computer Company (tabloid): LA 100, 101

Perception, machine: AI 99-100; and computer architecture, AI 102-103, 104-107, 108-110; memory, AI 108; speech recognition, AI 100-102; vision, AI 15, 16-29, 102, 104, 105, 106-107

Perceptron: *a prototype pattern-recognition machine modeled on the human nervous system.* AC 48-50, 51, 52, AI 12-14, 15, 109, HB 33, RO 18; A-units, AC 49; Mark I, AC 49-50, IC 45; R-units, AC 49; simulations of, AC 48

Pergo: TR 56

Peripheral device: *any device that is used for input or output functions in conjunction with a computer. See*

P

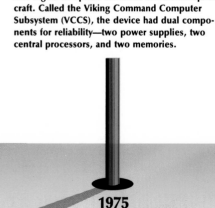

TELENET, the first commercial packet-switching network and a civilian counterpart to Arpanet, began linking customers in seven cities. The brainchild of Larry Roberts, the inventor of packet-switching, Telenet was the first of what are called VANs, or Value-Added Networks—so-named because of the extras they offer beyond the basic service of linking computers. Among the pluses that VANs provide are error checking and compatibility among dissimilar computers and terminals, as well as electronic mail services.

1975

VIKING PROBES TO MARS incorporated the first digital computer built into unmanned spacecraft. Called the Viking Command Computer Subsystem (VCCS), the device had dual components for reliability—two power supplies, two central processors, and two memories.

1975

Computers: basic parts of.

Peripheral processor: *a subsidiary processing element, such as an input/output controller or a coprocessor, that is designed to handle specialized tasks that would otherwise slow down the main processor. See* Supercomputers: centers for; Supercomputers: strategies for increasing speed.

Perkin-Elmer Corporation: CC 28, 29, PO 105

Perkins, Ed: MS 45

Perkins, Thomas: SO 70, 71

Permutation: CS 88, 104, *105*

Personal computers: *See* Computers, personal

Personal identification number (PIN): *a unique number or code that a customer enters into an ATM, for instance, to prove ownership of an account. See* ATM.

Personal Reader: HB 95

Pertec Computer Corporation: CB 101

PET (positron emission tomography) scans: CI *46,* 90

Petrofsky, Jerrold: IO 96-97

Phalanx Gatling gun: MF 95

Phelps, Byron: RV 19

Philbrick, George: AC 11-12, 15-16, 24, 27, IC 13

Philco: LA 42

Philips: and compact disk, MS 101-102, 103; and videodisk, MS 98-100

Phillips, Charles: LA 42

Phoenix Software Associates Ltd.: PC 24, 25

Phonemes: RO *66-67*

Phonemics: AI 101

Phone phreaks: CS 16

Phonetics: AI 101

Phonetic typewriter: AC 63-64, IC *123*

Phong, Bui Tong: CI 50

Phong shading: CI 50

Phony Pony: RO 68

Photinos: CC 106, 108

Photodetector: *a device that senses light and converts it into an electrical signal.*

Photodetectors, electronic: charge-coupled devices (CCDs), CC 32, *33-35, 36-37;* photomultipliers, CC 32, *100;* vidicons, CC 32

Photographic plates and film: CC 15, 31

Photolithography: CB *84-85, 88-89,* CM 62-65, 75, *82-83,* 104, *106;* photoresist, CM *80, 82-83*

Photon: *the smallest increment of electromagnetic energy; most commonly applied to light. See* Optical switch.

Physical attacks on computer systems: CS 35, 42, 44. *See also* Terrorist attacks on computer systems

FRACTAL GEOMETRY, a branch of mathematics unthinkable without number-crunching computers and their ability to display high-resolution graphics, was invented by Benoit Mandelbrot. The new geometry produces figures such as this "snowflake," which exhibits the complexity of shapes found in nature even though it results from a mathematical formula. Among other applications, fractal geometry has been used to study such infinitely irregular natural forms as mountains, clouds, and coastlines.

1975

THE FIRST FAULT-TOLERANT COMPUTER was the Tandem-16 from Tandem Computers. Tailored for on-line transaction processing and built to run during repair or expansion—and despite data errors or hardware failures—the computer had multiple processors linked on a buddy principle: Each processor had another's application program in memory, and if one failed, its buddy automatically stepped in. The Tandem-16, renamed the NonStop System, was embraced by the banking industry and widely used in ATMs.

1975

Physical defenses: CS 41

Physics applications: PO 102

Pi: calculation of, PM *34*, 35-36

Pick-and-place robot: control, RO 54; with sensors, RO 42

Pickering, Edward Charles: CC 15, 16, 42

Pickering, William H.: SP 87, 94

Pico: *the prefix denoting the one-trillionth part. See* Optical computer: light transmission.

Pierce, John: CO 86, 87, IO 101

Piezopolymer tactile sensors: RO 80

Piggybacking: CS 41

Piner, Stephen: IO 36

Pinguin: MF *68*

Pioneer 10 and *11:* SP 115, 118

Pipeline architecture: CI 113

Pipelining: *a processing technique that allows a CPU or a processor to work on more* than one instruction at a time, in assembly-line fashion. In its simplest form, pipelining involves fetching a new instruction from memory during each phase of the instruction cycle. PC 99, 101, *102-103*, PO 33, *58-59*, 61, 74, *94*, 96

Pirating: SW 63. *See also* Software

Pit: MS 99, *110*

Pittman, Tom: LA 102

Pitts, Walter: AC 47, AI 11, 12

Pixar: CI 90

Pixel: *short for picture element; one of the thousands of points on a computer screen from which digital images are formed.* AI *17*, CI 22, HB 63, IO 53

PL/I (Programming Language One): IC 56, LA 50, 67, 73, 81, SC 27, 35

PL/M: SO 102-103

Plaintext: CS 104

Plankalkül: IC *19*, LA *9-10*

Plant evolution: computer model of, RV 21, *22-29*

Plasmas: RV 104-105

Plotters: CI 16, *26*, 27, IO *32-33*

Pneumatic actuators: RO 51

Poe, Edgar Allan: CS 89

Poggio, Tomaso: AC 66

Pogo-stick hopper: RO 61, 69, *76*

Pointers: PC *34-35*

Polar-coordinate robot: RO 52

Polarization: *the direction of vibration of light waves. See* Self-Electro-optic-Effect Device (SEED).

Polarization of light: MS *112-113*

Polling: *the process of testing each source of input in sequence to see if it has data ready, and testing each output port in sequence to see if it is ready to receive* output. IO 28-29

Pollution: modeling effects of, PO 78-79, *80-81*, *82-83*

Polya, George: AI 34

Polyphemus: AC 13, IC *13*

Poniatoff, Alexander M.: MS 36

POP-2: LA 71

Pople, Harry: AI 41, HB 74

Popplestone, Robin J.: LA 71

Portable computers: Compaq, IC *108*, PC 23, *25;* laptop, PC *26;* Osborne, PC 22-23

Port protection device (PPD): *a microprocessor-driven box that answers a telephone and requires a valid password before connecting a caller to the computer.* CS 69-71; circumventing, CS 71

Ports: *connectors for attaching peripherals to the main board of a computer. See* Input/output: ports.

A COMPUTER THAT COULD READ ALOUD, the Kurzweil Reading Machine turned print into spoken words for the blind. Equipped with the first optical character reader, the machine scanned a page in less than a minute, then passed the results to a voice synthesizer equipped with more than a thousand pronunciation rules.

1976

LEARNING BY EXAMPLE became practical with AQ11, a program developed by Ryszard Michalski at the University of Illinois to recognize soybean diseases. He fed it symptoms of 290 diseased plants along with a human expert's diagnosis of each one. Comparing symptoms with diagnoses, AQ11 formulated rules for identifying soybean ills. The program later was applied to human medicine and physics.

1976

THE X.25 STANDARD for packet switching—the technique of dividing files into small parcels for transmission over a network—was approved by the International Telecommunications Union. X.25 led the way to similar international standards, or protocols, that simplified computer-to-computer communication and spurred development of data banks and electronic mail.

1976

Ports, parallel and serial: IO *24-25*, 27

Ports, vessel traffic systems: TR 91-93, 98

Position Location Reporting System: MF *99*

Positron Emission Tomography (PET): *a form of medical imaging in which positrons, or positively charged electrons, emitted by a radioactive substance injected into the patient provide data about the workings of the brain and other organs.* HB *22,* 23-24, IC *81*

Postes, Télécommunications et Télédiffusion (P.T.T.): CO 7

PostScript: PC *50-57*

Power, speed and: PO entire volume

Power supply: *a device for converting external alternating current into the direct-current voltages needed to*

run a computer's electronic circuits. See Computers, digital: structure and operation.

Power supply, auxiliary: CS 32-33

Power-supply problems: CS 30-33

PPG Industries: SO 77

Pragma A-3000 (robot): RO 34

Pragmatics: AI 101

Prime numbers: PO 7; mechanical number sieve, IC *11,* PO *8*

Princeton Plasma Physics Laboratory: RV 104-106; ICADA, RV 105-106; TFTR, RV 105

Princeton University: MS 84, PO 97-98; Institute for Advanced Study, CC 88, MS 12

Printer: *an output device that prints computer results in numbers, letters, or graphic images on paper.*

CI 16, *27,* IO *56-59;* ball-mechanism, IO *15;* buffer, IO *57;* daisy-wheel, IO 45-46, *56;* dot-matrix, IO 46, 56, *57-59;* high-speed, IO 16-17, *18;* ink-jet, IO *58;* laser, IO 46, *59;* and security, CS *12;* and typewriters, IO 36, 42

Procedural languages: LA 71, 111

Procedures: LA 64-65

Process control: SW 85-86

Processor Technology: PC 9

Pro/Engineer: PC 97-98

Program: *a sequence of detailed instructions for performing some operation or solving some problem by computer.*

Program Controlled Article Transfer: RO 35, 36-37

Program counter: *a register that indicates the memory address of the next instruction in the program to be*

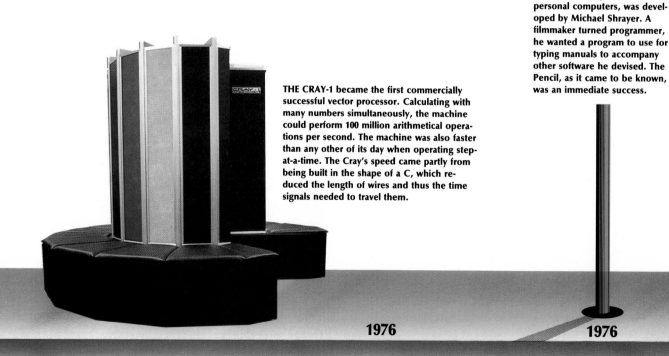

THE CRAY-1 became the first commercially successful vector processor. Calculating with many numbers simultaneously, the machine could perform 100 million arithmetical operations per second. The machine was also faster than any other of its day when operating step-at-a-time. The Cray's speed came partly from being built in the shape of a C, which reduced the length of wires and thus the time signals needed to travel them.

ELECTRIC PENCIL, the first word-processing software for personal computers, was developed by Michael Shrayer. A filmmaker turned programmer, he wanted a program to use for typing manuals to accompany other software he devised. The Pencil, as it came to be known, was an immediate success.

1976

1976

and Index; IO Input/Output; LA Computer Languages; MF The Military Frontier; MS Memory and Storage; PC The Personal Computer; PM The Puzzle Master; PO Speed and Power; RO Robotics; RV Revolution in Science; SC The Software Challenge; SO The Computerized Society; SP Space; SW Software; TR Transportation

P

executed by the central processing unit. See Programs. LA 29, 30

Programmable: *capable of responding to instructions that can be varied to solve different problems. See* Programming.

Programmable Implantable Medication System (PIMS): HB 101-102

Programmable Realtime Incoherent Matrix Optical processor (PRIMO): AC 91

Programmable Universal Machine for Assembly (PUMA): RO 40, 41

Programmers: number, SC 20; as security threats, CS 71-72. *See also* Employee attacks on computer systems

Programming: algorithms, LA *17-19;* automatic, SW 18; computer-aided, SC 39, 40-49, 51, 57, 62, 64-70; development of by enthusiasts, SW 57-61, 63; early electronic computers, SW 9, 12; with film strips,

SW 11; and manpower, SC 32; manual, IO 11-12, *13, 25;* with paper tape, LA 8, SW 11; and Plankalkül, LA 9-10; process of, SW 33, *42-47;* productivity enhancement in coding, SC 51, 54-57; productivity enhancement in design, SC 57, 60-63; productivity measurement, SC 52, 53, 54; with punch cards, SW 9-11; steps, SC 21; structured, SW 31; with switches, LA 9; and time-sharing, SC 36. *See also* CASE; Languages; Stored program computers; Systems programming; Validation

Programming language: *a set of words, letters, numerals, and abbreviated mnemonics, regulated by a specific syntax, used to describe a program to a computer.* characteristics, SW *38-39;* commands, SW *40-41;* higher-level, SW 17, 25-29, 33, 36-37; vs. natural

languages, SW *34-35. See also* Code; *specific languages*

Programming Languages (Sammet): LA 67

Programs: access to, SW 22-23; algorithms, SW 30; and ambiguity, SW 33, 34, 35, 110; basic functions, SW 75; large, LA 78; number for personal computers, SW 75; storage, SW 20-21, *22-23;* types, SW 19. *See also* Software

Program storage: internal memory, LA 14

Project Lightning: IC 38, MF 47

Project Matterhorn: RV 104-105

Project Tinkertoy: CM 22

Prolog: IC 75, LA 71, 111; and memory use, MS 82

PROM (programmable read-only memory): CB 83, MS 23, 28-29

Prosodics: AI 101

Prospector: SW 111

Prostheses: computer-aided design and manufacturing of, IO 77-78;

computer-designed, HB 18, 109; and computers, CI *106,* 107

Proteins: HB 10-11, 37, 42; analysis of structure, RV 81, *82-91;* and computer chips, AC *98-99, 102-103;* modeling, HB 34-35; and nanotechnology, AC 108

Protocol: *a set of strict rules governing the internal workings of a communications system.* CO 40; ASCII, CO 49, 54; Ethernet, CO 57, 62; Hayes-modem, CO 63; LAN, CO *58-61,* 62-63; MAP, CO 63-64; OSI, CO 56, 105, *106-121;* packet-switching, CO 54, 55-56; RS-232-C, CO *50-51,* 54; for satellites, CO 95; token-ring, CO 62; X.25, CO 55-56; X.75, CO 56

PROWLER: MF 69

Proxmire, William: RO 68, 103

Prudential Life: SO 13

Prueitt, Melvin: images by, CI *116-117*

Pseudorandom numbers: *a*

A ROBOTIC WALKER that could climb over obstacles and up shallow stairs was put through its paces at Ohio State University by Robert B. McGhee. His OSU Hexapod *(below),* a six-legged, insectlike vehicle, was linked by cable to a power supply and a computer that controlled its leg motors.

CP/M, an operating system for personal computers, was developed by computer scientist Gary Kildall *(left).* Widely adopted by computer makers, CP/M opened the door to software compatibility, making it possible for one version of a program to run on a variety of computers built around eight-bit microprocessors.

1976

1977

series of numbers produced by programs called random-number generators. The numbers are described as ''pseudo'' because they are created by a fixed procedure and thus are not truly random. See Random-number generators.

Public-key system: *a cipher that usually employs a pair of mathematically related keys, one that is public knowledge within the computer network, the other known only to its owner. The sender uses the receiver's public key to encrypt data, which may be decrypted only with the related private key.*
CS 99-102, 103, *112-117*; digital signature, CS 101-102, *116-117*; RSA, CS 101-102,

103; trap-door knapsack, CS 99-101
Puck: CI *18-19*
Pulsating stars: CC 87-88
Punch card: *a rectangular card on which data is represented as punched holes.*
CB 9, 10, 11, 12, 13, 14, IC *11*, IO 8-9, *10*, 11, *12*, 18, SO 14, SW 9-11; and Social Security Administration, SO 19
Punch-card tabulators: 1930s-1940s, RV 9-15
Purging: *in a computer's memory, the automatic erasure of stale information to create more storage space.* See Memory: purging and garbage collection.
MS 78
Puzzle solving: PM entire volume
Python missile: MF 72

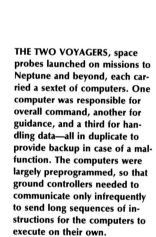

THE TWO VOYAGERS, space probes launched on missions to Neptune and beyond, each carried a sextet of computers. One computer was responsible for overall command, another for guidance, and a third for handling data—all in duplicate to provide backup in case of a malfunction. The computers were largely preprogrammed, so that ground controllers needed to communicate only infrequently to send long sequences of instructions for the computers to execute on their own.

THE APPLE II launched the personal computer industry. Shown below with Apple Computer cofounder Steve Wozniak, the Apple II became an instant success because it appealed to a broad range of users. Hooked up to a color TV, for example, it produced brilliant color graphics. Provided originally to enliven video games, they proved to be an asset in learning packages for children. Within eight years, more than two million Apple IIs were sold.

THE COMMODORE PET (Personal Electronic Transactor) was the first personal computer designed for a mass market. Although its memory was limited to 12K, the PET was simple to operate, came fully assembled with monitor and cassette deck for storing programs and data, and cost only $595.

1977

1977

1977

and Index; IO Input/Output; LA Computer Languages; MF The Military Frontier; MS Memory and Storage;
PC The Personal Computer; PM The Puzzle Master; PO Speed and Power; RO Robotics; RV Revolution in Science; SC The Software Challenge; SO The Computerized Society; SP Space; SW Software; TR Transportation

QMR (Quick Medical
    Reference): HB 74
Quadriplegics: computer aids
    for, HB 91-93, *98. See also*
    Mobility, human
Quality control: CM 65-67;
    automated, CM 66; in Japan,
    CM 70; statistical process
    control, CM 67, 70-71;
    testing, CM *86*-87; visual
    inspection, CM 66
Quantum-well device: *a semi-
conductor switch whose op-
eration depends on the ten-
dency of electrons to remain
trapped in one layer of the*
device until a pulse of en-
ergy frees them. See Self-
Electro-optic Effect Device
(SEED).
Quartz crystal: *a thin slice of
quartz that vibrates at a very
steady frequency in response
to an electrical current.*
CB 16, *17*, 111
Quasars: CC *12-13*, 58, 74;
    spectrum, CC *51*
Queue: SW *52*, 53
Quickdraw: PC 61, 64
Quicksort: SC 22
Quillian, M. Ross: AI 64-65
QWERTY keyboard: IO *40-41*

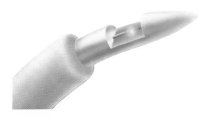

FIBEROPTIC CABLE saw its first commercial
service in an AT&T communications network
that linked three office buildings in downtown
Chicago. The network carried voice, video, and
data signals as light pulses through a cable
comprising a hair-thin glass core and a reflec-
tive coating to keep the light inside the glass
filament—both encased in a protective sheath.

BACON, a collection of programs named for Elizabethan scientist Sir Francis Bacon, rediscov-
ered fundamental laws of
science. Created by AI researcher
Herbert Simon and his colleagues
at Carnegie-Mellon University,
BACON programs repeatedly ex-
amined numerical data to find
relationships among the numbers. Given measurements of the
solar system, for example, BA-
CON correctly deduced that the
farther a planet's orbit from the
sun, the longer its year.

MAGNETIC RESONANCE IMAGING (MRI) gave
physicians their first detailed pictures of the
body's soft tissues. Made practicable by Godfrey Hounsfield, inventor of computerized tomography, MRI uses a computer to control an
intense electromagnetic field and radio waves
to produce images without exposing a patient
to the hazards of x-rays.

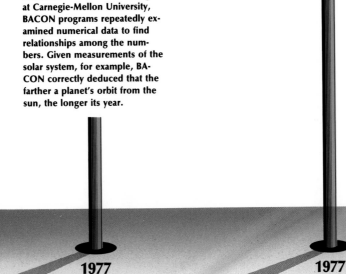

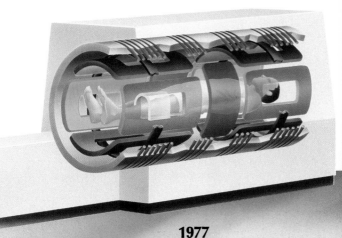

1977

1977

1977

Rabinow, Jacob: MS 45
Radar: altimetry, RV 99, *100-101;* antiradar missiles, MF 70-71; phased array, MF *26, 27, 28-29,* 94; and raindrops, RV *94, 95;* terrain-following, MF *75-77*
Radar, early-warning: MF 23, *24-25;* over-the-horizon, MF 30; phased array, IC *61,* MF *26, 27,* 29; sidelobes, MF *54-55*
Radar, electronic warfare against: analysis of source, MF *51;* burn-through, MF *58;* and chaff, MF *52-53;* counter-countermeasures, MF *58-59;* detecting and tracking, MF *50-51;* false echoes, MF *56-57;* frequency hopping, MF *59;* interrogation by, MF *50;* jamming, MF *53,* 97; use of sidelobes, MF *54-55*
Radiation therapy: and 3-D imaging, HB *112-113*
Radin, George: LA 50
Radio astronomy: early, CC 53-55; emissions, CC *7-8, 11, 13;* interferometry, CC 55-62, *78-83*
Radio Corporation of America: *See* RCA
Radioisotope thermoelectric generators (RTGs): SP 86
Radio Shack: SW 68. *See also* Tandy Radio Shack
Radio telescopes: aperture synthesis, CC 57-58, *78-79;* early, CC 53, *54, 56;* interferometry with, CC 55-62, *78-83;* One-Mile Radio Telescope, CC 57-58; satellite-based, CC *83;* single dish, CC 55; size and resolution, CC *76-77;* structure, CC *75;* VLA, CC 58, 59, 60, *80-81;* VLBA, CC 62
Radio uplink, loading software with: SP 62, 70
Radon, Johann: HB 19
Raibert, Marc H.: IC 109, RO 61, 62, 69, 76
Railinc: TR 76, 78
Railroads: TR 79, *80-89;* automobile shipping by General Motors, TR 77-78; classification (sorting) of rail cars, TR 77-78, *86-87;* early use of computers, TR 75; record keeping, TR 75-76; routing rail cars, TR 84; tracking of rail cars, TR *80-89;* TRAIN, TR 76, 78, 80, 82; UMLER, TR 80, 82
Railroads, commuter: TR *94-97;* computers, TR 94-97; fully automated, TR *103*
Rail yards: TR 75, *86-87*
Raindrops: dynamics of, RV 93, 94-95, *96-97*
Rajchman, Jan: MS 16, 18, 19, 21, 22

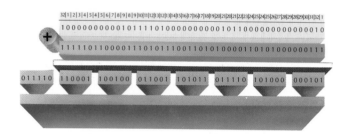

IBM'S DATA ENCRYPTION STANDARD (DES) was adopted to protect the confidentiality of unclassified computer data within agencies of the U.S. federal government. Available to the general public as well, the DES requires an eight-number key for scrambling and unscrambling data. With numbers ranging between zero and 127, there are some seventy quadrillion possible combinations, making it unlikely that the key to a message could be discovered by trial and error.

THE TRS-80 was the first desktop computer made by Tandy Radio Shack, a Texas-based chain of electronics stores. Along with the Apple II and Commodore PET, the TRS-80 led the shift from do-it-yourself kits to preassembled computers, ready to use out of the carton. Tandy and its competitors thus laid the foundation for a global market in personal computers that counts revenues in billions of dollars.

1977

1977

Ramanujan, Srinivasa: PM *35*, 36

RAM chips and graphics: CI 54

RAM (random access memory; read-and-write memory): CB *80-81*, 82, *83*, 111, 118, IO 26-27, MS 16, 22, 25, SW 20, 21, 22-23; checking, CB *118-119*; dynamic, MS *24*, *30-31*; static, MS 25, *32-33*

RAND Corporation: AI 31

Random-access memory (RAM): *a form of temporary internal storage whose contents can be retrieved and altered by the user; also called read-and-write memory. See RAM (random-access memory; read-and-write memory).*

Random-number generator: *a computer program that produces a scrambled series of numbers appearing to have no relationship to one another.* RV 35, *36-37*, 39

Random search: AI 37

RAND Strategy Assessment System (RSAS): MF *20-21*

Ranger, Project: SP 87; investigation, SP 94; midcourse correction, SP 88; *Ranger 1*, SP 88-89; *Ranger 2*, SP 89; *Ranger 3*, SP 89; *Ranger 4*, SP 89, 116; *Ranger 5*, SP 94; *Ranger 6*, SP 94; *Ranger 7*, SP 94, 116; sequencer, SP 88, 89, 95; stabilization of craft, SP 88

Raskin, Jef: PC 58, 60, 61-62

Raster graphics: coprocessors, CI 58-59; development, CI 49-54, 58

Raster Technologies: CM 101

Rather, Elizabeth: LA 106

Ratliff, Wayne: SW 70-71, *72*

Ratner, Mark: AC 97, 104

Raymond Engineering Laboratory: SP 38

Raytheon Company: CM 63; ReadyCode, SC 56

Raytheon Manufacturing Company: MS 37

RCA (Radio Corporation of America): CB 77, IO 26-27, LA 42, 44, MS 18, 22, 100, SO 20, 24; model, SP 110, 42;

Synthesizer, IO 100

Read: *the process by which the central processor of a computer examines data in memory or transfers data to memory from an input medium such as a floppy disk. See Disk drives.*

Reading Machine: HB 93-95, 96, IC *87*, IO 97-98

Read-only memory (ROM): *permanent internal memory containing data or operating instructions that can be read but not altered by the user. See ROM (read-only memory).*

Read/write head: *the part of a tape drive or a disk drive that both retrieves data from a tape or disk and records data on it. See Magnetic disk storage: read/write heads; Magnetic tape storage: read/write heads.*

Real number: *in computer science, a data type consisting of numbers written with a decimal point and/or exponent. See Data types.*

Real-time computing: *computer processing rapid enough to solve problems and control instruments as events occur.* IO 85

Reber, Grote: CC 53-54, 56

Record: *a data structure containing different but logically related items that are treated as a unit. See Data structures: records.*

Rectangular-coordinate robot: RO *52*

Recursion: LA 49, 69, *74-75*

Red Brigade: CS 35

Reddy, Raj: AI 100, 102, IC *80*

Red shift: CC 94

Redstone missile: SP 13

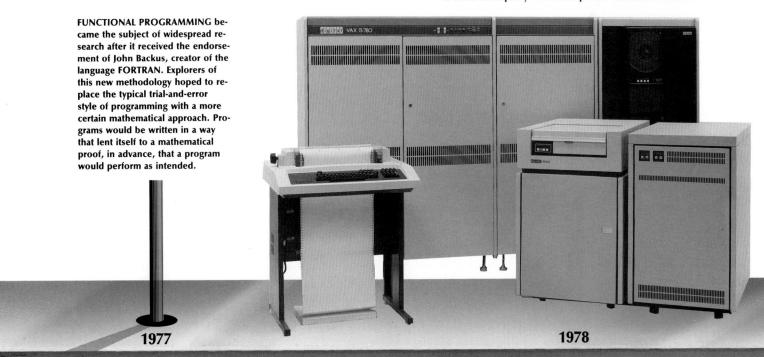

THE VAX 11/780 from Digital Equipment became the standard of comparison for a new breed of powerful minicomputers referred to as superminis. With the ability to address up to 4.3 gigabytes of virtual memory, the new VAX had hundreds of times the capacity of minicomputers without this feature.

FUNCTIONAL PROGRAMMING became the subject of widespread research after it received the endorsement of John Backus, creator of the language FORTRAN. Explorers of this new methodology hoped to replace the typical trial-and-error style of programming with a more certain mathematical approach. Programs would be written in a way that lent itself to a mathematical proof, in advance, that a program would perform as intended.

1977

1978

Reduction architecture: PO 102, 103

Redundancy of computers: SP 36; on Skylab, SP 59; on space shuttle, SP 65-66, 73, 74-83; on Viking, SP 98-99

Reeves Instrument Company: AC 24; REAC, AC 24

Reference monitor: CS 71, 73, 82-85

Register: *a special circuit in the central processing unit, such as an accumulator or program counter, that can either hold a value or per-form some arithmetical or logical operation.* CB 83, *112-113,* LA 24

Reines, Frederick: CC 98

Relational database: *a database that does not require prede-termined relationships among individual records but can reveal unanticipated connections or establish new ones at any time. See* Data-bases, relational.

Relay: *an electromagnetic switching device.* CB 37-38, 52, 58, 67; electro-mechanical, reliability of, RV 20

Remington Rand: CB 65, IO 16, 17, 36-37, LA 20-21; and ERA, PO 13; and Sperry, PO 13; UNIVAC, PM 59, SO 12, 20, SW 17. *See also* Sperry Rand

Remotely operated vehicles (ROVs): RO 102-105, *116-117*

Remote reconnaissance vehicle (RRV): RO 102

Rendering: CI 61; bump mapping, CI 70; image mapping, CI 70; ray tracing, CI 59, *68-69;* spatial texturing, CI *70-71*

Reservation programs: SO 40-41, 50-52

Reservations systems: PC 104-105

Resist: *a material used to shield parts of a chip during etching. See* Integrated cir-cuits: fabrication.

Resistor: *an electronic compo-nent that impedes the flow of current.* CM 23

Resnick, Daniel P.: CO 7

Resolution, human color and spatial: CI *52-53*

Resolvers: RO 48, 56, *57*

Retail merchandising, comput-ers in: SO 113, *114-121;* accounting, SO *116-121;* hierarchy of computers, SO *114-115;* in-store processor, SO *114-115;* inventory control, SO 113, 115, *116-117;* point-of-sale terminal, SO *114-115, 118-119*

Retinal chip: AC 66

Retinal-identification system: CS *52-53*

Revolute-coordinate robot: RO *52-53*

Reyes: CI 90

RF&P (Richmond, Fredericks-burg & Potomac): TR 75, 76

Rhyolite satellite: MF 46

Rice, Richard: SP 101

Richard, Ludie: SP 41, 42

Richardson, Lewis: SW 103

Richens, Richard: PM 67

Rifkin, Stanley: CS 17

RISC (Reduced Instruction Set Computer): IC 82, PC 91, 98, 99, 106; architecture, PC 100, *101;* pipelining, PC *102-103*

OSI, for open systems interconnection, was for-mulated by the Geneva-based International Or-ganization for Standardization to facilitate com-munication between computers made by dif-ferent manufacturers. The standard provides a seven-layer framework of protocols to be ob-served in the design of new hardware systems.

IMAGE PROCESSING for astron-omers took a leap forward with the Interactive Picture Process-ing System (IPPS). Developed by astronomer Don Wells for the CDC 6400 mainframe computer at Kitt Peak National Observa-tory, IPPS was a welcome alter-native to time-consuming batch processing. Wells's system per-mitted astronomers to produce their own computer-enhanced photographic images in a few minutes at the keyboard.

THE 5¼-INCH FLOPPY DISKETTE became the standard medium for personal-computer software after disk drives for the format were introduced by Apple Computer and Tandy Radio Shack. Similar in construction to the 8-inch floppies pioneered by IBM, this smaller version was devel-oped by Shugart Associates, a company whose founder, Alan Shugart, had guided the earlier IBM research.

1978 **1978** **1978**

Risk analysis: CS 28-29
Ritchie, Dennis: IC *65, 74,* LA 73, RV 78
Rivest, Ronald: CS 101, 112
RLL (Representation Learning Language): AI 81
Roach, John: PC 18
Road to Point Reyes: CI 6-7
Robert Abel & Associates: CI 80
Roberts, Edward: CB 95, 96, 97, *98,* 99, 100, 101, SW 62, 63
Roberts, Lawrence G.: CO 43-44, 46, 47
Roberts, Sheldon: CM *53*

Roberts, Thomas: CI 104
RoboSolid: PC 96
Robot: *a programmable device that is capable of manipulation, locomotion, or other work under computer control.*
Robot arm: actuators, RO 50, 51; coordinating more than one, RO *58-59;* end-effectors, RO *34, 35, 38, 39, 42, 43,* 49; programming, RO *54-55;* resolvers, RO *56-57;* structure, RO *48-49;* work envelopes, RO *52-53*
Robotic Aid: HB *98*

THE EINSTEIN X-RAY TELESCOPE was launched into orbit. Equipped with four specialized detectors, the satellite measured the strength of x-ray sources in the sky and captured sharply defined images of them. Computers played a role in every aspect of the operation, from scheduling observations to processing data beamed back to earth.

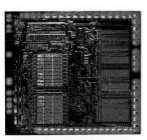

THE MOTOROLA 68000 microprocessor exhibited processing speed far exceeding that of its contemporaries, most of which had a word no more than eight bits long. This high-performance processor found its first use in powerful work stations intended for graphics-intensive programs common in engineering.

1978

1979

Robotic Industries Association (RIA): RO 8

Robotics: *the science of designing, building, and using robots.*
RO entire volume; research, RO 61-63, 68-70, 74-75, 78-80

Robots: RO 8, SW *100;* biological models for, RO *71-73;* definition, RO 8-9; effect on daily life, RO 112; effect on employment, RO 46; effect on nature of human jobs, RO 46; in hostile environments, RO 8, 101-105, 115, *116-121;* in space, AI *114-119;* status in 1940, RO 9. *See also* Teleoperators; Walking robots

Robots, programmable industrial: RO 33-39; growth of use, RO 40; limitations, RO 41; malfunctions, RO 41; miniature, RO 39-40;

programming, RO *54-55;* with sensors, RO 42; uses, RO 40-41

Rockwell International: SP 65, 74

Rockwell International Corporation: SO 99

Rogers, Carl: AI 58, HB 75

Rollwagen, John: PO 41, 48, 91, 96, 106

ROM (read-only memory): CB *82,* 83, 111, IO 26-27, MS 23, 24-25, *28-29,* SW *21,* 22; and bootstrap, CB *112-117;* PROM, CB 83. *See also* CD-ROM

Rosen, Harold: CO 89

Rosenberg, Charles: AC 61, HB 33, IC 119

Rosenblatt, Bruce: RV 41

Rosenblatt, Frank: AC 48-*50,* 51, 60, AI 12-13, 15, 109, RO 18

Rosenblith, Walter: RV 60, 64, 65

Rosenblueth, Arturo: RO 17

Rosin, Joseph: HB 106-107

ROSS: MF 11

Ross, Douglas T.: LA 68

Rosseland, Svein: CC 87

Rossi, Bruno: CC 66

Rothmueller, Ken: PC 60, 61

Rotterdam, port of: TR 92-93, 98

Rounding: RV *16;* ordered, RV *17*

Roussel, Jeanne: CM 65

Routing network: *in multiprocessors and multicomputers, the communications system that allows processors to exchange data and that sets priorities when processor demands conflict.*
PO 64-65

Royal McBee: PM 108; LGP-30, SW 26

RS-232: *a mechanical and electrical standard that permits the transfer of information*

between computers and communications equipment and that is also used to connect terminals, printers, and other peripheral devices.

RS-232-C: CO *50-51,* 54, IC 63

RSA system: *a public-key cipher for commercial data that is based on the products of prime numbers. The initials stand for Rivset, Shamir, and Adelman, the designers.* CS 101-102, *112-117*

Rubin, Vera: CC 98, 106

Rubinstein, Seymour: SW 69, *71*

Ruggio, Stanley: CI 37

Rule-based program: AI 39

Rumelhart, David: AC 55

Ruoff, Carl: RO 79

Russell, Steven: SW 60

Rvachev, Leonid A.: HB 70

Rydz, John: SO 91, 98

Ryle, Martin: CC 57, 58

Ryti, Carla: PM 28

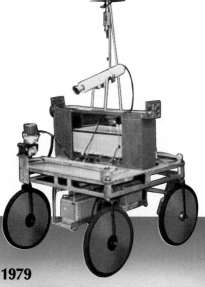

THE SELF-STEERING STANFORD CART relied on route-planning programs and artificial vision to make its way through rooms deliberately filled with clutter. Though the wheeled robot succeeded in avoiding obstacles indoors, it was slow; the cart took as much as fifteen minutes to travel three feet. Outdoors, it made an even poorer showing. Sunlight overwhelmed the on-board video camera, and shadows were interpreted as barriers to progress.

ADA, a language for military computers, was developed for United States and NATO armed forces by an international team of programmers led by the French computer scientist Jean Ichbiah. Named after Lady Lovelace (known to her friends as Ada), the language became the required vernacular for most American military software, replacing a jumble of programming tongues.

THE MULTIPLE-MIRROR TELESCOPE, or MMT, began operations atop Mount Hopkins in Arizona. One of the world's most sensitive telescopes, the MMT would be useless without computers. They swing the telescope to track celestial objects across the night sky, align its six seventy-two-inch mirrors on a common target, and collect optical data that has led to the discovery of a number of new quasars—distant, brilliant objects thought to be infant galaxies.

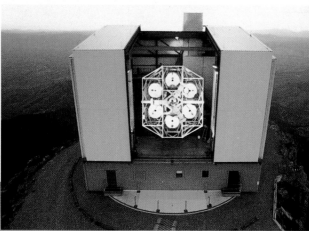

1979

1979

1979

Sabotage: CS 40

SABRE (Semi-Automated Business Research Environment): CO 42-43, IC *54*, SC 64, SO 40-41, 50-51, 52

SAC: *See* Strategic Air Command

SADARM (Sense and Destroy Armor): MF 79-80

SAGE (Semi-Automatic Ground Environment): CI 14, CO 18, 19, IC *38*, IO 13, MS 20, PO 68

Sagger missile: RO 111

Salisbury, Ken: RO 79

Salsberg, Arthur: CB 96

Salt, James: MF 72, RO 110

Saltzman, Barry: PM 110

SAM (Script-Applier Mechanism): AI 69-70

Sammet, Jean: LA 42, 43, 67, 68

Samos satellite: MF 37

Samplers: CM 100-101

Sampling: *the process of taking the value of a signal at regular intervals, often used when converting analog signals, such as voltage, into digital ones. See* Samplers.

Samuel, Arthur: AI 73-75, IC 28

Sanchez, Bruce: PC 93

Sandberg-Diment, Eric: CS 33

Sanders, Jerry: CM 54, 73

Sanders, Wendell: PC 58

Sandia National Laboratories: CM 93

Sandza, Richard: CS 10

Satellite imaging: CI *40-45*, 50-51

Satellite remote sensing: clouds, PM *12-13*; ozone, PM *8-9*; winds, PM *6-7*

Satellites, capacity: CO 94, 100; communication, CO 79-80, 85-89, *90-93*, 94-97, 100; data transmission, CO *92-93*, 95-97, 100; earth stations, CO 79, 97; geostationary, CO 85, 86, 89, 94

Satellites, reconnaissance: MF 36-37, *38-39*; electronic signal monitoring, MF 45-46; images, MF *38-43*

Satellite transmission of data: CS *94, 95, 96-97*

Saturn: SP 99-101

Saturn V rocket: SP 41

Sauthoff, Ned R.: RV 106

SBS (Satellite Business Services): CO 96-97

Scalar processing: *the conventional procedure for executing program instructions, requiring a separate instruction cycle for every operation.* PO 33, 61

Scale chart: AC 109

Scaler: *an analog-computer circuit that multiplies or divides values by a fixed number called a constant. See* Differential analyzers: mechanical.

Scaling: *the practice of using one value to represent a*

WORDSTAR, the first blockbuster program for microcomputers, was a word processing package introduced by MicroPro International. Written by house programmer John Barnaby *(above),* WordStar could display characters as fast as they were typed and line-for-line as they would appear when printed.

VISICALC, the program that made a business machine of the personal computer, was developed for the Apple II by Harvard M.B.A. candidate Daniel Bricklin *(background)* and programmer Robert Frankston. An electronic version of the financial-planning aid called a spreadsheet, VisiCalc (for visible calculator) automated the recalculation of a spreadsheet's conclusions after a change in its assumptions. The program was a huge success, selling more than 100,000 copies its first year on the market.

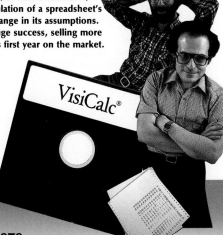

1979

1979

larger or smaller one. See Analog computers.
Scan codes: PC 30
Scanner: LA 87, *88-89*
Scanner (language): LA 68
SCARA robots: RO 52
Scelbi Computer Consulting: CB 94
Schank, Roger: AI 68-71, 75, 109
Schawlow, Arthur: CO 100
Scheinman, Victor: RO 39, 40
Scherbius, Arthur: CS 90
Scheutz, Georg: CB 13, IC 9
Schirra, Wally: SP 34, 38, 116, 117
Schlüsselzusatz: CS 91-92
Schneider, Jerry Neal: CS 63
Schottky, Walter: CM 98
Schreier, Ethan: CC 67, 68, 69
Schreyer, Helmut: CB 54-55
Schwarzschild, Martin: CC 87-88
Science, revolution in: RV entire volume
Scientific studies: PO 19, *20-29*
SCI Systems: PC 15
Scott, Alwyn: AC 105
Scott, David: SP 39, 117, 118

THE F-16 FALCON showcased fly-by-wire technology, which operated the aircraft's control surfaces by means of signals from digital computers. In this arrangement, which was later built into civilian planes, electronic sensors measure the pressure exerted by a pilot on the control stick and rudder pedals. This information is digitized and fed to computers that transmit commands to actuators for ailerons on the wings, and for the rudder and elevators at the tail.

A MANUAL OF CHIP DESIGN was cowritten by Xerox computer scientist Lynn Conway *(below, left)* and Caltech professor Carver Mead *(inset)*. Titled *Introduction to VLSI Systems* (VLSI stands for very large scale integration and refers to chips having more than 600,000 circuits per cubic inch), the book demystified the planning of these complex integrated circuits. Used as a textbook on campuses and in companies nationwide, it vastly expanded the ranks of engineers capable of creating such chips.

CADUCEUS, an automated medical advisor, was the joint effort of computer scientist Harry Pople and internist Jack Myers. The software, which grew out of the pair's pioneering work with medical expert systems, could assist a doctor in diagnosing a patient's illness and in selecting appropriate tests and treatments as the case progressed.

1979

1979

1980

Scott, Michael: PC 46, 47, 60, 61

Scott, Peter: PM 112

Sco X-1: CC 67

Screen buffer: CI *16*

Scripps Clinic: CI 112

Script: *a framelike structure used to represent a sequence of events.* AI 69-70

Sculley, John: PC 63, 65, 66-67, 68

Scytale: CS 88

SDI: *See* Strategic Defense Initiative

Seagate Technology: MS 52

Search: *a procedure for automated problem solving in which a computer seeks a solution by selecting among various possible alternatives. See* Search: methods. SW *54;* in database system, SW *81;* methods, AI *36-37*

Searle, John R.: AI 71

Sears, Roebuck and Company: PC 16

Seasat: RV 99, 102

Seattle Computer Products: SO 108

Seawolf missile: MF 72

Sector: *a wedge-shaped division on a disk that subdivides each track, facilitating access to specific pieces of data. See* Magnetic disk storage.

Security, computer: *See* Computer security

Security systems: CS 11, IO 82-83; business of, CS 11, 16; cost, CS 20, 42. *See also* specific systems

Seeber, Robert (Rex): RV 18

SEED: *See* Self-Electro-optic-Effect-Device

Seering, Warren P.: RO 40, 41

Seireg, Ali: CI 101, 107-108

Seismic analysis: PO 7, *26-27,* 43-44, 73-74

Seismic graphics: CI 90

Seismology: RV 47, *48-57;* analysis of the earth's crust, RV *52-53;* analysis of the earth's mantle, RV *56-57;* earthquake simulation, RV *54-55;* signal processing, RV *48-49*

Seismometer: RV *48-49*

Seitz, Charles: PO 102

Sejnowski, Terrence J.: AC 54, 61, AI 109, HB 33, IC *119*

Selectron tube: MS 16

Self-Electro-optic-Effect Device (SEED): *an optical switch in which beams of light trigger electronic events that cause the light to be either transmitted or absorbed, thus turning the switch on or off.* AC 95-97, IC *119,* PO *118-119*

Semantics: AI 60-61, 64-65, 68-71, 101; nets, AI *62-63*

Semaphores: SO *42-43*

Sematech: CM 74

Semiconductor: *a material with properties of both a conductor and an insulator. Common semiconductors include germanium and silicon.* CB 68, 69-70, CM 19-20, 93; doping, CB 68, 69-70, 72-73, *86-87;* gallium arsenide vs. silicon, PO 112; optical, PO *118-119;* research, CB 69, 70-72; structure and function, PO *108-109. See also* Gallium arsenide; Germanium; Silicon; Transistors

Semiconductor switch: *the fundamental component of all electronic computers, composed of semiconductor material and capable of turning a current on or off. Semiconductor switches store and transmit information expressed as zeros and ones. See* Switches.

Sense amplifier: MS 31

S

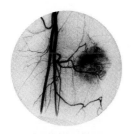

DSA (Digital Subtraction Angiography) revealed blood vessels with unprecedented clarity. The process depends on the comparison by computers of a pair of blood-vessel x-rays, one made with an x-ray-absorbent dye injected into the bloodstream and one without the dye. In the DSA image of a femoral artery above, a gray patch of diffuse blood indicates the presence of a tumor.

1980

A HARD DISK FOR MICROCOMPUTERS was introduced by Seagate Technology, a firm founded by Alan Shugart. Designed to fit in the space occupied by a standard floppy-disk drive, the Seagate hard disk held five megabytes of data, thirty times the amount stored by a typical floppy disk supplied with a personal computer of the era. Within a decade, storage capacity of hard disks for microcomputers—dubbed mini-Winchesters after the fourteen-inch drives produced by IBM—would increase to hundreds of megabytes.

1980

EURISKO, Greek for "I discover things," was a general-purpose expert system that reasoned by means of rules of thumb called heuristics. Douglas Lenat, father of Automated Mathematician, created the system, which counted among its feats the design of new and complicated microcircuits.

1980

Sensor: *an information pickup device that converts physical energy such as temperature or light into electrical signals, which may be translated for use by the computer.*
analog, IO 20-21; in cars, TR *28-29*

Sensor pills: HB 107

Sentinel: MF *68*

Sequencer: *a timing device, used prior to the introduction of computer controls, that initiates activities in a planned order.*
SP 88, 89, 95; reprogrammable, SP 95, 96

Sequent Computer Systems: Balance B21, PC 104; S81, PC 104

Serial: *pertaining to data or instructions that are processed one bit at a time rather than in groups of bits.*

See Architecture, computer; Von Neumann

Serial access: *a method of retrieval in which a computer must search sequentially through stored data to find a specific piece of information. See Memory.*

Serial processing: *the standard method of executing a program on a conventional computer, in which instructions are processed in a step-by-step, sequential fashion; opposed to parallel processing.* CB 109

Serial processor: *a conventional computer composed of a memory connected by a data bus to a central processing unit that performs operations sequentially. See Serial processing.*

Service Bureau Corporation: PO 18

Servocontrol: *a feedback control method in which the actual position of a device's parts is continually compared with the desired position, and appropriate corrections are made. See Feedback.*

Servomechanisms: RO 11, 14, 15-17

Sewing machines: SO 91, 98-99

SHAFT (Society to Help Abolish FORTRAN Teaching): LA 99

Shakespeare, William: PM 61

Shakey (robot): IC *64*, RO 70, 77

Shamir, Adi: CS 100, 112

Shandarin, Fergei: CC 102

Shane, Michael: PC 24

Shannon, Claude: AI 12, CB 36-37, *54*, IC *12*, 22

Shapiro, Stuart: PO 74, 75

SHARE: LA 48, 50, SO 17, 18; Advanced Language Development Committee, LA 50

THE FIRST OPTICAL DATA-STORAGE DISK held 1.3 gigabytes of information, almost sixty times the capacity of a typical microcomputer Winchester disk of the time. Called WORM (Write Once, Read Many), the technology was initially offered by Philips. Data is stored as indelible marks burned into a thin metal layer by laser beam. Because these scars cannot be erased or overwritten, WORM disks are best suited to storing information that might expand, but that is rarely altered—financial records, library documents, and the like.

1980

S

Shaw, David Elliot: PO 103-104, 106

Shaw, J. C.: AI 31, 32-33, 35, 100, IC 34, 36

Shaw, Robert: PM 110-111

Shearson Lehman Hutton: PC 91-92

Sheep shearer (robot): RO 113

Sheffield, HMS: MF 71-72, RO 110

Shell: *a UNIX program that manages the interaction between the system and the user. It interprets requests from the user, calls up programs from memory, and executes them.* RV *74-75*

Shepard, Alan: SP *18*, 116, 117

Shewhart, Walter: CM 71, 72

Shin Aitoku Maru: TR 24, 25, 26

Shipboard applications: Automated Manifest System, TR 71; controls, TR 23, 25, 26; electronic charts, TR 55-56,

64-65; engines, TR 23; fuel savings, TR 26; navigation and control, TR 56; planning, TR 56; and sailpower, TR 23-26. *See also* Navigation

Ships: designing, PC 94-95, TR 24

Shoch, John: CS 72, IC 101

Shock absorbers: automobile, TR *34-35*

Shockley, William: CB *57*, 70, *71*, *72*, 74, CM 17, 19, *20*, 29, 52, *53*, 98, IC 20, 27, MS 9

Shockley Eight: CB 74, CM 53

Shockley Semiconductor Laboratories: CM 52-53

Sholes, Christopher Latham: IO 36, 37, 40

Sholokhov, Mikhail: PM 61-62

Short Code: IC 23, LA 11, 14, 21-22

Shorter, Edward: PM 18

Shortliffe, Edward: AI 40, HB 72, IC *74*

Shrayer, Michael: IC 88, SO

102, SW 68-69

SHRDLU: AI 60-61, IC 72

Shrike missile: MF 70

Shrimp boats: TR 98

Shubik, Martin: PM 105

Shugart, Alan: MS 51, 52

Shugart Associates: MS 52

Siegel, David M.: RO 80

SIG (special-interest group): LA 73

SIGINT (signals intelligence): MF 45-46

Signal processing: AWACS, MF 98; electronic transmissions, MF 45-46; sound, MF 32,

34-35, 36

Signal processing, video: MF 37, *38-43;* color synthesis, MF *41*, 45; distortion and contrast correction, MF 44; image changes, MF 45; thermal imaging, MF *39;* three-dimensional imaging, MF *42-43*, 44

Signature, digital: CS *116-117*

Signature-identification system: CS 48-49

Signetics: CM 53

Silent Don, The (Sholokhov): PM 61-62

THE COMPUTER WORM was invented by John Shoch at Xerox's Palo Alto Research Center as a tool to increase computer efficiency. Schoch's short program searched a large computer network for temporarily idle processors and put them to work. Useful as they may be, however, worms pose a threat to computer security. If they are written by a miscreant, worms can be made to erase information from computer memories and cause other mischief.

THE FIRST PORTABLE COMPUTER, the Osborne I, was announced by journalist and entrepreneur Adam Osborne, who demonstrated the machine in the backseat of a car *(above)*. Complete with monitor and disk drives, the device weighed twenty-four pounds and used CP/M, the dominant operating system of the day. Thanks to shrewd deals with software firms, its $1,795 price included programs worth $1,500, making the computer immensely popular. However, a series of poor business decisions led to bankruptcy for Osborne Computer Corporation in September 1983.

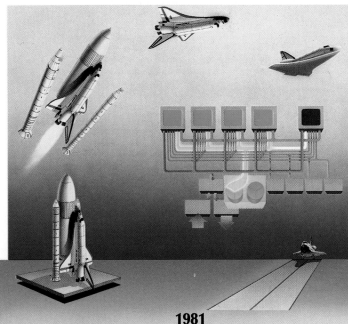

THE FLY-BY-WIRE SYSTEM in the space shuttle used five IBM computers. Four of them ran identical programs from the mission's Primary Avionic Software System (PASS), an arrangement that offered quadruple redundancy. The fifth was for emergencies; loaded with software called the backup flight system, it monitored the work of the other four and stood by to take over if they failed.

1980

1981

1981

Silicon: *an abundant semiconductor element from which computer chips are made.* CB 69, CM 19; as choice for semiconductor products, CM 23, 57; crystals (ingots), CB 72, 86; doping, CM 19-20, 23, *84-85;* etching, CM 57, 62, *83;* and gallium arsenide, CM 93, 98; insulating, CM 57; polysilicon, CM 42, *80-83;* transistor, CB 72, IC *32;* wafer manufacture, CM *58-61;* wafers, CB *86-87*

Silicon compilers: CM 33, 102-104, IC *104*

Silicon Desert: CM 54

Silicon dioxide: CM 22; etching, CM 57, 62; formation of layer, CM 57, *80-81;* impurities in, and MOSFETs, CM 29-30

Silicon Mountain: CM 54

Silicon Prairie: CM 54

Silicon Valley: CB 95, CM 52-54, SO 66, 70

Silverman, Brian: PO 104

SIMD (single instruction/multiple data): PO 105

Simmons, Adrian: SW 106

Simon, Herbert A.: AI 31-33, 34, 35, 39, 57, 77, 100, IC *34, 36*

Simstar: AC 28-30

Simula: IC 58, SC 20, 89, 102-103; Simula 67, SC 103-104

Simulation: *a computer program that manipulates the most significant variables in a problem or situation to show how change in one variable affects the results; a re-creation of the situation by means of realistic sound and visual displays.* CC 109, *110-119;* cloud-in-cell method, CC 105, 107, 109, *112-114;* compressed time, AC 25; correlation function, CC 119; and dark matter, CC 98, 102, 103, 105; of galaxies, CC 97; of motion of moon, CC 86-87; with object-oriented programs, SC 71, 72-83, 103; particle-mesh method, CC 105; of stars, CC 87-89; of universe, CC 85, 89, 95-97, 102, 103, 105-106, 107-108, 109, *110-119;* using analog devices, AC *17-23,* 24-26; using hybrid devices, AC 27-30; VLA, CC *80-81*

Simulators: driving, IO *80-81;* flight, SW 106-107, 108; fluid flow, SW 113, *118-119;* space shuttle, SP 21, *22-31;* war, SW 108-109

Singer Company: SO 89, 91, 98-99

Single-key system: *a cipher that encrypts and decrypts data with the same key. See* Encryption of messages and data: single-key.

Sketchpad: CI 31-35, IC *51*

Skidmore, Owings & Merrill, computer-aided design: CI 91, *92-99*

Skyflash missile: MF 72

Skylab: CC 71, RV 99, SP 59, 118; Apollo telescope-mount digital computer (ATMDC), SP 59-60, 62, 63, 64; attitude and pointing control system (APCS), IC *76,* SP 59, 61; problems with, SP 60-64; software, SP 60, 61, 62

Slaughter, Edward: PO 102

Slavery in U.S.: PM 21-22

Slide rule: AC 9-10; diagnostic, HB *71*

Small Astronomy Satellite-1: CC 68. *See also Uhuru*

Small-scale integration (SSI): *fewer than ten logic gates on a chip. See* Integrated circuits: density of components.

Smalltalk: IC *71,* IO 74, *75,* PC 59, SC 20, 89, 101; development, SC 104-105; Smalltalk 80, SC 105

Smarr, Larry: CC 104

Smart buildings: IO 82

Smart card: CS 30-*31*

TELECOMPUTING came to France with the opening of Teletel, an electronic telephone directory accessible over telephone lines. From a modest experimental start, with only 600 suburban Parisian homes connected, Teletel grew within six years to include three million subscribers and 6,000 entertainment, shopping, information, and banking services including credit-card transactions. While most participants gained access to the network by means of an easy-to-use Minitel terminal *(below, left),* others logged on from personal computers.

IBM INTRODUCED THE PC, touching off explosive growth in the personal-computer market. IBM built its first microcomputer in one year—almost overnight, by IBM standards. To pull off the feat, the computer giant relied on outside suppliers for most of the PC's parts, including its microprocessor, the Intel 8088.

MS-DOS (Microsoft Disk Operating System) debuted as the operating system for the IBM-PC. The software assured the future of Microsoft, the company founded six years earlier by Bill Gates and Paul Allen. As sales of the PC and compatible machines grew, MS-DOS eclipsed the previously dominant operating system, Gary Kildall's CP/M, and unleashed a burst of software development.

1981

1981

1981

and Index; IO Input/Output; LA Computer Languages; MF The Military Frontier; MS Memory and Storage; PC The Personal Computer; PM The Puzzle Master; PO Speed and Power; RO Robotics; RV Revolution in Science; SC The Software Challenge; SO The Computerized Society; SP Space; SW Software; TR Transportation

S

Smart Weapons Program: MF 80

Smith, Alvy Ray: CI 89

Smith, Burrell: PC *49*, 62

Smith, C. R.: SO 40

Smith, Desmond: AC 94

Smith, Fred: SO 112

Smith, George E.: CC 32

Smith, Michael: AI 41

Smith, Peter: AC 92, 94

Smith, R. Blair: SO 40

Smithsonian Astrophysical Observatory: CC 19

Society, computerized: SO entire volume

Soffer, Bernard: AC 91

SofTech: LA 81

Software: *instructions, or programs, that enable a computer to do useful work; contrasted with hardware, or the actual computer apparatus.*
SC 19, SW entire volume; Aegis, MF 96; and astronomy, CC 108; AWACS, MF 96; commercial production, SW 61, 62, 63, 68-74; challenge, SC entire volume;

communications, CO 56; compatibility with hardware, SC 26; complexity, SW 30, 32; complexity measurement, SC 53-54; controlling MMT, CC *48-49*; cost, SW 29-30; crisis, LA 78-79; engineering, SC 60; everyday life, SW 91, *92-99*; frontiers, SW 101-112; industry, SC 20-21; library of modules, SC 55; logical inconsistencies, SC 6-7, 28-29; medical diagnostic, HB 18; ownership rights, SW 61, 62, 63, 68; for parallel processors, SC 107; personal computer, CB 26, 97, 99, 103, PC 19, 47, 61, 63, 65; piracy, CS 64; public domain, SW 68; rate of production, SC 19-20, 51-52; SDI, MF 109-110. *See also* Copy protection; Image processing; Programming; *specific applications;* Validation

Software, microcomputer: *See specific applications*

Software, scientific: fast Fourier transform, RV 42-44; FORTRAN, RV 41; MACSYMA, RV 45-46; MATHLAB, RV 44; Monte Carlo method, RV 32, 35, 38-40

Solar cells: SP 86

Solar Maximum Mission satellite: SP 70

Solar system exploration: *See* Voyager

Solid-state: *pertaining to electronic devices, such as transistors, made from silicon and other solid substances as opposed to vacuum tubes or electromechanical relays. See* Transistors.

Solid-state tactile sensors: RO 80

Solomon, Leslie: CB 96, 97

Sonar: active, MF 31, *32-33*, 36; passive, MF 31, *32-33*, *34-35*, 36; sensors, RO 75

Sony Corporation: and compact disk, MS 101-102, 103

Sorts: SW *54-55*

SOS (Share Operating System): SO 18

SOSUS (Sound Surveillance System): MF 32, *34*

Sound, characteristics of: IO *112-113*

Sound, underwater: MF 31-32, 35; filtering noise, MF 32, 36

Sound effects: SW 65

Source: *in a MOS transistor, the area of semiconductor material that supplies current-carrying electrons; equivalent to the emitter in a bipolar transistor. See* Switches.

Source, The: CO 21, 27

Source code: *the lines of programming in a high-level language that are fed to a compiler or interpreter to be translated into machine code*

THE VERY LARGE ARRAY, twenty-seven radio-telescope dishes arranged in a *Y* having arms ten miles long, delivered resolution comparable to one dish twenty miles wide. Computers handled 200 VLA functions, from aiming the dishes to compiling the data. A revolutionary new software package, called the Astronomical Image Processing System (AIPS), was devoted to transforming into pictures the 20,000 bits of radio data arriving at the Very Large Array every second.

1981

Southern Railway Company: LA 41

Space, computers and: SP entire volume

Spacecraft, robot: RO 7-8, 111-112

Spacecraft systems, shuttle: IO 83-84

Space exploration: AI 111; scenario, AI *112-119*

Space research: and development of microchip, CM 25-26; and soldered circuitry, CM 21-22

Space shuttle: CB *8*, MS 22, SP 64-67, 70-71; *Challenger*, SP 21, 70, 71, 120, 121; *Columbia*, SP 67, 70, 119, 120; computers, SP 65-66, 67, 73, *74-83*; data buses, SP 75, 74-80; gyroscopic sensors, SP *74*; HAL/S, SP 66; mechanical controls, SP *82-83*; multiplexer-demultiplexer (MDM), SP *75*,

78-79; primary avionics software system (PASS), IC *101*, SP 76, 78-79; repair of Solar Maximum, SP 70; software, SP 65, 66, 67, 70, 73, 74, 76, 78-79, SW 7, 107-108; and space station, SP 71; tape software storage, SP *76-77*; timing of computers, SP 67, *78-79*, *80-81*

Space stations: SP *55, 68-69*, 71; and artificial intelligence, SP 71-72; and space travel, SP 72

Spacesuits, experimental: IO *102-105*

Space Telescope Science Institute: CC 90

Spacewar!: IC *48*, SW 60

Spada, Frank: AC 25

SPADOC: MF 27-28

Sparks, H. L.: PC 16 AC

Spatial light modulator (SLM): *a device whose optical prop-*

erties change in response to an outside stimulus, such as an electric current; the liquid crystal display of a calculator is one example. AC *74-75*, 90-91

Special cases: testing, SC 10-11

Speckle interferometry: CC 29-31

Spectral-hole technology: MS 108

Spectrograph: Hubble Space Telescope, CC *93*; MMT, CC *50-51*

Spectrum 32: HB 77-78

Speech recognition: AC 63-64, AI 100-102, RO *64-67*; simultaneous translation, AC 64. *See also* SUR

Speech synthesis: AC *32-35*, 61-62, SW *96-97*

Speech synthesizer: HB 90-91; and musical synthesizer, HB 94

Speed: CM 89-93, 97-108; and

density, CM 89; of electric current, CM 90; and gallium arsenide, CM 93, 99; and power, PO entire volume; superconductivity, CM 90; and wiring paths, CM 94

Speedcoding: IC 31, LA 21, 39, SO 15, 16

Spencer, Christopher: RO 34-35

Sperry 1100/84: SO 7

Sperry Rand: CI 36, LA 42, 44, PO 13, SC 21, SO 20, SW 17

Sperry Rand Univac Division:

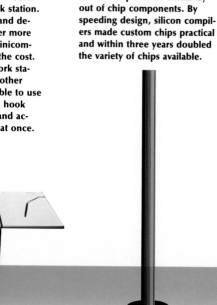

THE SILICON COMPILER was invented by David Johannsen *(above)*. Actually a computer program, a silicon compiler translates a description of the desired chip into an actual layout of chip components. By speeding design, silicon compilers made custom chips practical and within three years doubled the variety of chips available.

DBASE II brought the power of database-management software to personal computers. Written by NASA engineer Wayne Ratliff *(above)*, dBase II enabled microcomputers to organize large files of information such as subscriber lists, inventories, and payrolls. The program was founded on relational database principles enunciated by Edgar Codd almost a decade earlier.

THE FIFTH GENERATION PROJECT, an ambitious $700 million computer-research effort in Japan, was announced. Its aim: to capture the lead in the world computer market. One of the project's objectives was to produce a computer sixty-five times as fast as a Cray-1, the benchmark of the day for high-speed computing. Another was to radically improve the artificial-intelligence capabilities of computers.

THE DN 100 from Apollo Computer was the first work station. It provided engineers and designers with a computer more powerful than some minicomputers at a fraction of the cost. Later generations of work stations from Apollo and other companies would be able to use standard PC programs, hook into supercomputers, and accomplish several tasks at once.

1981　　　**1981**　　　**1981**　　　**1981**

and Index; IO Input/Output; LA Computer Languages; MF The Military Frontier; MS Memory and Storage; PC The Personal Computer; PM The Puzzle Master; PO Speed and Power; RO Robotics; RV Revolution in Science; SC The Software Challenge; SO The Computerized Society; SP Space; SW Software; TR Transportation

PO 8, 13, SW 17; LARC, PO 8-9; UNIVAC 1, PO 7; UNIVAC 1103, PO 31

Sperry Univac: CM 91, 92

Spevack, Marvin: PM 60

Spiegel, Edward: PM 110

Spiess, Ray: AC 28

Spine robot: RO *71*

Spinrad, Hyron: CC 36

Spitzer, Lyman, Jr.: RV 104

Spooling: SO 30

Sports: *See* Biomechanics

Sports applications: SW 113, *119*

Sposato, Steve: SC 56

SPOT satellite: MF 40, PM 32

Spot welding: RO 40

Spray painting: RO 40-41, 47, *48-59*

SPREAD (Systems Programming, Research, Engineering, and Development): SC 24-26

Spreadsheet: *software that simulates electronically the rows and columns of a ledger sheet, with a capacity for defining mathematical relationships between figures in particular positions on the ledger; used for accounting and for financial analysis and modeling.* PC 69, SW 69-71, 72, *78-79;* calculations, PC *78-81;* data compression for, MS 76; formatting, PC *76-77;* graphics, PC *84-85;* linking, PC *82-83;* Lotus 1-2-3, PC 12, 19, 69; memory use, PC *74-75;* scrolling, PC *72-73;* structure, PC *70-71;* VisiCalc, PC *9-10*

Spread spectrum: MF 99

SPRINT (Special Police Radio Inquiry Network): SO 39, 47-49

Sputnik I: TR 49

Sputnik I, II, III, and *V:* SP 13, 87, 116

Sputtering: CM 80

SQL (Structured Query Language): SO *58-61*

SRI: *See* Stanford Research Institute

SSEC (Selective Sequence Electronic Calculator): RV 18-20, 40

Stachnik, Robert: CC 30

Stack: SW *53;* interrupt, SO 36

Stafford, Thomas: SP 38, 116, 117, 118

Stallman, Richard: CS 11

Standard antiaircraft missiles: MF 95

Standard ARM (Antiradiation Missile): MF 70

Standard Oil of California: LA 50

Stanford Research Institute (SRI): AI 71, IO 14, 64, LA 82, 83, PC 59, RO 70, 77, SW 88-89, 111; International, AI 71, LA 82, 83, RO 70, 77; and videodisk, MS 98

Stanford University: AC 46, AI 9, 57, HB 79, 106; Artificial Intelligence Laboratory, RO 39, 62, 74; Stanford/JPL hand, RO *76,* 79; Stanford Cart, IC *96,* RO 74, *77*

Starr, Arnold: RV 59, 63

Stars: computer models of, RV 21

Star Wars: CI 76, 89

Star Wars: *See* Strategic Defense Initiative

State-based analysis: *See* CASE

Statement: *an instruction in a high-level program that tells the computer what to do.* LA 54

State University of New York at Stony Brook: CC 29, 30

Static electricity: CS 29-30

Static routing: CO 76-77

Statistical process control: CM 67, 70-72

Statistics: mapping, PM 22

Steady State theory: CC 94

MODULA-2 improved on Pascal, the high-level language written by Niklaus Wirth to teach the art of programming. Wirth developed the new language to overcome his original creation's shortcomings, such as its lack of adequate provision for input/output. Modula-2 permitted programs to be compiled in sections (modules), a timesaving feature compared with Pascal, which required that a program be recompiled in its entirety after the slightest change.

1981

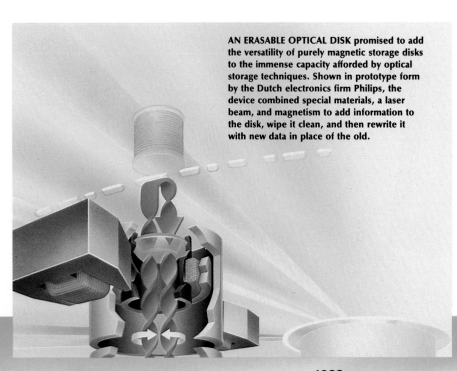

AN ERASABLE OPTICAL DISK promised to add the versatility of purely magnetic storage disks to the immense capacity afforded by optical storage techniques. Shown in prototype form by the Dutch electronics firm Philips, the device combined special materials, a laser beam, and magnetism to add information to the disk, wipe it clean, and then rewrite it with new data in place of the old.

1982

Steering: four-wheel, TR *32-33*
Stellarator: RV 104-105
Stepper (step-and-repeat camera): CM 62-63; wafer, CM 64-65
Steuding, Hermann: SP 12
Stevens, Louis: MS 50
Stibitz, George R.: CB 37, *54, 58*, CO 14-15, IC 12, 13, IO 11
Stockebrand, Thomas: RV 62
Stoft, Paul: RV 70, 71
Storage: *devices such as disks and tapes that store data either magnetically or opti-*

cally. Although they are slower-working than a computer's internal electronic memory, storage devices provide virtually unlimited capacity and preserve data indefinitely.
MS 7, *24-25;* memory and, MS entire volume; speed of, MS 7, 8
Storage devices: cathode-ray tube, SW 14; mercury delay line, SW 12, 14
Stored program computers: SW 12-14; first, SW 14

Strachey, Christopher: CI 9
Strategic Air Command (SAC): MF 23
Strategic Computing Program: IC 114, MF 110
Strategic Defense Initiative (SDI): MF 107-110, 111, *112-121;* battle management, MF 109, *112-113;* decoy detection, MF 107-108, *115;* distributed systems and software, SC 36-38; interceptors, MF 107, *118-119;* laser weapons, MF *108, 116-117;* sensors, MF *114-115*
Strategic Defense Initiative Organization (SDIO): MF 107, 108
Streeter, Richard: CS 59
Stretch: PO 9-*11,* 16
String: *a series of characters, often a name or word. See* Data types.
STRIPS: RO 70

Strom, Stephen: CC 30
Structured analysis: SC 60-61
Structured programming: LA 78, SC 60, 98-99
Stunt boxes: PO 72
Submarines, weapons against: MF 95. *See also* Sonar
Subroutine: *a self-contained section of a program that can be separately prepared and referred to by a single name. When the name of a subroutine appears as a statement in a program, the entire group of statements it represents is executed.*
LA 15, 64-65, SW 16-17
Subset, language: LA 67
Substitution: CS *104*
Sumitomo Bank: MS 107
Sumlock Comptometer Company, Ltd.: SO 90
Sun Microsystems: PC 90, 96-97; SPARC-station 1 PC, 98
Sunnyvale, California: CM 52

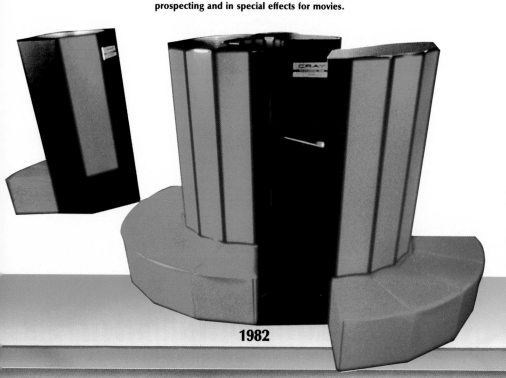

THE CRAY X-MP employed parallel processing to achieve a speed of 420 megaflops (million floating-point operations per second)—almost double that of competing machines. Designed by Steve Chen, the X-MP was essentially a pair of Cray-Is yoked together to work on different parts of the same problem simultaneously. The computer was intended primarily for weapons research, but it soon found application in oil prospecting and in special effects for movies.

1982

LOTUS 1-2-3, melding the spreadsheet capability of VisiCalc with graphics and data retrieval, was designed by Mitchell Kapor *(above)* to work with the sixteen-bit processor of the newly introduced IBM PC. Those advantages combined to get 1-2-3 off to a roaring start; 60,000 copies were sold before the program had been on the market a year.

1982

Supercockpit: MF 81, *82-91;* air-to-air combat, MF *86-87;* attacking, MF *88-89;* en route, MF *84-85;* flying damaged, MF *90-91;* takeoff, MF *82-83*

Supercollider: RV 107, *108-117;* computer tasks, RV 108; control of acceleration, RV *110-111;* control of magnets, RV *112-113;* data collection and analysis, RV *114-117*

Supercomputer: *a term applied to the fastest, most powerful computers at a given time. Supercomputers typically are used to solve scientific problems that involve the creation of mathematical models and the manipulation of large amounts of data.*
SW 103; access to, PO 97-98; and array processors, PO 75; centers for, PO *46-47,* 97-98; early history, PO 8-18; growth of market, PO 43-45; increased competition, PO 45; and models of universe, CC 85-86, 103, 104, 105, 107; speed comparisons, PO *42-45,* 91; strategies for increasing speed, PO 33, 49, *54-65;* uses, PO 7-8, 43-44; wafer-stack, MF 110; world reaction to Japanese challenge, PO 89-90

Superconductivity: CB 78, CM 90-91; Josephson junction, CM 91-92; magnets, CM 91; temperatures, CM 90, 91, 92-93

Superconductor: *a material that, when cooled to within a few degrees of absolute zero, can conduct a current with no electrical resistance. Superconductor switches control current flow with a magnetic field and consume very little power.*
in computers, IC 124, PO *114-115*

Supermarket applications: SO *92-97, 106-107; SW 94-95*

SuperTracker: SO 109-111

Surgery, reconstructive: and 3-D imaging, HB *110-111*

Surge suppressors: CS 32

S

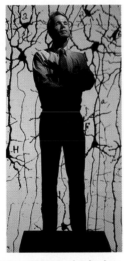

JOHN HOPFIELD of Caltech rehabilitated the concept of neural networks, savaged more than a decade earlier by Marvin Minsky and Seymour Papert in their book *Perceptrons.* Hopfield viewed memory as energy levels in the brain, a theory that seemed to fit with the electrical behavior of neural networks.

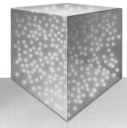

THE CLOUD-IN-CELL METHOD of modeling the evolution of the universe was developed by cosmologist Adrian Melott and physicist Joan Centrella. Their approach calculated the effects of gravity on one million subatomic particles represented as clouds distributed through a space representing a tiny chunk of the universe. When run through a computer, this simulation grew enormous patterns of matter similar to the clustering of galaxies observed in the actual universe.

APPLE COMPUTER'S LISA sharply cut the time needed to learn the use of a computer. For example, a spreadsheet that required twenty hours' practice on an Apple II could be mastered in an hour on this machine. The difference lay in a mouse, invented fifteen years earlier; it permitted a user to operate the computer by pointing at functions on the screen rather than having to remember complicated commands. Although the Lisa was a technological milestone, its price of $10,000 was so high that it proved a commercial failure.

1982

1982

1983

SUR (Speech Understanding Research): AI 100

Surveillance devices: CS 41

Surveyor, Project: SP 87; sequencer, SP 95; *Surveyor 1*, SP 95, 117; *Surveyor 5*, SP 95

Sutherland, Ivan: CI 14, 31-*32*, 33-35, 37, IC *51*, IO 73

Swift, David M.: RV 96

S.W.I.F.T. (Society for Worldwide Interbank Financial Telecommunication): CS 87, SO 86, 87

SWIRL (Strategic Warfare in the ROSS Language): MF 16, 17

Switches: PO 107; biological, CB 78; electrical and electronic, CB *68-69*; Josephson junctions, CB 78; junction diode, PO *109*; and new semiconductors, PO *112-113*; optical, CB 78, PO *116-119*; superconducting, PO *114-115*; transistor, PO *110-113*. *See also* Electrical computer circuits; Electronic components

Switching network: crossbar, PO *64*

Sydnes, Bill: PC 13, 14

Sylvania Electric Products: LA 42

Symbolic logic, program to prove theorems: AI 31-33

Symbolic manipulator: RV 44-46. *See also* MACSYMA

Symbolic substitution: AC *78-79*, 97

Symbolic substitution logic: *a method for processing data optically that substitutes an output pattern for an input pattern.*

Symbol table: LA *33*, 89, *92*

Synaptics: AC 67

Synchrotrons: CM 107

Syncom: CO 94

Syntax: *the rules for arranging words and symbols in a programming language in a manner that is understandable to the language's compiler or interpreter.* AI 101; approach to language, AI 56, 59-61; and BNF, LA 48, 49; and keywords, LA 57

SynthaVision: CI 80-81

Synthesizer: *an electronic device for the production and control of sound. See Music, synthesized.*

Synthetic-aperture radar (SAR): AC 89, SP *90-91*

System dynamics: IC 37, PM 99, 104; business models, PM 99, 104; world model, PM 104

Systems analysis: SC 39, 57; process-oriented, SC 62-63

Systems programming: SC 22, 23; organizing, SC 31-33; System/360 development, SC 23-27, 30-34

System/360: history, SC 23-27, 30-34

System unit: CB 110; board, CB 110, *111*

Systolic Acousto-Optic Binary Computer (SAOBiC): AC *88*

SYSTRAN: IC 65, PM 76-77

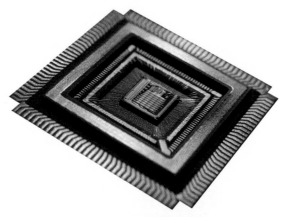

THE COMPAQ PORTABLE COMPUTER was the first of the so-called PC clones—machines that ran the same software as the IBM PC. Houston-based Compaq Computer Corporation, the firm organized expressly for the purpose of developing this new computer, benefited from a temporary scarcity of IBM's immensely popular microcomputer. Customers unable to find PCs snatched up $111 million worth of Compaq's twenty-eight-pound portables in the year following the machine's introduction. Two years later, the company had revenues in excess of $500 million.

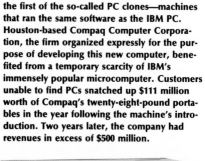

MIDI, a set of standards for computerized electronic instruments and the exchange of data between them, was agreed upon by major manufacturers of music synthesizers. Conformance to MIDI (Musical Instrument Digital Interface) has made it possible for musicians to link synthesizers one to another— and to personal computers that have been equipped with a special socket called a MIDI port.

VERY HIGH SPEED INTEGRATED CIRCUITS (VHSICs), fabricated by techniques that allowed circuit elements to be made smaller and placed closer together than ever before, were introduced by the Cleveland-based company TRW. The first VHSIC chips held only 13,000 transistors but were capable of twenty-five million switching operations per second.

1983

1983

1983

Tabulator: *a machine that processes punch cards.* CB *13*, 14, 51, 52

TAC (Tactical Air Combat) Brawler: MF *16*, 72

TACAMO (Take Charge and Move Out) aircraft: MF 100

Tactile sensors: RO 79-80. *See also individual headings*

Tamaya: PM 28

Tandem Computers: SO 65, 70-78; and banking industry, SO 74-76; growth, SO 77-78; Guardian Operating System, SO 74; and manufacturing industries, SO 77; NonStop System, IC *86*, SO 74; and securities business, SO 77; T/TOS, SO 73, 74; Tandem-16, SO 73-74

Tandon Corporation: PC 15

Tandy, Charles: CB 104

Tandy Radio Shack: CB 103, PC 68; TRS-80, CB *99*, 103-104, IC *92*, PC 9, 18

Tanks: antitank weapons, MF 67, 70, 79-80; M-1 Abrams, MF 65; reactive armor, MF 67, 70

Tape Record Coordinator (TRC): SO 19

Tarkington, Fran: SC 64

Tarkington Software, Inc.: SC 64

Task: *a single step of an operating-system job. See* Operating systems: components.

Taslitz, Steve: MS 107

Tate, George: SW 70-71, *72*

TAUM-METEO translation system: PM 77

Taylor, Edward: SW 109-110

Taylor, Gary: PM 62

Taylor, Norman: PO 68

Taylor, Richard: CI 75, 80, 83

Taylor, Robert: IO 66, 72

TDMA (time-division multiple access): CO *92-93*, MF 99

Teach pendant: RO 54, *55*

Teal, Gordon: CB 72, *96*, IC 32

Tecmar, Inc.: PC 18-19

Tejeda-Flores, Miguel: CI 83

Tektronix: CI 38, PO 71

Telecommunications networks: CO 29, *66-77*; analog and digital signals, CO *30-31*; codecs, CO *36-37*; commercial, CO 47-48; compatibility in, CO 40, 43, 49, 54-57; modems, CO *34-35, 50-53*; multiplexing, CO *32-33*; and personal computers, CO 57; protocols, CO 40. *See also* ARPA; LANs; OSI; Packet switching; Time-sharing

Telecommunications Research Establishment, England: CM 19

Teleconference: CO 28

Teledyne Brown Engineering: MF 28

Telegraph: CO 9; and multiplexing, CO 13-14

PHILLIPE KAHN, a former professional saxophone player and student of Pascal inventor Niklaus Wirth, renewed interest in the Swiss computer scientist's language with a compiler called Turbo Pascal. Kahn, a Parisian transplanted to Silicon Valley, had written the compiler for his own convenience in developing software for the Apple II. Speedy, inexpensive, and capable of producing compact programs, Turbo Pascal sold so widely that it became the standard version of the language and yielded instant riches for Kahn.

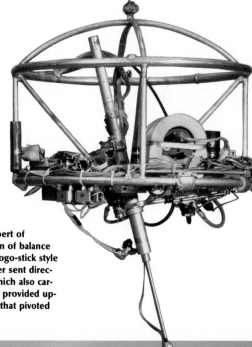

A ONE-LEGGED ROBOT, designed by Marc Raibert of Carnegie-Mellon University to study the problem of balance in walking machines, hopped across the floor pogo-stick style at approximately five miles per hour. A computer sent directions to the robot through an umbilical cord, which also carried compressed air and pressurized oil. The air provided upward thrust; the oil went to hydraulic actuators that pivoted the leg to keep the contraption upright.

1983

1983

Telenet: CO 47-48, 49, 54, IC 85

Teleoperators: RO 29, 102, 115; anthropomorphic, RO *120-121*; master-slave devices, RO *118-119*; underwater, RO *116-117*

Telephone: CO 13-14; cellular, CO *22-25*; conversion to digital, CO 29, *36-37*; and optical fibers, CO 103; organization of network, CO *16-17*; and satellites, CO 94

Telephone applications: SW *96-97*

Telephone banking: SO *82-83*

Telephone system, manipulation of: CS 16

Telepresence: RO *120*

Telescope mounts: computer controlled altitude-azimuth *vs.* equatorial, CC 22, *43*, *46-47*

Telescopes: CC 17; automated photoelectric, CC *20-21*;

multiple mirror, CC 43, *44-51*; multireflector, CC 17-19, 22; satellite mounted, CC 28-29, *90-93*; segmented, CC *24-27. See also* Mirrors; Radio telescopes

Teletel: CO 7, IC 102

Teletypewriter: *See* Keyboards

Teletypewriting: CO 9, 12-13; and multiplexing, CO 14

Teletypewriting Exchange (TWX): CO 15, 20

Television graphics: CI 83, 89

Televisor: MS 97-98

Telharmonium: IO 98, 100

Teller, Edward: MF 106, RV 33; quoted, CB 62

Telstar: CO 79-80, 88

Template matching: AI *26-27*

Terman, Frederick: RV 68

Terminal: *a device composed of a keyboard for putting data into a computer and a video screen or printer for receiving data from it.*

and access to computers, CS *12, 13*

Terminal Control Areas (TCA): TR *110-111*

Terrain Contour Matching (TERCOM): MF *75-77*, 78-79, RO 27

Terregator (robot): RO *76*, 79

Terrorist attacks on computer systems: CS 35, 40, 41, 42; in Italy, CS 40; in Japan, CS 40; in United States, CS 35

Teukolsky, Saul: PO 74, 75

TEX: HB 90

Texas Instruments (TI): CB

THE KURZWEIL 250, a computerized keyboard developed by inventor Raymond Kurzweil *(above),* reproduced the sounds of thirty different musical instruments, including the piano, trumpet, and guitar. The key to the machine's versatility was a memory bank in which the complex tones of the assorted instruments were stored in the form of mathematical models. Kurzweil produced his synthesizer at the urging of blind musician Stevie Wonder, an admirer of Kurzweil's earlier reading machine.

APPLE'S MACINTOSH COMPUTER won the hearts of computerphobes with a mouse-driven graphical interface that was as easy to learn as the Lisa's, which appeared the preceding year. Based on Motorola's 68000 microprocessor, Macintosh reaped the benefits of a multimillion-dollar marketing campaign that trumpeted the machine's simplicity compared with IBM-style PCs. Within six months, Apple sold more than 100,000 of the new computers.

TALKING COMPUTERS became a reality with Digital Equipment's DECtalk, a device that converted text to speech by means of a 10,000-word phonetic dictionary and several hundred rules of pronunciation. DECtalk is used mostly by businesses to handle telephone inquiries. Typically, callers enter their questions with touch-tone codes, then hear DECtalk read answers drawn from a company database.

1983

1983

1984

and Index; IO Input/Output; LA Computer Languages; MF The Military Frontier; MS Memory and Storage; PC The Personal Computer; PM The Puzzle Master; PO Speed and Power; RO Robotics; RV Revolution in Science; SC The Software Challenge; SO The Computerized Society; SP Space; SW Software; TR Transportation

73-74, 76, 96, CC 32, CM 22, 23, 24, 26, 54, CS *43*, PO 33, SO 90; ASC (Advanced Scientific Computer), PO 34, 39; DDP (Distributed Data Processor), PO 103; Information Engineering Facility, SC 64; and microcomputers, PC 10; speech synthesis chip, SO 99-100; TMS 1000, CB *82-83*, IC *80*
Text files: compression, MS 76-77
Texture analysis: AI *22-23*

Theft of chips: CM 56
Thermal imaging: MF *39*
Thesaurus Linguae Graecae: PM 60
Thinking: AI 108-109
Thinking Machines Corporation: AI 109, PO 105-106
Thisted, Ronald: PM 61
Thomas, Lewis: HB 17
Thomas, Lowell: LA 68
Thomas J. Watson Astronomical Computing Bureau: RV 12
Thompson, Ken: IC *65*, LA 73
Thorpe, Charles E.: RO 75

Thrashing: MS 83
3C273: CC *12-13*
3C326.1: CC 37
3-D graphics: CI *50*. See also Modeling; Rendering
3D/International: PC 95
Three-dimensional imaging: MF *42-43*, 44
Three-dimensional views inside body: of brain, HB *114-115*; and cancers, HB *112-113*; creating, HB *103-105*; and orthopedic medicine, HB *108-109*; and reconstructive surgery, HB *110-111*
Three-dimensional vision: AI *20-21*
3M Corporation: HB 97, MS 98
Three Mile Island (TMI) nuclear plant: RO 101; teleoperators at, RO 102
Threshold gate: *in optical computing, a device that transmits light only when the beam exceeds a certain brightness. See* Nonlinear material.
Thumbwheel: IO *70*
Tide predictor: AC *10*

Tilton, John: CM 51
Time bomb: CS 14
Time-division multiplexing: *a transmission technique for digital information in which a communications channel is divided into time slots, allowing data from multiple sources to be interleaved and sent concurrently over a single communications link. See* Multiplexing: time division.
Time on the Cross (Fogel and Engerman): PM 22
Time-sharing: *the simultaneous use of a computer by more than one person.* AI 57, 58, CO 39-42, CS 9, 71, 92, IC 41, LA 71, 99, MS 78, SO 44-45, SW 27, 87-88; commercial, CO 39, 41-42; and DRI, PM 97; and Multics, SC 34-36; and personal computers, PM 98; special purpose, CO 42. *See also* On-line transaction processing; Telecommunications networks

THE 3 ½-INCH DISKETTE, called a microfloppy, garnered widespread acceptance after it was adopted by Hewlett-Packard and Apple Computer. Developed by Sony Corporation, the microfloppy was smaller than the standard 5 1/4-inch diskette, but it stored more data and was much sturdier. A rigid plastic jacket enclosed the flexible disk, and an access door sprang shut to protect the magnetic surface when the diskette was removed from its drive.

1984

1984

ETAK, the first computerized navigation system for cars and trucks, displayed a video map on a dashboard-mounted screen. Developed by a small California engineering company, Etak used dead reckoning from a known starting point to estimate a vehicle's location. Sensors counted wheel revolutions to record distance traveled, while an electronic compass determined direction. A computer installed elsewhere in the vehicle correlated this data with an electronic map.

Timing: of signals on chip, CM 34

Tinbergen, Jan: PM 93, 94

Tindall, Bill: SP 14, 17, 45, 46

Tinkertoy computer: PO *104*, 105

Tiny BASIC: LA 101

Titanic: LA *7, 8*, RO 103

Titus, Jonathan: SO 101

Tokamak Fusion Test Reactor (TFTR): RV 105

Tokyo Institute of Technology: RO 77; Titan III, IC *112*, RO *77*

Toma, Peter: PM 76

Tomahawk missile: RO *26-27*, 111

Tomography: HB 19-20; seismic, RV *56-57*. *See also* Computed tomography; Magnetic resonance imaging; Positron emission tomography

Tomovic, Rajko: RO 76; hand, RO *76*

Top-down model: CC 98, CC 102, 103

Top-down school: AI 7, 14

Top-down theory: *an approach* to AI based on the belief that human intelligence is best simulated by complex programming that mimics the human thought process. See Top-down school.

Torode, John: SO 103

Torres y Quevedo, Leonardo: AI 8

TOW (Tube-launched, Optically-tracked, Wire-guided) missiles: MF 67

Townes, Charles: CO 100

Toys: and microprocessors, SO 99-100

TPF (Transaction Processing Facility): SO 51

Traces: and parallelizing compilers, SC 110, 112-117

Track: *the narrow band on a disk or tape where data is stored. A disk track is either one revolution of a continuous spiral filling the whole disk or one of a series of concentric circles; tape tracks run the length of the tape. See Magnetic disk storage; Magnetic tape storage.*

Trackball: *a ball, mounted and*

THE IBM PC-AT ran several times faster than the company's earlier personal computers. Intended for data-intensive business use, the AT (for Advanced Technology) was based on Intel Corporation's new 80286 chip. Customers could order this computer with a twenty-megabyte hard disk drive, as well as a drive for improved, 5¼-inch floppy disks that held 1.2 megabytes of data.

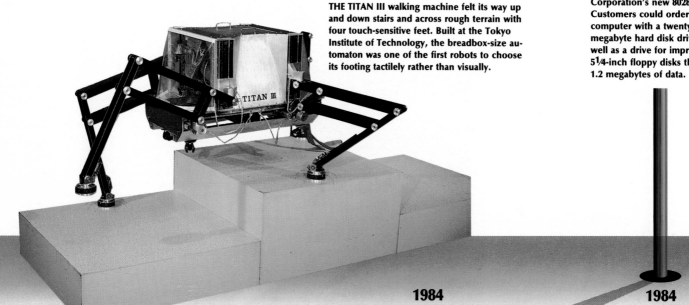

THE TITAN III walking machine felt its way up and down stairs and across rough terrain with four touch-sensitive feet. Built at the Tokyo Institute of Technology, the breadbox-size automaton was one of the first robots to choose its footing tactilely rather than visually.

1984

1984

rotated in a box, used to direct the movement of a cursor on a display screen. IO 70, *71*

Tracking and Data Relay Satellite: CC *90*

TRADIC: CB *97*, IC *33*

Traffic: *See* Automated traffic management

Traffic Alert and Collision Avoidance System (TCAS): TR *116-117*, 118

Traffic-control software: SW 85-86, *98-99*

Traffic lights: TR 106

Trageser, Milton: SP 43

TRAIN (TeleRail Automated Information Network): IC *66*, TR 76, 78, 80, 82, 88

Tramiel, Jack: CB 103, 107, PC 9

Transaction: *the exchange of a piece of information between a computer and a human user. See* Transaction

processing.

Transaction monitor: SO 41

Transaction processing: SO 39

Transients, electrical: CS 30-32

Transistor: *a semiconductor device used as a switch or an amplifier.* CB 57, 67, 70-72, IC *32*, MS *27*, SO 21; advantages, CB 72; AND gate, CB *75*; bipolar, CM 20, 28, PO *110*; CMOS circuits, CM 30-31, *42-43*; cost, CB 72, 78; fabrication, CB 72-73, *88-89*, 96; field-effect, CB 97; first commercially successful, CB 73; gallium arsenide, CM 98, PO 113; HEMT, PO *113*; highly miniaturized, CB 78; invention of, and computer, CM 17-18, 19; junction, CB *68*, 71-72, CM 19, 20, 23-24, IC *27*; MOS, CB 77-78, 97, CM 29-30; MOSFET, CM 29, PO 110-*111*; n-MOS, CB *88-89*,

CM 29; NMOS, CM 29; n-p-n and p-n-p, CM 28; operation, CB 67; optical, AC 91, 95; planar, CB *69*, 72, 74, CM 23-24, IC *41*; PMOS, CM 29; point-contact, CB 70, IC *20*; power usage, CM 28, 30; silicon and germanium, CM 19, 57, 62; structure, CB *68*, *69*, 70; structure of, CM 20, 29; and supercomputers, PO 9, 10; unipolar, CM 29. *See also* Integrated circuits

Transit: TR 49-50

Transit, infrared: PM 31

Translation: *See* Machine translation

Translator program: *software that converts programs written in high-level languages into the binary code of machine language. Translators are either interpreters, which convert instructions one at a time, or compilers, which*

COMPACT DISKS became available for computers. Called CD-ROM (for compact disk-read only memory), this optical storage medium could hold 550 megabytes of data and came prerecorded with information. An early publication was *Grolier's Electronic Encyclopedia* (above), a nine-million-word reference that occupied less than a fifth of one disk.

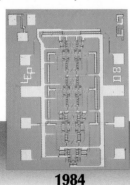

GALLIUM ARSENIDE became the basis for high-speed integrated circuits introduced commercially by California manufacturing firms. Chips made of this semiconductor, like the French prototype shown here, had long been known to conduct electrons three to six times faster than silicon circuits, while consuming less power. But gallium arsenide remained a laboratory curiosity until new manufacturing techniques made its use practical.

1984

COMPUTER VIRUSES were the subject of an urgent warning from professor Fred Cohen of the University of Southern California. Small programs that make copies of themselves, viruses infect any computer connected to a contaminated device—a disk drive or another computer tied into a network, for example. Cohen's speech at a computer-security conference sparked the first public alarm over viruses, which may harm data and programs in computers they infiltrate.

1984

1985

translate an entire program before execution begins. See Compilers; Interpreters.

Translators: SW 19. *See also* Compilers; Interpreters

Transmission media: CO *10-11;* copper wires, CO 80, 82, 103; microwaves, CO 80, 81-89, 94-97, 100; optical fibers, CO 80, 81, 100-104; satellite, CO 79-80, 81, 85-89, 94-97, 100

Transmitter: *a device that sends data over a communications link; also a device that translates electronic signals into electromagnetic waves. See* Transmission media.

Transpac: CO 48

Transphasor: *a type of optical transistor devised by Desmond Smith in 1981.* AC 94

Transponder: TR 98, 99, 113;

and collision avoidance, TR 116-117

Transportation applications: TR entire volume

Trap door: CS 14, 64-65, 68

Trap-door problem, and encryption: CS 100-101

Traveling-salesman problem (TSP): PM 32- 34, SW 102

Traveller TCS: AI 82-83

Tree, search: AI *36-37*

Treybig, Jim: SO 66, 70, 71-72

Triple I (Information International, Inc.): CI 80, 81-82, 83

Tripoli, U.S. air raid, 1986: MF 61-62

Trojan horses: CS 18-19, 59, 60, 66-68, 72, *78-81,* 85

TRON: CI 75, 76, 77, 80-*81,* 82

Trumpler 14 and 16: CC *8-9*

Truncation: RV *16;* ordered, RV *16*

TRW: CI 36, MF 100, SC 54-55;

neural networks, AC 65, *66-67*

TSP: *See* Traveling-salesman problem

Tukey, John: RV 42-43

Turbo Pascal: IC 109, LA 103

Turing, Alan M.: AI 7, CB *54,* 56-58, 64, IC *12,* 24, MS 10, SW 13, 14, *15,* 16, LA 16

Turing Award, SC 85

Turing machine: SW *15*

Turkana: RV 95-98

Turner, Frederick Jackson: PM 19

Twain, Mark: CC 106, IO 37

TWIRL (Tactical Warfare in the ROSS Language): MF 11, 15

TX-0: IC *35,* IO 35, 38, PO 68, RV 60, 62, SW 58

TX-1: RV 60

TX-2: CI 31, 32, 33, IC *37,* IO 39, RV 60, 62

Tymshare: SO 45

Tymnet: CO 48-49

Typewriters: IO *36-38,* 42-43

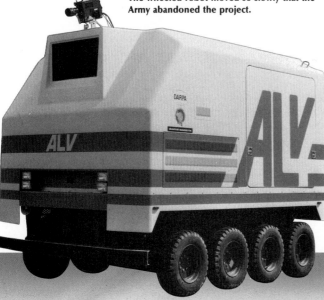

THE AUTONOMOUS LAND VEHICLE (ALV), an experiment in unmanned reconnaissance, was built for the U.S. Army by the Martin Marietta Corporation. The ALV was designed to find its way with the help of TV cameras, inertial guidance sensors, sonar, and laser range finders. The wheeled robot moved so slowly that the Army abandoned the project.

1985

AMERICA'S STRATEGIC COMPUTING PROGRAM got under way. A $600-million endeavor funded by DARPA, the Pentagon's technical research agency, the five-year effort was aimed at boosting computing speeds a hundredfold through the use of fast, gallium arsenide chips and parallel processing.

1985

Uhuru: CC 68-69, 70, IC *68*

Ulam, Stanislaw: IC 17, RV 32-35, 38

Ultra: CB 55-56, CS 91

Ultrasound imaging: HB 23, *54-55*

Ultraviolet: *a band of electromagnetic radiation with a higher frequency and shorter wavelength than visible light.*

Ultraviolet emissions: CC 7, *9, 11*

Ulysses mission: SP 101

UMLER (Universal Machine Language Equipment Register): TR 80, 82, 88

Uncapher, Keith: CO 47

Underwater robots: RO 103-105, *116-117*

Unimate (robot): IC 48, RO 38-39

Unimation, Inc.: IC 48, RO 37-40, 42, 106

Uninterruptable power supply (UPS): CS 32-33; personal

computers, CS 33

Union Carbide Corporation: LA 50

Union Carbide Electronics: CM 53

Unipolar transistor: *one through which current is carried either by electrons or by holes, but not by both. See Switches.*

UNIPRINTER: IO 17

UNISERVO: IO 16

Unisys, and Aegis: MF 94

United Airlines: Apollo system, PC 104-105; Open Systems Manager, PC 105

United States: early space missions, SP 13; military, CB 52, 53, 59, 73, 74, 76; reaction to Japanese challenge, PO 89-90, 97; space program, CB 73, 76

U.S. Army: National Training Center (NTC) war games, MF *8-9;* War College, RO 111;

SW 108

U.S. Census: MS 8, PM 19, 20; of 1890, RV 9; of slaves, PM 21

U.S. Census Bureau: CB 13, 14, 64

U.S. Coast and Geodetic Survey: AC 10

U.S. Coast Guard: and CAD blueprints, PC 94-95

U.S. Customs Service: ACS Financial System, TR 72; Automated Broker Interface, TR 70; Automated Commercial System, TR 70-73; Automated Manifest System, TR 71; Automated Quota System, TR 72; Cargo Selectivity System, TR 71; and customhouse brokers, TR 67, 69; early computer systems, TR 68-69; Early Implementation System, TR 69; information flow within, TR 68; Office of Automatic

THE CRAY-2 SUPERCOMPUTER had four processors, twice the number in its predecessor, the X-MP. Even smaller than earlier Crays, the Cray-2 packed six miles of wiring into a four-foot-tall chassis that was filled with a Freon-like refrigerant to prevent overheating. Froth in the coolant earned the first Cray-2 the nickname Bubbles.

1985

CUSTOM CHIPS called ASICs (application-specific integrated circuits) were pioneered by Ensoniq, a Pennsylvania manufacturer of electronic keyboards. By replacing 120 off-the-shelf components with a single custom-designed chip built exclusively for sound synthesis, Ensoniq was able to produce a better keyboard and sell it for one-fourth the price of the competition.

1985

Data Processing, TR 68; Summary Selectivity System, TR 72; tracking cargo, TR 67-73

U.S. Defense Department: and development of Ada, LA 79-84; software problems, LA 78-79

U.S. Federal Aviation Agency (FAA): TR 100, 109

U.S. Geological Survey: PM 32

U.S. Internal Revenue Service: SO 7, *10-11*, 22

U.S. Navy: SO 77; ship defense system, MF 94-96

U.S. Postal Service, Merrifield, Virginia, facility: RO *108-109*

U.S. Social Security Administration: SO 19-20

UNIVAC (Universal Automatic Computer): CB 54, *57*, 64-65, IC *27*, IO *14*, 16, 17, 36, LA 11, 21, PM 59, SO 12, 13; 491, CO 39; and tape, MS 37; UNIVAC 1, SW 16, 17,

18; UNIVAC 1107, SC 103. *See also* Sperry Rand

Universal product code (UPC): *a twelve-digit bar code used by grocery stores and other retailers. See also* Bar codes. IC *77*, SO 50, 92, 94, SW *94-95*

University of Arizona: CC 17, 19, 23, 36

University of California at Berkeley: AI 68, RV 80

University of California at San Diego: AC 46, PO 97-98

University of Colorado: AC 46

University of Illinois: AI 73, PO 97-98

University of Manchester: IO 13

University of Michigan: ICPSR, PM 19

University of Moscow: RO 68-69

University of New Hampshire: RO 105

University of Pennsylvania: HB 70; Moore School of Electrical Engineering, CB 63, IC 19, MS 10; and ENIAC, CB 59, 63, IO 11, MS 8, SW 9; Wharton School of Business, PM 95

University of Pittsburgh: HB 72, PO 98

University of Southern California: AC 46, HB 79, RO 63

University of Southwestern Louisiana: PO 103

University of Tokyo: PO 91

University of Toronto: AC 46

University use of database system: SO *54-63*

UNIX: *a general-purpose, multiuser, interactive, time-sharing operating system popular within education and research institutions.* IC 65, LA 73, 76, RV 73, *74-77*; adaptability, RV 80; C

version, RV 73; development, RV 78-79; and MS-DOS, PC 96-97; operating system, PO 98

Unmanned spacecraft, computers: SP 86

UPC: *See* Universal Product Code

Uranus: SP 99-101, 108-109, *110-111, 112-113*

U.S.S.R., early space missions: SP 13, 87, 94

Utah/M.I.T. hand: RO *76*, 79, 80

Utilities: SW 19

INTEL CORPORATION'S IPSC (Intel Parallel Super Computer) harnessed 128 microprocessors, each connected to six of its neighbors. By working in concert, the microprocessors could quickly solve huge scientific problems. Intel modeled the iPSC on the Cosmic Cube, a sixty-four-processor computer built by Caltech's Charles Seitz and Geoffrey Fox as an inexpensive means to supercomputer power.

THE HIGH SIERRA FORMAT for storing data and directories on CD-ROMs was adopted by more than a dozen computer and electronics firms at a meeting in Nevada's Sierra. Their agreement to codify CD-ROM storage brought compatibility to a new area of the industry, where previously each compact-disk publisher had devised a unique storage plan, and no machine could read them all; using the High Sierra Format would ensure that any computer or CD player could read any CD-ROM disk.

1985

1985

V-2 (missile): SP 9, 11, 13
V-2 rocket: analog computer, AC 14-15, IC *14*
Vacuum tube: *the earliest form of electronic switch, eventually replaced by the transistor.*
CB 54-55, 60, *67-68*, CM 17, IC *9*; and Colossus, CB 58; and ENIAC, CB 59, 60, 68; reliability, RV 19
Vail, Alfred: CO 9
Validation: entire program, SC 16-17; functional testing, SC 7, *8-11*; structural testing, SC 7, *12-15*
Valley, George E.: CI 13
Value-added network (VAN): *a data network that supplements basic communications services acquired from a common carrier with additional features that correct transmission errors and ensure compatibility between dissimilar computers and terminals. See* VAN (value-added network).
VAN (value-added network):

CO 48, 49
Van Dam, Andries: CI 35, 60, 114, IO 66
Van Geen, John: CO 20-21
Vanguard I: SP 13, 116
Vannier, Michael: CI 106, 107
Van Wesel, Adriaen: PM 44-45
Variables: global and local, LA 65
Variable stars: study of, CC *20-21*
Varian V74: CC 42
Vaucanson, Jacques de: AI 8
VAX 11/780: RV *66*, 80
Vector graphics, early development: CI *30-31*, *32*, *33-34*, *35*, *36*, *37*, 38
Vector processing: *a parallel-processing technique in which an instruction is invoked once and then is executed on an entire list, or vector, of numbers.*
PO 33-34, *60-61*
Venera 1: SP 87, 103, 116
Venus: mapping, SP *90-91*; missions to, SP 85, 87, 89, 101. *See also* Mariner, Project

THE 80386, a thirty-two-bit microprocessor from Intel, packed 275,000 transistors onto a single chip. The 80386, used in personal computers, boasted near-mainframe speed and power. It could perform as many as four million operations per second and handle up to four gigabytes (billion bytes) of memory. Yet it was compatible with Intel's earlier processors—including the 8088 built into the IBM PC—and could run almost any software written for them.

THE ADAPTIVE SUSPENSION VEHICLE took its first walk. Built at Ohio State University for the Defense Department, the three-ton, seventeen-foot-long behemoth stood on six hydraulically operated legs guided by seventeen onboard computers. Controlled by an aircraft-style joystick, the ASV was equipped with a seventy-horsepower engine that enabled the machine to travel at about eight miles per hour.

1985

1985

Verhoog, Pieter: PM 23
Very Large Array (VLA): CC 58, *59*, 60, *80-81*, IC *103*; software, CC 60
Very-large-scale integration (VLSI): *the placement of 5,000 or more gate equivalents or more than 16,000 bits of memory on a single chip. See VLSI.*
Very Long Baseline Array (VLBA): CC 62, IC 58
Very Long Baseline Interferometry (VLBI): CC 61-62, IC 58

Very long instruction word: *See* VLIW
Verzuh, Frank: AC 15
Vessel Traffic Systems (VTS): TR 92; English Channel, TR 91-92; Rotterdam, TR 92-93, 98
Veterans Administration: HB 102, 106
VHSICs (Very High Speed Integrated Circuits): IC *108*, MF 48, 100
Vias: CM *10-11, 116-117*
Videodisk: MS 97-100, 109, *110-115*, 116, *117*;

manufacture, MS 99-100; random access, MS 100-101. *See also* Compact disk; Optical storage
Video display: character-based, PC 31, *32*; graphics-based, PC 32, *33*; memory-mapped video, PC *40-41*
Video display unit: SW *21*
Video games: CI 49, IC *72*, SW *64-67*, 106-107
Viehe, Frederick W.: MS 21
Vietnam War: guided bomb, MF *70*, 71; radar-guided missiles, MF 70
Viking: SP 86, 98; landers, RO 111; *Viking 1* and *2*, SP 98-99, 118; Viking command computer subsystem (VCCS), IC *85*, SP 98, 99
Virtual memory: *a technique for handling programs too large to fit all at once into a computer's memory. Pro-*

grams and data are divided into pages or segments that are sorted on disk or tape and loaded into memory only as needed for the program's execution. IC 51, MS 74-75, 82-84
Virus: *a program that copies itself into new databases and computers whenever its program is invoked.* CS 18, 19, 72, IC *113*, SC 58-59
Virusafe: SC 59
VISA: SO 49
VisiCalc: CB *99*, 103, IC *97*, PC 9, 11, 17, SW 69-70, 72
Vision, machine: AI 102, 104, RO 19; beam-break system, RO *20-21*; bin-picking, RO *24-25*; color analysis, AI *24-25*; connectivity map, AI 26, 27; difficulties, AI *28-29*; edge detection, AI *18-19*, 105, *106-107*; in exploratory

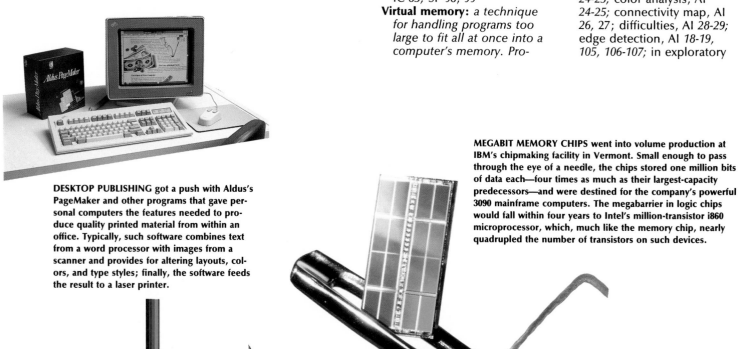

DESKTOP PUBLISHING got a push with Aldus's PageMaker and other programs that gave personal computers the features needed to produce quality printed material from within an office. Typically, such software combines text from a word processor with images from a scanner and provides for altering layouts, colors, and type styles; finally, the software feeds the result to a laser printer.

MEGABIT MEMORY CHIPS went into volume production at IBM's chipmaking facility in Vermont. Small enough to pass through the eye of a needle, the chips stored one million bits of data each—four times as much as their largest-capacity predecessors—and were destined for the company's powerful 3090 mainframe computers. The megabarrier in logic chips would fall within four years to Intel's million-transistor i860 microprocessor, which, much like the memory chip, nearly quadrupled the number of transistors on such devices.

1985

1985

and Index; IO Input/Output; LA Computer Languages; MF The Military Frontier; MS Memory and Storage; PC The Personal Computer; PM The Puzzle Master; PO Speed and Power; RO Robotics; RV Revolution in Science; SC The Software Challenge; SO The Computerized Society; SP Space; SW Software; TR Transportation

situation, RO *30-31;* feature extraction, AI *26-27;* image formation, AI *16-17;* navigating system, RO *26-27, 30-31;* object recognition, AI 15, *16-29;* optical processing, RO *28-29;* quality control, RO *22-23;* relational approach, AI *26-27;* template matching, AI *26-27;* texture analysis, AI *22-23;* in three dimensions, AI *20-21. See also* Navigating robots

Vision: computer-aided, HB 93-96, 107; and neural networks, AC 66

VLIW (very long instruction word): SC 107; compilers, SC 108-117

VLSI (very-large-scale integration): CB 78, CM 18, PO 96-97; design of circuits, CM 31-32

Voice-entry terminal: IO 95-96

Voice-identification systems: CS 43, *50-51*

Voice recognition: *the translation by a computer of spoken commands into digital instructions. See* Voice-entry terminal.

Voice synthesizers: HB 18

Voltage regulators: CS 32

Volume rendering: HB *103-105*

Von Braun, Wernher: SP 9, 12, 13, 33-34, 39, 41, 72, 86, 87

Von Karman, Theodore: SP 86

Von Neumann, John: AC 7, AI 102, CB *56,* 61-62, *63, 64,* CC 88-89, CO 15, 42, IC 17, *27,* MS 12, 16, PO 33, 49, 103, RV 32, 33, 35, 38, SC 88, SW *12-13,* 25, SW 102; architecture, AI *104-105,* CB *63,* 77; computer architecture, AC 7, 8. *See also* Architecture, computer

Von Neumann architecture: *the conventional computer design, composed of a memory connected by a bus to a central processing unit that performs operations sequentially. See* Architecture, computer: von Neumann.

Von Neumann bottleneck: *an operational slowdown in conventional computer designs, caused by the funneling of information into a single channel between the CPU and memory.*

Vortex satellite: MF 46

Voxel: *short for volume element, the cube of data collected by any of several medical imaging techniques and representing the density of tissue at one specific location in the body. An image is created by assigning colors or shades of gray to voxels in relation to their density values.* HB *48-49,* 104

Voyager: SP 86, 99-101; attitude, SP 106; communications, SP 104, *105, 107,* 113; computers, IC 90, SP 100, 101, *107;* image processing, SP *109, 110-111;* photography, SP *109, 110-111, 112-113;* requirements for Uranus, SP 100-101, *108-109; Voyager 1,* SP 99-100, 102, 103, 115, 118; *Voyager 2,* PM 15, RO 7-8, SP 99-101, 102, 103, *104-113,* 115

Vydec Corporation: IO 43

V

NETTALK, a neural network simulated on a minicomputer, learned to read English aloud. The work of Terrence Sejnowski *(left)* of Johns Hopkins University and Charles Rosenberg of Princeton, NETtalk was supplied with a training text and a recording of the material spoken by a six-year-old boy. In just twelve hours, NETtalk matched its pronunciation to the child's with 95 percent accuracy. Subsequently, the network scored 78 percent reading an unfamiliar text.

AN OPTICAL TRANSISTOR, a component central to digital optical computing, was patented by David Miller of AT&T Bell Labs. Called the Self-Electro-optic-Effect Device (SEED), the transistor is a light-sensitive switch in which a weak beam of light controls the passage of a much stronger one. A SEED consists of thin layers of gallium arsenide and gallium aluminum arsenide stacked in a multitiered sandwich about the size of Lincoln's chin on a penny.

1986

1986

Wabot 1 and 2 (robot): RO 69

WAC Corporal rocket: SP 87

Wafer: *a thin, round slice of semiconductor material, usually silicon, on which hundreds of chips are made at once.*
CM *64;* effect of size, CM 63; manufacturing, CM *58-61;* quality control of processed, CM 65-66; stepper, CM 64-65

Waldron, Kenneth J.: RO 68

Walker, Paul: MF 80

Walking: computer-aided, HB 102

Walking robots: RO 61-63, 68, *76-77, 81;* creeping gait, RO *82-83;* dynamically stable, IC 109, RO 61, 69-70, 81; rough terrain, RO *88-89;* running gait, RO *86-87;* statically stable, RO 68-69, 81; walking gait, RO *84-85*

Wallace, David: PM 61

Walleye bomb: MF *70-71*

Walt Disney Studios: RV 68

Walton, Thomas: SP 40

Wang, An: IO 43, MS 17, 19, 20, 21

Wang, Li-Chen: LA 102

Wang Laboratories: IC *76,* IO 43, 45

Warburton, J. A.: CC 57

War games: MF *6-21;* aircraft, MF *16-17;* army, MF *8-15;* electronic warfare, MF *10-11;* European scenarios, MF *14-15, 18-19, 20-21;* Idahex, MF *14-15;* JANUS, MF *12-13;* naval, MF *18-19;* and political factors, MF 20; satellite defense system, MF *6-7*

WarGames: CS 65

Warner, Homer: HB 61

Warren, Jim: LA 101-102

Washington University Medical Center: CI 106

Watanabe, Tadashi: PO 91, 96

Water hazards: CS 33

Watermark magnetics: CS 30-31

Watson, James: HB 42

Watson, Thomas J., Jr.: CB 51, 52, IO 18, 61, *63,* MS 50, PO 10, 11, 16, SC 23, 24, 33

Watson, Thomas J., Sr.: CB 51-52, 65, PM 59, RV 11, 19; reaction to Mark I, RV 15

Watson, Thomas J., Astronomical Computing Bureau: RV 12

Watson Scientific Computing Laboratory: RV 18

Waveguide: *a conduit for radio and light waves. Optical fibers serve as waveguides of light; metal tubes are used to guide radio waves.*

Waveguides, optical: AC 86-87, 92

Waxman, Bruce: RV 63, 65

Waybill: TR 84

Wayne, Ron: CB 107

Weapons: brilliant, AC 89, MF 63, 64; directed-energy (DEWs), MF 107, *108,*

MASSIVE PARALLELISM was achieved in the Connection Machine. Designed by inventor Daniel Hillis, the computer was originally built with some 16,000 processors. Later models had more than four times as many such devices, each with its own small memory and linked with the others in a flexible network that could be altered by reprogramming rather than by rewiring. Able to execute several billion operations per second, the Connection Machine could outstrip any rival computer when working on problems that could be parceled out among its many processors.

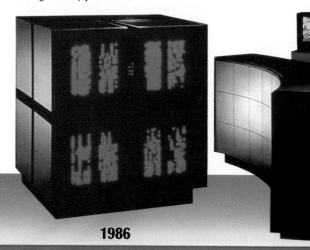

1986

COMPAQ'S DESKPRO 386 was the first thirty-two-bit personal computer built around Intel's 80386 chip. The Deskpro 386 was powerful enough to take on chores of computer-assisted design, engineering, and manufacture, as well as other demanding graphics work formerly reserved for minicomputers. Within three years, the company would follow its Deskpro 386 with stepped-up models that ran twice as fast as the original.

1986

116-117; kinetic-energy (KEWs), MF 107, 108, *118-119*
Weapons, smart: MF 25, 80; air-to-air radar-guided missiles, MF 72-73; AMRAAM, MF 72-73; antitank, MF 67, 70; automatic target recognition, MF 66-67; controversy over, MF 63-64; cruise missiles, MF *75-77*, 78; DIVAD, MF 64-65; early remote control weapons, MF 62-63; Exocet, MF 71-72; fire-and-forget, MF 71-72; ICBMs, MF 73-74, 78; LANTIRN, MF 66-67; naval, MF 31, 71-72; Paveway II, MF 61-62; SADARM, MF 79-80; sensors for, MF 62; smart rocks, MF *118-119*; TOW, MF 67
Weapons research: PO 8, 43, *44*
Weary Willie: MF 62-63
Weather: PM *10-11*; forecasting, SW 101, 102-*104*, 105-106; radar, computerized, TR *118-119*. *See also* Meteorology, computer modeling
Weaver, Warren: AI 55, PM 67, 77
Webb, James: SP 43, 44
Webber, Jim: SC 54, 57, 67
Wegstein, Joseph: LA 42-43, 45, 48
Wehrung, John: AC 105, 106
Weidenhammer, James: MS 38
Weiffenbach, George C.: TR 49
Weitz, Paul J.: SP 61, 118, 120
Weizenbaum, Joseph: AI 58-59, 71, HB 75, 76, IC *60*
Wells, Don: CC 37, 38, 42
Werbos, Paul: AC 55
Westar: CO 94
Western Electric: RO 11
Western Union: and multiplexing, CO 13-14; satellite, CO 94; and telecommunications network, CO 47
Westinghouse-Bettis Atomic Power Laboratory: LA 37, RV 41
Westmoreland, William: MF 80
Westphal, James: CC 36
Westworld: CI 76
Weyerhaeuser Company: PC 92-93; ExcelleRate, PC 93
Wharton Econometric Forecasting Associates (WEFA): PM 97, 98, 99
Wharton School of Business, University of Pennsylvania: economic forecasts, PM 95
Wheels, disadvantages of: RO 62-63
Whipple, Dick: LA 101
Whipple, Fred: CC 19
Whirlpool (M51): CC *10-11*
Whirlwind: CI 9, *12*-14, CO 18, IC *25*, IO 12, *13*, 38, LA 21, MS 18, 19, 20, PO 67-68
Whitaker, William: LA 79, 80, 81
White, Edward: SP 37, 46, 116, 117

A NEURAL NETWORK ON A CHIP was created by Bell Laboratories' Hans Peter Graf, Richard Howard, and Lawrence Jackel. Unlike most earlier neural networks, which were software simulations run on digital computers, this device has circuitry laid out to function as neurons rather than as logic elements for executing conventional computer programs. The special-purpose chip recognizes handwritten numbers from zero to nine.

A COMPUTERIZED COCKPIT gave crews of Europe's A320 Airbus jetliner the fly-by-wire capabilities first developed for military jets. During flight, on-board computers display instrument data on three pairs of small screens as another computer handles the plane's control surfaces. Additional computers guide the airliner along a preprogrammed flight path.

1986

1987

White, Simon: CC 106, 107, 108

Whitney, Gary: PC 95; The Whitney Group, PC 95

Whitney, John, Jr.: CI 83, 84

Whitney, John, Sr.: CI 76

Widrow, Bernard: AC 50, 52

Wiegand, Sam: SO 74

Wiener, Norbert: AI 10-11, 12, CO 15, IC 22, PM 67, RO 14-17, 18

Wigginton, Randy: PC 62

Wigner, Eugene: quoted, CB 61

Wilhite, Tom: CI 77, 80

Wilkes, Maurice V.: CB 63, 65, IC 22, IO 14, 38, LA 14, 21, SW 14

Wilkie, Dan: PC 15

Wilkins, Maurice: HB 42

Williams, Al: SC 30

Williams, Donald: CO 89, 94

Williams, F. C.: IO 14, SW 14

Williams, Fred: MS 12; tube, MS 11, 12, 16

Williams, Ronald: AC 55

Williams, Samuel B.: CB 37, CO 14, 15

Williams tube: *a computer-memory device that stores binary data as dots and dashes on a CRT screen.* IC 19, MS 11, 12, 16

Wilson, Kenneth: PO 74, 75, 76

Wilson, Robert: CC 95

WIN (WWMCCS Intercomputer Network): MF 101

Winchester, Ian: PM 20

Winchester drives: IC 77, MS 51, 52. *See also* Magnetic disk storage

Window: *a partitioned section of a video screen that displays the contents of a data file or the workings of an application program, while other data or programs are visible on other portions of the screen. See* Word processors. PC 40-41, 59, SC 92-97; hypermedia: PM 82-83

Wind patterns, oceanic: PM 6-7

Windshear: TR 120-121; Low Level Windshear Alert System, TR 120-121

Windstar Sail Cruises: TR 24; and fuel savings, TR 26; ships of, TR 24-26

Winningstad, Norman: PO 72, 73, 75, 76

Winograd, Terry: AI 60, IC 72

Winston, Patrick H.: AI 75-76, 84

Wire-frame graphics: CI 30-31, 92-93, 94, 98, 102, 103, 109

Wire length: and flow of electrical pulses, PO 39, 96-97

Wiring: automobile, TR 11,16

Wiring paths: CM 94-97

Wirth, Niklaus: IC 67, LA 76, 77-78, 83, 103-104, SW 29, 39

WIS (WWMCCS Information System): MF 102

Wolter, Hans: CC 70

Woltosz, Walt: HB 90

Women as "computers": CC 15

Womersley, J. R.: SW 13

Wonder, Stevie: HB 94, IO 98

Wood, Benjamin: RV 11

Woods, Gary: SP 40

Woods, Robert, Jr.: PM 18-19

Woods Hole Oceanographic Institution: RO 102

Word: *the basic storage unit of a computer's operation; a sequence of bits—commonly from eight to thirty-two—occupying a single storage location and processed as a unit by the computer.* CB 36

Word-Cruncher: PM 60

Word processing: *the use of a computer for creating, displaying, editing, storing, and printing text.* IO 35-36, 43, 45, SW 50, 53, 68-69, 76-77; for ideographic languages, IO 44-45; soft-

APPLE'S MACINTOSH II was the first Mac to include sockets for add-on circuit boards. A feature of almost all computers except the Mac, such sockets permit a computer to be fitted with additional memory, for example, or to be connected to a variety of peripherals. The Mac II had two other advantages over its predecessors: It had a faster microprocessor, and it came with a math coprocessor, a chip tailored for speed in number crunching.

PERSONAL SYSTEM/2, IBM's new generation of personal computers, took a step toward Apple's Macintosh family with a new operating system named OS/2. Among other features, it permitted the use of a mouse to manipulate data and programs, much as the Mac does. The PS/2 line comprised four models. The most powerful of them employed Intel's 80386 microprocessor, while more modest examples contained earlier, less capable chips.

1987

1987

W

ware, IO 45. *See also* Editors, program; Printers; Typewriters

Word processors: PC 29; display, PC 31, *32-33;* formatting documents, PC *36-37;* for handicapped, HB 90-92, 93; mail merge, PC *42-43;* memory use, PC *30-31;* pointers, PC *34-35;* and reading machine, HB 95; spelling checkers, PC *38-39;* windows, PC *40-41. See also* Desktop publishing

Words +, Inc.: HB 90

WordStar: IC 97, SW 69, 71

Work factor: CS 90

Work stations: PC 90; and personal computers, PC 96

World War II: and development of robots, RO 9-11, 14-17; guided weapons, MF 62-63; and navigation, TR 44-46

WORM (write once, read many) disk: *an optical disk on which a user can write information. Once the data is recorded, it can be read repeatedly but never changed or erased.* IC 100, MS 103-104, 108, *118-119,* 121; card format, MS *119*

Worms: CS 64, 72, IC 101

Wozniak, Steven: CB 104-105, 106-107, 108, IC *90,* PC 45, *46,* 66, 68, SW 68, *71*

Wright Aeronautical Corp.: AC 16

Write: *the process by which a computer records data in memory, external storage, or display devices. See* Disk drives.

Wurst, Jack: SO 98

WWMCCS (Worldwide Military Command and Control System): MF 101-102

WYSIWYG: PC 36

A VOICE-OPERATED TYPEWRITER was demonstrated by Teuvo Kohonen *(below)* of Finland's Helsinki University of Technology. Based on neural networks, the typewriter recognized as much as 97 percent of the speech uttered by persons who had "trained" the system by dictating 100 words to it.

HYPERCARD provided quick, natural access to great volumes of data. Developed by William Atkinson *(above)* for the Macintosh, the program enables the user to browse through information by association, the way the human mind does. Hypercard pointed the way toward the future development of so-called hypermedia software, which might combine literature with music, art, and film.

CEDAR promised simpler parallel processing through a system developed by David Kuck at the University of Illinois *(below)*. Like other parallel computers, Cedar employs multiple processors to work on many parts of a problem simultaneously. But Kuck's machine goes a step further. It alleviates the difficulty of programming such computers by including software that automatically arranges data and instructions to suit the parallel system.

1988

1988

1988

X.25 communications protocol: CO 55-56, IC 87

X-29: *See* Grumman Aerospace Corporation X-29

Xerox PARC (Palo Alto Research Center): CO 57, IO 67, 72, 73-74, 75; Alto, CI 60, IO 74, 75, PC 59-60, SC 104; Ethernet, CO 57; graphics program, IO 66; PARC, PC 59, 60; Star, PC 60; Star 8010, IO 74

X-ray: *a band of electromagnetic radiation that has a wavelength between ultraviolet and gamma rays.*

X-ray astronomy: CC 63; early, CC 63, 66-67; emissions, CC 6-7, 9, 13, 74; satellite-based, CC 67-68, 69, 70-74

X-ray binaries: CC 70

X-ray crystallography: RV 81, 82-91

X-ray fluorescence spectroscopy: PM 46-47

X-ray lithography: CM 106, 107

X-ray telescopes: early detectors, CC 66, 67; Einstein, CC 71, 72, 73-74; focusing, CC 70, 71, 72, 73; microchannel plate, CC 73

X Window: PC 107, 108-119; protocol, PC 112-113; software, PC 110-111; system manager, PC 114-115; window manager, PC 116-117

SUPERCONDUCTIVITY may hold the key to swifter, more densely packed integrated circuits. Until recently, this resistance-free state had been observed only in a handful of substances at extremely low temperatures. But in the late 1980s new compounds that superconducted at warmer temperatures were discovered. Thus far, none of these substances have been made into commercially useful computer products, but research in this area has accelerated.

OPTICAL COMPUTING, already applied as analog processes in the field of signal processing, shows promise for the future as a means of digital computing. Light is attractive as a computing medium because it travels faster than electrons, can carry more information, and is naturally parallel. That is, many information-carrying light beams can be handled simultaneously by a single processor (a lens is a simple example) because light rays do not interfere with each other as electrical pulses do. However, many obstacles lie in the way of optical computing, and few expect a general-purpose optical computer before the turn of the century.

THE NEXT COMPUTER, developed for universities by Apple cofounder Steven Jobs (below), was hailed as innovative on three counts: it was the first personal computer to incorporate a drive for an optical storage disk, it had a built-in digital signal processor that equipped the computer for tasks such as voice recognition, and it was designed to simplify programming through the use of object-oriented languages.

THE GIGACHIP, an integrated circuit comprising one billion transistors, is the next challenge for the semiconductor industry. To achieve this goal, chip fabricators must shrink, by a factor of four, the one-micrometer features of the million-transistor chip. The results would be worth the effort. A gigachip, for example, could fulfill the promise of supercomputer on a chip, complete with multiple central processing units, input/output ports, and large amounts of memory, as well as special processors for graphics and number crunching.

1988

and Index; IO Input/Output; LA Computer Languages; MF The Military Frontier; MS Memory and Storage; PC The Personal Computer; PM The Puzzle Master; PO Speed and Power; RO Robotics; RV Revolution in Science; SC The Software Challenge; SO The Computerized Society; SP Space; SW Software; TR Transportation

Yale University: AI 68
Yamaha: IO 107
Yannes, Bob: CM 99-100
Young, John: SP 37, 47, 67, 70, 116, 117, 118, 119, 120
Young, Richard: PC 16
Young, Ronald: RO 106
Yourdon, Edward: SC 60

Z-2: CB 100
Z4: LA 9
Zel'dovich, Yakov: CC 98
Zenith Electronics Corporation: PC 15, 68
Zierler, Niel: IC 31, LA 21
Zilog Z-80: CB 104, IC 79, SO 102, 103
Zimmerman, Joel S.: CS 28
Zuse, Konrad: CB 38, 53-*54*, 55, 58, 64, IC *14*, 19, IO 12, LA 9-10, 11, SW 11, 13; Z1, CB 38; Z2, CB 38; Z3, CB 53-54, IC *14*; Z4, CB 54, 64
Zwicky, Fritz: CC 28, 97, 98

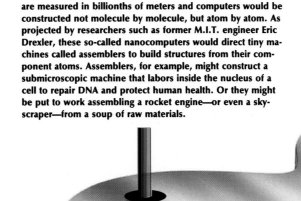

NANOTECHNOLOGY delves into a realm where dimensions are measured in billionths of meters and computers would be constructed not molecule by molecule, but atom by atom. As projected by researchers such as former M.I.T. engineer Eric Drexler, these so-called nanocomputers would direct tiny machines called assemblers to build structures from their component atoms. Assemblers, for example, might construct a submicroscopic machine that labors inside the nucleus of a cell to repair DNA and protect human health. Or they might be put to work assembling a rocket engine—or even a skyscraper—from a soup of raw materials.

MOLECULAR COMPUTING is a branch of research that envisions tiny, ultrafast computers made with techniques borrowed from organic chemistry and medicine. One proposal foresees biochips comprising millions of molecule assemblages grown through a sequence of chemical reactions. Researchers have already produced molecules that behave like diodes, which permit current to flow in one direction but not the other. The hope is that memory cells and logic gates made of molecules will follow.

Picture Credits

The sources for the illustrations that appear in this book are listed below. Credits from left to right are separated by semicolons, from top to bottom by dashes.

Cover, 4, 5, and time-line art throughout by Matt McMullen. Alphabet art throughout by Greg Harlin from Stansbury, Ronsaville, Wood, Inc., photographed by Larry Sherer. 6, 7: The Science Museum, London (4); National Portrait Gallery, London. 8, 9: The Science Museum, London; Culver Pictures; Ann Ronan Picture Library, Taunton, Somerset; The Science Museum, London; Quesada/Burke, New York; art by Mark V. Robinson. 10, 11: Adam Lubroth, courtesy Escuela de Ingenieros de Caminos, Canales y Puertos, Madrid; courtesy International Business Machines Corporation; The MIT Museum; Richard Bonifield. 12, 13: The Royal Society of London; courtesy AT&T Archives; Alfred Eisenstaedt for *Life*; Per A. Holst; courtesy AT&T Archives. 14, 15: Courtesy Marshall Space Flight Center; courtesy Professor Konrad Zuse, Hunfeld, West Germany; The MIT Museum; courtesy J. V. Atanasoff, copied by Thomas E. Molesworth; art by Mark V. Robinson; British Crown Copyright, courtesy Brian Johnson, London. 16, 17: Courtesy International Business Machines Corporation; art by Stansbury, Ronsaville, Wood, Inc., photographed by Larry Sherer. 18, 19: The Computer Museum, Boston; Erwin Böhm, Mainz, courtesy of Professor Konrad Zuse, Hünfeld, West Germany; The Computer Museum, Boston. 20, 21: Courtesy AT&T Bell Laboratories; art by Mark V. Robinson; courtesy International Business Machines Corporation. 22, 23: John Wiley and Sons, Inc.; A. E. January; The Archives of the Computer Laboratory, Cambridge University; The Science Museum, London, and UNIVAC; Manchester University. 24, 25: The Science Museum, London/© N.P.L.; courtesy Unisys Corporation; courtesy The Mitre Corporation Archives. 26, 27: Private collection; courtesy Unisys Corporation; The Institute for Advanced Study, Princeton, New Jersey; courtesy AT&T Archives. 28, 29: The Moore School of Engineering, University of Pennsylvania; Leni Iselin for *Fortune*; The Computer Museum, Boston; G. W. A. Dummer, Malvern Wells, Worcestershire. 30, 31: A. E. Glennie, Aberdeenshire; courtesy International Business Machines Corporation; art by Peter Sawyer; Bob Veltri, courtesy Special Collections Library, Virginia Polytechnic Institute, Blacksburg. 32, 33: Art by Stephen R. Wagner, photographed by Larry Sherer; courtesy International Business Machines Corporation; courtesy AT&T Archives. 34, 35: Dan McCoy/Rainbow; courtesy International Business Machines Corporation; The Computer Museum, Boston. 37: The MIT Museum (2). 38, 39: Courtesy International Business Machines Corporation; courtesy Texas Instruments; courtesy International Business Machines Corporation. 40, 41: Courtesy International Business Machines Corporation; courtesy National Semiconductor; The MIT Museum; courtesy National Semiconductor. 42, 43: The MIT Museum; Bank of America Archives; courtesy Control Data Corporation, Historical Archives. 44, 45: Lawrence Livermore National Laboratory Computer Museum; courtesy AT&T Archives; Arvin/Calspan; The MIT Museum. 46, 47: Courtesy International Business Machines Corporation; courtesy AT&T Archives; courtesy International Business Machines Corporation. 48, 49: The MIT Museum; art by Stephen R. Wagner, photographed by Larry Sherer; courtesy MIT Lincoln Laboratory. 50, 51: Cambridge *Evening News,* Cambridge; NASA, no. 107-KSC-67C-919; The MIT Museum. 52, 53: © Art Matrix, Dr. Hubbard Fractal Research Facility, Cornell Theory Center, International Business Machines, National Science Foundation; chart by Time-Life Books; courtesy International Business Machines Corporation. 54, 55: Courtesy Dartmouth College Library (2); courtesy International Business Machines Corporation; Mark Sexton (2). 56, 57: Courtesy General Motors Corporation; courtesy Lawrence R. Klein; David Edward Dempster; © 1980 Digital Equipment Corporation. 58, 59: Rune Myhre, Oslo; Stanford University; courtesy International Business Machines Corporation. 60, 61: The Computer Museum, Boston; The MIT Museum; courtesy National Semiconductor; The MIT Museum; art by William J. Hennessy, Jr., photographed by Larry Sherer; art by Matt McMullen. 62, 63: Art by Al Kettler, photographed by Larry Sherer; courtesy Douglas C. Engelbart; courtesy Raytheon Corporation (2); art by Tyrone Huntley, photographed by Larry Sherer. 64, 65: AP/Wide World Photos; courtesy SRI International; The MIT Museum; courtesy AT&T Archives (2). 66, 67: Art by Stephen R. Wagner; art by Douglas R. Chezem, photographed by Larry Sherer; art by Peter Sawyer of Design Innovations; inset John Walsh/Photo Researchers, Inc.—J. Anthony Tyson from AT&T Bell Laboratories and Pat Seitzer from Cerro Tololo Inter-American Observatory, Chile (2); courtesy Niklaus Wirth, Zurich. 68, 69: NASA, no. 71-H-481; art by Steve Bauer/Bill Burrows Studio; © 1985, reprinted by permission of Intel Corporation. 70, 71: Courtesy International Business Machines Corporation; courtesy AT&T Archives; courtesy Hewlett-Packard; courtesy Xerox Corporation. 72, 73: Michael Alexander for *People;* art by Al Kettler; The Computer Museum, Boston. 74, 75: Thorn EMI Central Research Laboratories, Hayes, Middlesex (2); Stanford University; courtesy Alain Colmerauer, Marseille; courtesy Intel Corporation. 76, 77: Photo courtesy of Wang Laboratories Inc.; NASA, no. 74-

HC-75; courtesy International Business Machines Corporation; bar-code art by Time-Life Books—art by Tyrone Huntley. 78, 79: Art by Wayne Vincent; S. Schwartzenberg, Center for Computer Research in Music and Acoustics; Xerox Corporation; © 1985, reprinted by permission of Intel Corporation; courtesy Hewlett-Packard; courtesy Zilog, Inc. 80, 81: Robotics Institute, Carnegie-Mellon University; © 1989 Phillip A. Harrington/Fran Heyl Associates; courtesy of Dr. Harry Chugani and Dr. Michael E. Phelps, UCLA School of Medicine; © 1984 Forrest M. Mims III. 82, 83: © William Thompson, Microsoft; Dan Cunningham; courtesy International Business Machines Corporation; courtesy Douglas B. Lenat; art by Sean Daly. 84, 85: Jeff Wilson, FPS Computing; courtesy Federal Aviation Administration; The MIT Museum; NASA/JPL. 86, 87: From *The Fractal Geometry of Nature* by Benoit B. Mandelbrot, published by W. H. Freeman, San Francisco, © 1982; Stone and Steccati Photographers; Martin L. Schneider. 88, 89: Paul Shambroom, courtesy Cray Research, Inc.; © 1988 Rick Browne; Department of Photography, Ohio State University. 90, 91: Commodore Business Machines, Inc.; courtesy Apple Computer, Inc.; art by Stephen R. Wagner; art by Peter A. Sawyer from Design Innovations; art by Stephen R. Wagner. 92, 93: Art by Sam Haltom; courtesy Radio Shack, a division of Tandy Corporation; courtesy Digital Equipment Corporation, Maynard, Massachusetts. 94, 95: Art by William J. Hennessy, Jr.; art by Matt McMullen; NASA; courtesy Motorola, Inc. 96, 97: Robotics Institute, Carnegie-Mellon University; Smithsonian Institution, photo no. 80-20234; Paul Hirschberger for *Fortune*; disk photographed by Dan Cunningham; Simpson Kalisher. 98, 99: © George Hall/Check Six, 1985; Peter Yates— Jon Brenneis; Dr. G. A. Johnson, Duke Medical Center; courtesy Seagate Technology. 100, 101: Art by Stephen R. Wagner, photographed by Larry Sherer; courtesy Paperback Software International; art by Joseph Milioto. 102, 103: Vioujard/Gamma, Paris; courtesy International Business Machines Corporation; art by Lili Robins. 104, 105: Ashton-Tate; courtesy Hewlett-Packard Company's Apollo Computer Subsidiary; © Fredrich Cantor; art by Stephen R. Wagner. 106, 107: Paul Shambroom, courtesy Cray Research, Inc.; © 1989 Andrew Popper; Max Aguilera-Hellweg/Onyx; art by David Jonason/The Pushpin Group; Chuck O'Rear. 108, 109: Reprinted with permission of Compaq Computer Corporation, all rights reserved; courtesy TRW Inc.; Ed Kashi; © 1984 Marc H. Raibert. 110, 111: © 1986 John Goodman; courtesy Digital Equipment Corporation, Maynard, Massachusetts; courtesy Apple Computer, Inc.; art by Matt McMullen; courtesy ETAK, Inc. 112, 113: Professor Shigeo Hirose, Tokyo Institute of Technology; courtesy International Business Machines Corporation; courtesy L.E.P., France; art by Thomas Miller; courtesy Grolier Electronic Publishing, Inc. 114, 115: Courtesy Martin-Marietta; Paul Shambroom, courtesy Cray Research, Inc. 116, 117: Courtesy Intel Corporation (2); Kevin Fitzsimmons/NYT Pictures. 118, 119: Courtesy Aldus Corporation; courtesy International Business Machines Corporation; The Salk Institute; courtesy AT&T Bell Laboratories. 120, 121: Steve Grohe, courtesy Thinking Machines Corporation; reprinted with permission of Compaq Computer Corporation, all rights reserved; picture supplied by AÉROSPATIALE-Photo Meauxsoonne, Toulouse. 122, 123: Courtesy Apple Computer, Inc.; courtesy International Business Machines Corporation; Pekka Kuparinen; © 1984 Matt Herron/Black Star; Center for Supercomputing Research and Development, University of Illinois at Urbana-Champaign. 124, 125: Diana Walker for *Time*; art by Al Kettler.

Acknowledgments

For their help in the preparation of this volume, the editors thank: **In Japan:** Mieko Ikeda, Tokyo; **In France:** George Gourrier, Chef de Division Composants et Microcircuits IIIV, L.E.P., Limeil-Brévannes; Bruno Janet, France Telecom, Paris; **In the United States:** District of Columbia—Paul Ceruzzi, Smithsonian Institution; Pennsylvania—Pittsburgh: Hans Moravec, Carnegie-Mellon University; New York—Valhalla: Barbara Henniger, International Business Machines Corporation.

Time-Life Books Inc.
is a wholly owned subsidiary of
TIME INCORPORATED

Editor-in-Chief: Jason McManus
Chairman and Chief Executive Officer:
J. Richard Munro
President and Chief Operating Officer:
N. J. Nicholas, Jr.
Editorial Director: Richard B. Stolley

THE TIME INC. BOOK COMPANY

President and Chief Executive Officer:
Kelso F. Sutton
President, Time Inc. Books Direct:
Christopher T. Linen

TIME-LIFE BOOKS INC.

EDITOR: George Constable
Executive Editor: Ellen Phillips
Director of Design: Louis Klein
Director of Editorial Resources: Phyllis K. Wise
Editorial Board: Russell B. Adams, Jr., Dale M.
Brown, Roberta Conlan, Thomas H. Flaherty, Lee
Hassig, Jim Hicks, Donia Ann Steele, Rosalind
Stubenberg
Director of Photography and Research:
John Conrad Weiser

PRESIDENT: John M. Fahey, Jr.
Senior Vice Presidents: Robert M. DeSena,
James L. Mercer, Paul R. Stewart, Joseph J. Ward
Vice Presidents: Stephen L. Bair, Stephen L. Gold-
stein, Juanita T. James, Andrew P. Kaplan, Carol
Kaplan, Susan J. Maruyama, Robert H. Smith
Supervisor of Quality Control: James King

PUBLISHER: Joseph J. Ward

Editorial Operations
Copy Chief: Diane Ullius
Production: Celia Beattie
Library: Louise D. Forstall

Correspondents: Wibo van de Linde (Amsterdam);
Elisabeth Kraemer-Singh (Bonn); Lance Keyworth
(Helsinki); Christine Hinze and Judy Aspinall (Lon-
don); Trini Bandres (Madrid); Christina Lieberman
(New York); Dag Christensen (Oslo); Maria Vin-
cenza Aloisi (Paris); Ann Natanson (Rome); Dick
Berry (Tokyo). Valuable assistance was also pro-
vided by: Christina Lieberman and Elizabeth
Brown (New York).

UNDERSTANDING COMPUTERS

SERIES DIRECTOR: Lee Hassig
Series Administrator: Gwen C. Mullen (acting)

Editorial Staff for *Illustrated Chronology and Index*
Designers: Cynthia Richardson (principal),
Lorraine D. Rivard
Index Coordinator: Elizabeth Graham
Associate Editors: Marion Briggs (pictures),
Robert A. Doyle, Allan Fallow, John Sullivan (text)
Researchers: Scarlet Cheng, M. Tucker Jones,
Stephanie Lewis
Writers: Margery A. duMond, Esther Ferington
Copy Coordinator: Anne Farr
Picture Coordinators: Katherine Griffin, Robert H.
Wooldridge, Jr.
Editorial Assistant: Susan L. Finken

Special Contributors: Martin Mann, Kathy Wismar
(text). The master index for the Understanding
Computers series was compiled from the indexes
of the individual volumes, which were prepared by
Mel Ingber.

THE CONSULTANTS

GWEN BELL is director of exhibitions and collections
at the Computer Museum in Boston.

GREGORY W. WELCH is exhibit developer at the
Computer Museum in Boston.

MICHAEL R. WILLIAMS, a professor of computer science at the University of Calgary in Canada, wrote *A
History of Computing Technology.*

Library of Congress Cataloging in Publication Data

Illustrated chronology & index.
  (Understanding computers)
  Contains index to entire series (Understanding computers),
glossary terms, and a time line in computer science.
  1. Computers—History—Indexes. 2. Computers—Dic-
tionaries.
I. Time-Life Books.   II. Series.
Qa76.17.I35 1989   004   89-4619
ISBN 0-8094-6070-X
ISBN 0-8094-6071-8 (lib. bdg.)

For information on and a full description of any of the Time-
Life Books series listed, please write:
Reader Information
Time-Life Customer Service
P.O. Box C-32068
Richmond, Virginia 23261-2068

Time-Life Books Inc. offers a wide range of fine recordings,
including a *Rock 'n' Roll Era* series. For subscription information, call 1-800-621-7026, or write TIME-LIFE MUSIC, P.O. Box
C-32068, Richmond, Virginia 23261-2068.